Social Mobility and Change
Among
Tibetan Refugees

Social Mobility and Change
Among
Tibetan Refugees

Dr. Monu Rani Gupta

Raj Publications
New Delhi - 110002 (INDIA)

Social Mobility and Change Among Tibetan Refugees

First Published in 2005

ISBN 81-86208-43-7

Published by : ***Poonam Goel***
Raj Publications
4855/24, Ansari Road,Daryaganj
Delhi - 110009
Tel. : 011- 55392533 Res. 011-27143321
Email : rajpublications@rediffmail.com

Laser Typesetting : Aarati Computers,
Delhi-110 009

Printed at : Balaji Offset Printers,
Delhi

PRINTED IN INDIA

Contents

जवाहरलाल नेहरू विश्वविद्यालय
JAWAHARLAL NEHRU UNIVERSITY
NEW DELHI - 110 067

Centre for the Study of Social Systems
School of Social Sciences

Foreword

This work by Dr. Monu Rani Gupta is a significant contribution towards providing an in-depth understanding of the amazing story of a refugee community recovering itself in terms of religion, culture, language and self respect despite the challenge from an authoritarian and aggressive power like People's Republic of China. Dr. Monu Rani Gupta has been successful in presenting a sociological analysis of a complex reality like the Tibetan settlements and their dynamics in the Indian context.

The study is organised in 9 parts dealing with the following aspects — i) Tibet, Tibetan and the Chinese invasion, ii) refugees iii) family and marriage iv) women and society v) religion, vi) education, vii) economy, viii) polity: the democratic ideal, and ix) conclusion (including the role of mass media).

Each part is appropriately structured internally and logically integrated with the other sections of the book. I consider it as a significant contribution in making sense of the Tibetan story in India as well as towards sociology of forced migration and its socio-cultural consequences. I am confident that this work will be found meaningful by the students of Tibetan society and culture. It will be also relevant to understand the problems and prospects of refugee communities in the modern world system where a nationality without its own state becomes extremely vulnerable and marginal in socio-political and economic terms. Through this contribution Dr. Monu Rani Gupta has furthered the process of understanding the social changes among Tibetans Refugees which was initiated by scholars like Girija Sakalani, Anand Kumar, Heimendorff, Hubertus von Welck, and Dagmar Bernstorff.

21 Jan., 05 — **Anand Kumar**

Preface

The story of Tibetans in exile is an amazing example of civilizational residence and cultural revival. According to the Dalai lama," I retrospect, for the past forty years. We Tibetans in exile have not been deficient in upholding our identity and preserving our religion....As inheritors of this Tibetan nationality, I think we in exile, owing to our freedom has been quite useful for the past forty five years in the preservation of our rich Tibetan religion, culture and language. This is a big achievement for us. In 1959, when the conditions were so desperate, we never thought that such things would happen after forty years. Nor did we think that we would have so many people throughout the world expressing genuine concern and support for the Tibetan cause. However, since we have the truth on our side, we have been convinced that the truth would prevail. And with this conviction, we have put a lot of efforts and continued our work. But at that time it was not possible for us to estimate that we would achieve the present results."

(Speech in the Assembly of Tibetan People's Deputies, 9 Sept. 2004)

This expression of satisfaction about the consequences of quest for survival through "freedom in exile' by the most representative voice of the Tibetans around the world is rooted in the Indian settings of the Tibatan refugees. Because out of the Total exiled Tibetans, more than 80 percent (85,000 persons) are settled on the Indian soil in various states including Karnataka, Himachal Pradesh, Uttar Pradesh, Uttranchal, Sikkim, West Bengal, Orissa, Madhya Pradesh, Maharashtra, Arunachal Pradesh and Ladakh regions of Jammu & Kashmir. Among the others 14,000 are in Nepal, 7,000 are in U.S.A. and Canada, 3,200 in Europe, 1600 in Bhutan, 1000 in Taiwan, 250 in Australia and New Zealand and 100 in Japan.

The spiritual and temporal head of the Tibetan community His Holiness the 14th Dalai lama has made India his 'Little Potala'. All the basic NGO's of Tibetans in exile has also established their headquarters in India. The spiritual head of their 4 major seats are also in exile in India. Tibetan Diaspora have emerged as a success story of the twentieth century due to their partnership with India despite the intensity of chinese presentation and wide spread globe indifference upto 1989 when the Dalai lama was recognized as a symbol of compassion, non-violence and universal responsibility.

— **Anand Kumar**
School of Social Sciences, JNU

1

Introduction

The present work falls within the realm of sociology of dynamics which includes change and mobility of Tibetan community after refugehood and tries to analyse the social change brought with in their system in various aspects. There is no doubt that the society has constantly been changing at fluctuating speeds.

Change is an incessant process of social evolution. How ever it does not follow any prescribed design of growth. Often its speed is either too fast or too slow. The form and structure of social life is dicated by this movement and flow of change. Whenever the level of dissatisfaction expends to such a level as would permit a breakdown of stability and systematic evolution, this gives way to change.

In order to understand the social phenomenon properly it is essential to look back over the history of people, their origin and their past evolution.

Family organisation, caste and community structure, factory categories have been analysed in respect of their changing role and status. Even the principle and its implications to the system as a whole have been analysed in various studies related to social change.

Concept and Theories of Social Change

The theories of social change have been too impressive, too general and too simplified. The aims of these theories is to explain social change occurring in the known human societies. They support all the principles of change like evolution, invention, diffusion, imitation, challenge and response, class conflict and so on[1]. To Morris Ginsberg, social change is a change in social structure, eg: the size of the society, the composition or imbalance of its parts and the type of its organisation. "Examples of such changes", he believes, "are contraction in the size of the family, or rather the domestic units, which has occurred, and is occurring in many societas, the breaking up of economy with the rise of cities, the transition of "estate", the social classes, or to go back to earlier stages, the growth of the system is publicly administrative justice, replacing former personal or group retaliation. The term "social change must also include change in attitudes or beliefs, in so far as they sustain institution and change with them. The field of inquiry is thus very wide"[2].

Comte advanced the concept of fixed stages - from 'theological to the 'scientific' - through which society must progress[3]. Spencer in his 'cosmic' philosophy, proposing that every society goes through fixed and immutable stages not because of deliberate human effort but as a consequences of a cosmic design free from his control, replaces the idea of social development by human endeavour with inevitable revolutionary development in directions dicted by natural law[4].

Gumplowicz[5] proposed theoritic variations on the Darwinian concept of the 'survival of the fittest,' the fittest being defined as the most effective social system or element thereof.

Durkheim[6] advanced a concept of social change involving two stages - the traditional, 'mechanical solidarity' and the recent, 'progressive division of labor'. It is similar to the concept of Tonnis. But Durkhim's 'Collective representation' replaces Tonnis concept of 'rational self-interest ensuring group solidarity'.

Theorists like Weber, Tonnies and Simmel using the western society as their model argued that society is moving from one stage is another relentelessly, which was essentially than the better one. Webes's theory of bureaucracy[7] and Tonnis theory of geminschaft, gesellschaft[8] subscribed to the evolutionary principle of the irreversible movement of society in a specified directions.

Early twentinth century British social- scientists, such as Graham wallas, Leonard Hobbouse and Morris Ginsberg, reliving Spenceces's tradition, juxtaposed that social change was inevitable and held that its direction is from simple, to highly differentiated, but at the same time highly integrated forms of organisation[9].

Simultaneously, a group of French social thinkers and reformers, constructing on the theories of saint Simon and Rousseau, argued that government is always and everywhere hostile to change, since it invariably represents the parasitic class of social elite having a vested interest in preserving that traditional forms of social life. Enabling them to live at the expence of the masses. They saw progress in the per se elimination of the government[10]. Holding that society is moving inevitably through predetermined phases or stages as a consequence of a mystic force called historical imperative[11].

Marx believed that in each stage, society is divided into two classes - those owing the means of production and those deprived of them. This result in antithetical class-interest and the pursuant struggle, which becomes the most extreme in the capatalist phase and culminates in the class-war[12]. The outcome is a revolution which the "expropriators are expropriated"[13].

The Fabian socialists, on the other hand rejected the idea that is to bring evolution of a good society, revolution is neccessary, and held that the transition from capatalism to socialism would and should be gradual and peacemeal[14].

Grand Theories of Social Change

"A grand theory is a broad conceptual scheme with systems of interrelated propositions that provide a general frame of reference for the study of social processes and institutions"[15].

Parson's general system theory and Sorokin's theory of socio-cultural dynamics are examples of grand theories.

These grand theories of social change are of two types:

1. Progress and evolution theory expounded by Spencer, Hobhouse, Comte and Marx. The basic assumption in the idea of this theory is that the conditions at the present day are due to the consquences of some changes that have been taken in the past. These theories are also known as linear theories.
2. *Cyclical theories* - Tonybee and Sorokin the exponents of the theory explained that different cultures in human history have passed from the rising phase to the declining phase, showing that change is cyclic.

Sorokin[16], provides the historical explaination of change contended that all socities fluctuate through time and between two polar extremes - "the ideational" (the good) and "the sensate" (the bad). He believed that all socities swing from one pole to another but the whole of the social system did not move in one co-ordinated way.

Another concept "Re-birth" has propounded by Tonybee[17]. He called it "The response to the challenge of imminent destruction."He believed that society in a manner somewhat analogous to the physical maturation of an organism, having approached maturity, develops organisational rigidity, causing it to become stiff.

Another theory of change states that societies change, not towards perfection, but towards extinction. This belief is supported by drawing an analogy between society and living organism. The apparent rise and subsequent decline of the civilizations of the past is all too easily adequated with the life cycle of the individual human being, who is born, grows to maturity and then dies.

Giovanni Battists Vicco and Edward Gibban provided the first applications of this cydical theory in the eighteenth Century.

Spengler[18] in the earlier twentieth century, advanced another application of this concept by arguing, that the west, which have given birth to industrial society was now loosing vigour and beginning to stagnate, only to be replaced by the vigour of the emergent Asian Society.

The particularistic theory of change involves the assumption that in each instance social change is the product of some particular variable, or "cause" Every change in the "cause" will produce a concomitant change in the society. It is a realization that theory must be based on adequate fact that led to the formation of middle range theories. These theories are restricted to emperical level. Such as population change, marriage and family dynamics, special aspects of industrialization, religious organization etc.

The chief exponent of the middle - range theory is R.K. Merton. Some middle range theories are theories of reference group, the theory of social mobility and the theory of formation and change of social norms.

Anthropologists have suggested that change follows a certain process with which technical experts and social scientists should be familiar.

G. Elliot Smith advocated the idea of culturally dominant centers, and developed into a concept of social change.Following this, cultural anthropologists were split into two camps-

(a) the diffusionists - they tried to trace everything cultural to some particular centre; and

(b) the parallelists - they were inclined to think that people had independently developed their own cultural devices.

Rogers[19] refers change as brought by three factors-

(1) Intention - the process by which the new ideas are created or developed.

(2) Diffusion - the process by which new ideas are communicated through a given social system.

(3) Consequence - the change occuring with in the system as the result of the adoption or rejection of the innovations.

In modern times, the broader cultural base, made possible by widening of contacts and communications between people, has to an ever-changing rate of change.

Foster sees the upper class as the first adaptors of change. The lower class imitate the upper classes and gradually the change follows[20]. There is no second thought to the fact that there is no single path of change for all developing countries.

Another anthropological approach to the study of social change explains 'diffussionism', as important variable in the study of change. Here diffusionism tends to explain change in one society by finding its origin in other. A.L. Kroeber was one such thinker who analysed this theory[21].

Another approach in the study of social change is similar to that of functional approach. It studies equilibrium and the conditions under which stability is maintained as against those under which it is undermined[22].

Change is Essential - Change is an essential element of life. Every group, every society or community is undergoing some changes or the other. The study of social change has always been important in sociology.

As Johnson writes, "Broadly speaking, there are two kinds of processes going on in a socisl system; process that maintain the structure of the system and processes that change the social system, but they may also help to maintain it. In the face of new circumtances, the social system may need to adapt structure to some extent in order to survive[23]. It shows that system is forced to change in order to maintain its continuity or itself. All socities are primatively repugnant to change. Though most of recorded social history men have apparently considered that change per se is undersirable and the ideal social condition is stability[24]. Stability evidently has not only been the social ideal but also the normal condition[25].

Social stability is achieved through persistance. As parsons writes, "a social stucture is a natural persistence system. It maintain its continuity despite internal changes from movement to movement, year to year, just as living organism, inspite of metabolic changes, it is dynamic[26].

Thus social change and social stability are both features of any social system. Continuity and change goes hand in hand as it is no doubt that the society has constantly been changing at fluctuating speeds.

It is not possible, for all individuals in the society to accept the change and tolerate its speed and character. There are few who suffer from considerable dissatisfaction. Every individual has its own level of tolerance and the quantity of dissatisfaction is directly related to their tolerance power. As lack of satisfaction increases, tolerance power tends is decrese and at this hour, the process of change is increasingly seen as inadequate, improper and tardy. Various groups of the society whether conservatives or the radicals should adjust themselves to the changing conditions. If either or both groups fail to acheive mutual understanding with one another, conflict becomes inevitable. This can also result in the struggle between both the ends which can lead to disintegration of the society. Change is a powerful source of conflict and its nature is complex, difficult to understand and explain.

Among the forces that are capable for changing elements of social structure, can be distinguished in two large groups -

(1) Exogamous - those that originate outside a social structure.

(2) Endogamous - those that are generated by the structure itself.

For the former, the exogamous structure change, or exogamous factors are used and for the latter that of the endogamous structure change, endogamous factors are used[27].

M.J. levy has introduced the similar contrast. The related factors for change may be internal factors or external factors or it is sometimes the combination of both the factors.[28] Levy was most interested and concerned with the cases related to the external factors of change.

Becker's own theory of change is based upon his belief in the predictive power of the human mind equipped with effective tools and concepts. Like M.J. Levy and Becker accepted the importance of internal forces such as class conflict as well as external forces such as crises as being important in initiating change.

The concept of competition and conflict between species, and the invasion of an ecological area by a new species with attended changes, has also been drawn upon to explain social change. This has been done by drawing an analogy between human society and the plant and animal world.

For Becker invention is one of the source which produce change in the society. Taking of the similar lines, Ogburn[29] advanced the theory of 'social lag'. He suggests that social changes always originate in the invention of a new of doing something or of something new to do. Falling in line with Tarde and Marx, he argued that inventions occur most often in the field of material technology. The result is that a strain or stress, is set-up between the new techniques and the various organizational aspects of the social system, changes in which come slowly, leading to a disequilibrium between the two, called "cultural lag".

Providing another explaination Hornel Hart[30] in an effort to restate the old ideas of social progress using Tarde's concept of invention held; culture accumulates through the addition of new inventions at an accelerative rate which leads to linear accelerative social change invariably directed at increasing efficiency or effectiveness.

Some other thinkers, using the North - South dichotomization explained observed differences between societies by arguing that climate determined a people's character. Making the first use of geographic factors Ellsworth Huntington[31] argued, only as existing geographic conditions change, the societies will be changed, unless the people should migrate to some new geographic location.

Biologically, it is believed that people of the world are divided into races which have markedly different interest abilities to develop and maintain social life, and the norms and quality of social life that a people lead are indications of their social qualities. Consquently, deteriorative changes may logically be traced either to mongrelization by the infusion of inferior social stock on the running out of the social qualities, while rising ones can be traced to the flowering to the latent racial greatness or to the appearence, presumably through the evolutionary process, of superior biological qualities in the formely undistinguished population.

It is to be remembered that social change is not in any sense a product of the society per se, or a consequence of some universal and unvarying law of social life. Further, the changes that may occur in a society are fairly comparable to those violations of the normal organic processes that follow when, for reasons yet unknown, a cell goes wild-when it break from the "laws" that control its growth and reproduction and multiplying, disturbing the functioning of the entire organism. The forces that make for social change are, if the organic analogy pursued abnormal - violation of the normal process by which the social system is transmitted from generation of members.

A change in society comes as a foreign and unwanted agent, not neccessarily of destruction, but always of disturbances to the established and organizationally preferred structures and processes of life.[32]

Societies always operate with the aim of self - maintainence and all types of organizations are inherently resistant to change. It is true as social change is the work of such individuals who are social deviants and acts as an anti - social elements in the society. This view is proposed in the theory of "Collective Behaviour" advanced by Robert. E. Park.[33] in 1921. According to Park change occurs due to the incidental consequence of the fortuitions have become desocialized through participation in mass killings. He explains that new modes of social conduct sometimes evolve and occasionally get established in the social system as the end product of the mass movement. However, it is by substituting 'individuals' for 'masses,'[34] In Park's theory that a more illustrative explaination of the process of change can be provided.

Acceptance of the special role of individual in breaking traditions makes a fuller appreciation of the process of social change possible. It is usually an outstanding individual who percieves the need of change, if that individual possesses the will and power to effect the change, society changes.

Oley Zenam, elaborating his 'power-will hypothesis, has evolved a useful concept of social change that helps explain the causation of violence in different forms.[35] According to him, through the factors contributing to social change are numerous,complex and intextricably interwined, one can roughly divide them into two categories-

(1) ecological (nominal objective)

(2) eiconic (phenomenal objective)

In general most historical changes can be traced to some combination of factors belonging to these two realms. Coincidence of 'will' derived from the eiconic realm and 'power' deviced from the ecological realm, represent sufficient condition for change involving decision making. Each of them taken seperately represents a neccessary condition for this type of social change.

Social change is a part of modernization. Cultural accumulation, invention, contacts with other cultures, diffussion, education and change per se are the sources of change. Values, technology, population and social movements and dynamic men are the factors of social change. Each of these factors does not by itself produce social change. Interaction between various factors produce social change. That is why the problem of causation has intrigued men in many ages and climes.[36]

The study of change has also been conducted in large-scale socities by many contemperory sociologists. An attempt has been made to draw conclusion about change in traditional society when process of modernization has been introduced in it.

Prof. Wilbert Moore and Arnold Feldman report that "there is a common care of structual elements found in industrial socities ranging from the more obvious features, such as factory system of production and increasing urbanisation, through," common cognitive orientation, such as the view of time and use of knowledge; and common value orientation, such as achievement orientation."[37]

Dialectical - Historical Approach

Dialectical historical approach in the study of social change is witnessed in the writrings of D.P Mukherjee's 'Diversities' (1958). The main focus is on the emergence of middle class under the impact of British Colonial rule. He sees change as a process of movement through conflict and Contradiction.[38] Another exposition of this approach in the writings of A.R. Desai (1959).[39] He analysis the process of change in India in context to the history of nationalism. The dialectical - historical concepts have also been used by Ramkrishna Mukherjee[40] in his study of 'The Rise and fall of the East India Company.'

According to Riseman, change in the ratio of births to deaths often brings about profound changes in a traditional society.[41] As the population grows, the death rate drops, agriculture improves and yield surpluses. These are periods of rapid social mobility, of the accumulation of capital,of invention and expansion. According to this theory the changes in the society leads to changes in the dominant social type.

When death rates follows birth rates downward, population become static or declines, agriculture is replaced by industry and industry in part by the service occupations, hours are short, materials and leisure abundant, at this time men finds that: "Increasingly other people are the problem, not the material enviorment."[42]

The United States after world war II may serve as an example.

Social Mobility

In the recent times the process of social mobility has become more impressive and active.

The important structural units that sociologists have used for the analysis of social stratification in India are caste, class, elite and professional - occupational categories. The treatment of caste in the studies become unavoidable as a standard to measure change with the refrences to other principles of stratification such as wealth and power.[43]

Mobility involves changes in position that bring about new contacts and stimulations. Therefore Sorokin defined mobility "as spatial change involving mental contacts."[44]

Mobility studies have mainly drawn their data from the studies of caste, class, occupation, leadership and elite structure.

In the field of social stratification, so in the other closely related aspect, social mobility, occupational mobility has been considered as a significant indicator by many sociologists like Sorokin, (1927); Mills (1960); and Ghurye, (1961). Though there are many others who do not accept the view that social mobility in ocupational terms is identical immediately with unidimensional vertical social mobility.

Damle[45] and Lynch have used the concept of "refrence group" to study caste mobility. The entire reference group approach to study mobility according to Damle and lynch, focus upon three aspects :

(1) The motivational structure, the aspiration of the members to move upward.

(2) Opportunity structure - the eligibility or indigibility of the members to move in a desired direction.

(3) The communication structure - which influence people's motivation for social mobility.

Damle lay stress on the first two aspects and lynch lay stress on the third aspect. Thus, all the three aspects provide a refrence group frame in the study of mobility.

Intergenerational Mobility

Mobility studies shows that father to son mobility steps are quite small. It is found very rare where son gets a job much higher or much lower that his father's occupational prestige or pay.[46]

The study of Milles (1960),[47] Blau and Duncan (1967),[48] lipset (1982)[49] never examine the downward mobility of sons with elite fathers into manual labour.

Another valuable study of N. Rogoff (1953) compares the distribution of fathers - son shifts in occupation for the two periods.[50]

The studies analysing the social mobility are confined to urban areas generally. Sovani, Apte and Pendse (1956), analysis of the mobility in Poona is an often quoted work. Taking caste and socio - economic status as control variables, they have analysed the intergenerational occupational vertical mobility.

One of the major contribution in the studies of downward mobility is by C.J. Richardson (1977).[51] Richardson explains that downward mobility arises due to the failure or inability of some middle class families to provide a social and economic foothold sufficient to maintain a similar status for their sons.

In the industrial society Blau and Duncan (1967)[52] Parkin (1972),[53] explained the occupation as the best indicator of class and social position in the stratification system.

One of the most important findings in the mobility study done by Lipset and Bendix (1959),[54] shows that men of high social origin are found sometimes doing jobs of low level mannual position and half the men of working class parentage hold jobs higher to their original position.

Such studies are quite near to the functionalist approach of social stratification. "Social inequality" to the functionalists (Davis and Moore; 1945) is "an unconsiously evolved device by which societies insure that the most important positions are filled by the most qualified person."[55] As functionalists argue that "not all jobs are equally important."[56] There is another form of social mobility available to the members of the Indian society i.e. mobility through renunication or by becoming Sanyasis.[57] Silverberg writes," for individuals in India there has always been a means of escaping the stratification system eg: as sanyasis or family ascities."[58]

Group Mobility

There are also various instance of group mobility. Achievemnt of individuals may lead the entire group upward or downward in the social stratum.

The works of Burton Stein (1968),[59] K.M. Panniker (1955)[60] stated that conquest and wealth were the two powerful determinants of social mobility. Panniker stated that claiming the Kshatriyahood by non - kshatriya castes most of the royal houses were established.

Similar studies conducted on changes in social mobility by Morans(1959)[61] and Surajit Sinha (1957),[62] where many tribals ascended to the position of royalty in India by claiming nationhood either by conquest or accmulation of power.

The studies mentioned are the examples of the mobility caused by external or exogamous factors like conquests and invasions.

Another important factor which determines the upward or downward mobility of the individual is education. The studies of Hauser and Daymount (1977),[63] Parelius and Parelius (1978),[64] Haveman and West (1972),[65] shows that more the education person has, more likely is the person to enjoy occupational and financial success. Education plays an important role in the occuring of changes in the society.

Theodore Braneld (1968)[66] while studying the two communities (Ebibara and Kawabara) of Japan throws light on the role of education which it plays in accelerating and retarding the changes in the society which was at that time undergoing a fast and often painful flux.

Various types of social change studies have been undertaken. Kuppuswamy mentions them as follows :

(1) Acculturation studies - which study the change taking place in a group which is open to outside influence.

(2) Studies in demographic and ecological change, which includes study of migration, population etc.

(3) Urbanisation studies - which deals with urban areas, their structure and so on.

(4) Social mobility and dynamics - These studies deal with change in social structure due to social mobility which is important in modern India.

(5) The study of institutional and community change - These include study of family, economic and political institutions and studies of rural community.

(6) Social movements - There are the social changes brought about by organised attempts by people in the form of religious, political or labour movements.

Various Views on Refugees

The various litrature on refugees covers three broad types od Individuals:

(1) Those who have become refugees due to economic causes,

(2) Those who become refugee due to political, religious or ethnic reasons, and

(3) Those who seek a refugee status due to war.

Recently the third type is more popular the war facing refugees. Traditional people, who because of their territory, are forced to flee to more or less inhospitable or unsympathetic areas.

Refugees

Many of the refugee studies related to the Indian context are generally based on refugees who seek their refugee status due to the partition of the country.[67]

R.N. Saksena's study on Punjab refugees in Dehra Dun was concentrated upon social attitudes. Similar on the lines was a study of Stephen keller which was also based on the former Punjab refugees from west Pakistan.[68]

Though both the studies mentioned above resulted due to forced movement of the population, But it is quite different from that of the status of Tibetan refugees. There was no question of granting new nationality to the Punjabi community nor they were met with 'coolness' and 'hostility' by the Indians.

Joseph Schechtman[69], the author of the 'Refugees in the world: Displacement and integration (1963) was concerned to the problem of Jewish refugees. He was himself involved in the Zionist movement.

The main objective of the study was to let the international community knew about the kind of life, the refugees lead, to bring about solutions for the betterment of their condition.

The study of Gardner Murphy focuses attention on the social and Psychological dimensions of the refugee condition. According to him " when populations are uprooted both on the societal and on the individual level, flight and compulsory displacement of population engender a considerable amount of contemporary feeling and this has tended to effect both societal attitudes and individual objectivity."[70]

The Author of the book' The Uprooted' written by Kanti Pakrasi, is mostly concerned with the Bengali refugees from East Pakistan (New Bangladesh).

"A study of socio-economic conditions and attitudes of displaced persons: A study of social tension in Bombay" by C.N. Vakil and P.H. Cabinetmaker is another notable study on the refugees.

While reviewing the literature briefly on the refugees, it can be concluded that mostly the studies related to refugees were based on -

1. The bad conditions faced by refugees in camps and settlements;
2. Suggesting measure for the betterment of socio-economic conditions of the refugees,
3. Results of uprooting and problems of social disorganisation.
4. Drastic and sudden changes among the refugees community due to interaction with the host's social system.

India has a long history of migrants, they have been coming and settling down due to one or the other reasons. The refugees situation is in no way new to India. She has received large number of refugees recently from Tibet and then from Bangladesh.

All the migrant groups are in constant process of assimilation in the Indian culture. Tibetan refugees have been considered as the most important and numerous group received by her, both from the view of humanitarian dimensions and political dimensions. They have been accomodated protectedly by the government of India in various settlement throughout the country. The literature available in Tibetans in Exile 1959-69, Dr. Anand Kumar

(1994) reveals all the earlier settlements and rehabilitation programmes conducted by Government of India in the early days of their asylum.

Tibetans have their own distinct culture but, inspite of forty three years living in a host country, they are still maintaining their own culture.

Tibetan literature contains plenty of mysterious stories about the land, such as studies conducted by Dr. Dawa Norbu (1987), R.D. Taring (1996), Rigzin Tsepak (1993) and Guiseppi Tucci's (1980). By the constant emphases on the occult and supernatural in the Tibetan myths, legends and holy literature have substantially added to the sense of strangeness associated with the land.

Then, there are many travellers, historians and Tibetans who wrote about Tibet and its people. Among such studies are - W.D. Shakabpa (1967), H.E. Richardson (1962, 1984), David Snellgrove (1980), R.A. Stein (1972), Heinrich Harrer (1953) and Charles Bell (1998).

Many authoritative books have been written on the social and cultural life of Tibetans.

Sir Charles Bell's "People of Tibet", G. Tucci's "Tibet : The land of snows", L.A. Woddell's, 'The Buddhism of Tibet', H. Hoffman's, 'The Religions of Tibet', G. Sandberg's, 'Tibet and Tibetans', D. L. Snellgrove's "Buddhist Himalayas and the cultural History of Tibet", R.A. Steins, "Tibetan Civilization", are some of the most important of these works.

Another important work on Tibet and its people is conducted by David Macdonld's (Touring in Tibet and Sikkim). It deals with the country and its people in all its aspects -physical, social cultural, historial, administrative and economic. It is in fact an encyclopaedia on Tibet.

But with the interaction with the host country, the traditional attitudes and beliefs, are passing through an important phase of change. In this context various studies indicate the process of change among Tibetans in India.

Few among such studies are conducted by A.V. Arakheri (1998), Ram Bahadur Chhetri (1990), Melvyn Goldstein (1978), T.C. Palakashappa (1976), Girija Saklani (1984), and Tanka. B. Subba (1990).

The study of Mundgod Tibetans been made by Palakshappa, an Indian sociologists (1976), contributed in the understanding of refugees, the stresses and strains faced by them, their rehabilitation, aspirations and problems of adjustment. He also noted that some Tibetan refugees have made money which they loan out on interest to the Indians (1978:106). This shows the growing confidence between the Indians and the Tibetans. It also indicates the growing affluence of the Tibetans in the settlement. The work emphasisses on the process of change and mobility occuring in the Tibetan community. However it lacks depths and details of the Tibetan society and culture.

Dr. Tanka. B. Subba studied the process of adaptation and rehabilitation among Tibetan refugees in the region of Sikkim and Darjeeling districts. He measures degree of adaptation in terms of social skill, occupation and income. They have a considerable degree of closeness with the local people who practice Buddhism. He pointed out that these Tibetan refugees have created a lot of self employment opportunities and alternative occupations. Due to interaction with the local people, these refugees have cultural traits. Besides all this, people themselves share a strong sense of pride in their tradition, culture and religion.

Another study made by Melvyn Goldstein (1978), of Mundakuppe settlement shows that, Tibetan interection with the Indians has been restricted to fleeing encounters in the market places and sporadic contact in employer/ employee situations where the Tibetans are in dominant positions.

He points out that, there has been virtually no assimilation to Indian cultural and social institutions. Their economic property and vigrous protection of cultural traditions is a fertile matrix of interethnic resentment, hostility and conflict. Goldstein nowhere indicates the amount of change in the Tibetan society and how the process of mobility took place after they seek asylum in India.

A study of persistance and change conducted by Ram Bahadur Chhetri (1990), in Pokhara, Nepal, is another important work in the field of adaptation of Tibetan Refugees. He study the changes in the economic life of Tibetans from nomadic herding to handicraft business. Changing pattern of family and marriage, various rituals and practices has made the study more interesting to those who study change. He also studies the process of adaptation of refugees in the totally new enviornment. Thus, Ram Bahadur Chhetri has taken up few social problems and therefore it cannot be called as the comprehensive study of Tibetan refugees.

Last, but not the least is the most important study conducted by Girija Saklani (1984). The field area of her study include S Dharamsala, Amdo settlement in Dehra Doon and Majnu - Ka - Tilla camp in Delhi.

She has observed changes in all the significant spheres of Tibetan social life; i.e: family, religion, social hierarchy, economic and political structures, etc.

Saklani pointed out that resistance to change is accepted by them as the main aim of their refugee existence. Therefore, the forms and patterns along with each and every sphere of change have been evaluated in terms of the preservation of cultural identity aim of the refugee community. She also contribute to the study of more practical problems related to rehabilitation of the Tibetan refugees.

As the study of Girija Saklani was conducted just after few years the Tibetans came in India, therefore, the study could not provide a wide distinction of change and mobility among them.

From the studies mentioned, it is clear that inspite, getting exposed to the modern world, Tibetans have managed to preserve their traditional socio - cultural institutions in various ways.

In the light of what has been discussed in the proceeding pages, the present work proposes the following objectives :

Objectives:

There are set of problems common to the study of social change. A great many discussions about social change bog down in unresolved argument about whether certain changes, say in the rate of social mobility, are "real changes" or merely "expression in a new form" of older well - documented charcteristics[71].

Firstly, it is to be specified as to what elements believed to be changing e.g., change in attitude or values or a person, his behaviour, his status or his occupation.

Secondly, it is neccesary to agree precisely about what will be objectively accepted as constituting "change".

Adopting a middle - range approach what Merton[72] refers to as "cummulative emperical research" it was tried to explain the consequences of social change in a Tibetan community.

There is no doubt that various studies have been conducted in different parts of the country by various sociologists and anthropologists, as noted while reviewing the literature. But there is a lack of detailed and systematic information about the life of Tibetan refugees changing in the cities of Dharamsala and Dehra Dun.

After reviewing the literature, it was found that most of the studies related of the Tibetan refugees places greater emphasis on one or the other, particular aspect of the community. This present study, however is a broad survey of all the aspects of change in the social life of Tibetan refugees resulting in mobility among them. Social mobility has to be analysed in terms of two principle types - vertical social mobility and horizontal social mobility. In this context of social mobility the present study deals with -

(a) Various channels of social mobility which permit individual to move up and down from one social stratum to another.

(b) Different mobility rates and factors responsible for the high and low rate of social mobility, and their implications on the various groups of the Tibetan community.

(c) The intergenerational mobility rates among the refugees.

As it has been found the changes occuring in the society are not accepted by all the members of that society. Whenever change and mobility occurs people show different attitudes, some may be positive and some others may be negative towards it. Thus, the present work deals with the effects of change and mobility on the human behaviour and psychology. It was also intended to find out whether social mobility proved "favourable" or "unfavourable" for the society.

This work is first and formost an emperical knowledge of how Tibetan refuges are effected by living in a society which is quite different from what they practised prior to refugehood, how they cope up with the Indian society which is stratified and a developing society. Being an outsider, the study will provide an impartial description of the life of Tibetans in exile who accomodated themselves to the new enviorment.

In this way, the work will further help the researchers and theorists to examine the relationship between refugees and their new social enviorment.

Another important aspects of the work is that it is primarily based on DehraDun and Dharamsala. Both these places witness their importance in the settlement of Tibetan refugees since they have migrated to India. Therefore, it was an important task to show that these two places still play a significant role in the life of Tibetan refugees. The facts about social change and social mobility with relation to these places are scarce and hard to come by.

This attempt will also help the planners and the researcher to think about them and plan better policies like providing better living facilities, planning welfare programmes, health and literacy programmes and so on.

References

1. Kuppuswamy - Social Changes in India. 1972.
2. Ginsberg, Morris. - Social Change. British Journal of Sociology. Vol. IX, 1958. (pg. 205).
3. Lapiere, Richard. T. - Social Change. Mcgraw Hills. 1965, New York. (pg. 5).
4. *Ibid.*
5. Gumplowicz, Ludwing - "Der Rassenkanpf, Innsbruck. Wagner. 1928.
6. Durkheim, Emile - "The Rules of Sociological Method, Free Press, New York, 1964. Passim.
7. Gertn, H.G. and C. Wright Mills - From Max Weber. Oxford University Press Oxford, 1946. Ch. VIII.
8. Tonnies, Ferdinand - Community and Society, East Lansings. The Michigan State University Press. 1957.
9. Ginsberg, Morris - The Idea of Progress. A Revolution, Boston. Beacon Press, 1953.
10. Fever, Levis, S. - Ideology and the Ideologists, Basil Blackwell, Oxford, 1975.
11. Marx, Karl Das Kapital, Kerr, Chicago, 1909.

12. *Ibid.*
13. Wayper, C. Li : Political Thought - B.I. Publication, N. Delhi. 1977. pg. 212.
14. Lapiere, Richard, T. - op cit. pg. 13.
15. Abraham, Francis, M. - Modern Sociological Theory - 'An Introduction'. Oxford University. Press.
16. Sorokin, Pitrim, A. - Social and Cultural Dynamics. American Book Company, 1937, New York. (pg. 41).
17. Tonybee, Arnold, J. - A study of History, Oxford University Press, Fairlaion - 1947.
18. Spengler, Oswald-The Decline of the West. New York, Alfered. A Knopf, 1939.
19. Rogers, Everett, M. - Modernisation Among Peasents. The Impact of Communication, New. York. Holt. Richart & Winston Inc. 1969.
20. Fairchild, H.P. (ed) - Dictionary of Sociology. 1962. pg. 14.
21. Etzioni and Etzioni - Social Change - Sources Patterns and Consequences. London, Basic Books Inc. Publishers. pg. 80.
22. *Ibid.* pg. 81.
23. Johnson, H.M. - Sociology - A Systematic Introduction. N. Delhi, Allied Publishers ltd. 1960. pg. 625.
24. Lapiere, Richard, T. - Social Change. New York, Mcgraw Hills. 1965. pg. 1.
25. *Ibid.* pg. 2
26. Parsons, T. - The Social System - New York, Free Press. 1964.
27. Daherndorf, Ralph - Class and Class Conflict in Industrial Society. London, Routledge and Kegan Paul. 1959. pg. 127.
28. Levy, M.J. - Some sources of the vulnerability of the structures of relatively non-industrialised societies to those of highly industrialised socities. B.F. Hostelititz (ed.) The progress of underdeveloped areas. Chicago. 1952.
29. Ogburn, William, F. - Social change with respect to culture & original nature; New York, Villing Press. 1950.

30. Hart, Hornel - The Techniques of Social Progress. New York, Halt Rinehart and Winston Pub. 1931.
31. Hutington Ellsworth. Climate and Civilization, Yale University Press. 1924, New Haven, Also, Hutington Ellsworth. Hainsprings of Civilization. John Siley, New. York. 1945.
32. Lapiere, Richard, T. op cit. pp. 38-39.
33. Park, Robert, E. & Erenest, W. Burgees. Introduction to the Science of Sociology. The University Press of Chicago. 1921. Chicago (pp. 865-952).
34. The Transformation of Rennaisant Europe and the Westernization of the oriental societies could be treated as illustrative examples in these cases.
35. Zenam, Oley - Terrorism and Violence in a light of a theory of Discontent and Frustation. In Livingston Marcus, H. Lee Bruce Kress and Marie. G. Wanck (eds.) International Terrorism in the Contemporary World. 1978 (pp. 245-47).
36. Prasad, Narmadeshwar - Change strategy in a developing society. Meerut, Meenakashi Prakshan.
37. Moore, Wilbert and Arnold Feldman - Industrialization and Industrilism Convergence and Differentiation, Transactions of the Fifth World Congress of Sociology, Clouvain: International Sociological Association. 1962. II: 165.
38. Mukherjee, D.P. - Diversities. Peoples Publishing House, Delhi 1958.
39. Desai, A.R. - Rural Sociology in India. 1959.
40. Mukherjee, R.K. - The rise and fall of the East India Company. Berlin 1958.
41. Inkeles, Alex - What is sociology. An Introduction to the Discipline and Profession Prentice Hall of India Pvt. Ltd. (op cit.) New Delhi, 1987. pg. 53.
42. Riesman, David - The Lonley Ground, New. York. Doubleday 1958. pg. 34.

43. *Ibid.* (pp. 3-6)
44. Sorokin, P. - Social Mobility - Harper and Brothers, New York, 1927.
45. Damle, Y.B. - Reference group theory and mobility in the caste system in James Silverberg (ed.) Social Mobility in the caste system in India. Morton and Co. the Hague. 1968.
46. Blau and Duncan - The American occupational structure. 1967, John Viley, New. York (pg. 28).
47. Miller, S.M. (1960) - Comparative Social Mobility (pp. 1-89).
48. Blau & Duncan - op cit.
49. Lipset - The Academic Mind at the top. The political behaviour and values of faculty elites. In public opinion quarterly, 46 (Summers) (pp. 143-168).
50. Rogoff - Recent trends in occupational mobility, Fress Press. 1953.
51. Richardson, C.J. Contemperory Social Mobility, Francis Printers (Pub. Ltd.), London. 1977.
52. Blau & Duncan - The American exceptional structure: New York. Wiley. 1967. (op cit.)
53. Parkin, F. - Class inequality and political order. Paladin, London. 1972.
54. Lipset and Bendix - Op. cit. (pg. 185).
55. Davis and Moore - Some principles of stratification - American Sociological Review. April, 10, 1945 (pp. 242-249).
56. Ibid.
57. Singh, Yogendra - op. cit. (pg. 117).
58. Silverberg - Social mobility in the caste system in India (pg. 128). Moutor, The Hauge. 1968.
59. Stein Burton - Social Mobility and Medieval South Indian Hindu Sect. - Social mobility in the caste system in India. Mouton, The Haque. 1968.

60. Panniker, K.M. - Hindu Society at the Cross Roads - Asia Publishing House, Bombay. (1955).
61. Drans, M. - A Tribe in search of a great tradition. The Emulation - solidarity conflict. Man in India. (1959).
62. Singh Surajit - Tribal cultures of Penninsular India as a discussion of little tradition in the study of Indian civilization. - Man in India (1957).
63. Hauser, R.M. and Thomas N. Daymont - Schooling, Ability & Earnings, Cross Sectional findings 8-14 yrears after high school graduation sociology of education, 50 July, 1977.
64. Parelius and Parelius - Sociology of Education. Englewood Cliffs, N.J. Prentice Hall. 1978.
65. Haveman, Ernest & P. S. West - The College Graduates American Today, Harcourt Brace, New. York. 1952.
66. Brameld, Theodore - Japan Culture, Education and Change in Two communities (pg. xv-xviii) by Holt, Pinchart and Wiston Inc. USA. 1968.
67. Saksena, R.N. - Refugees - A study in Changing Patterns. Asia Publishing House, Bombay. 1961.
68. Keller Stephen, L. - Uprooting and Social Change. The role of refugees in development. Published by Manohar Book Service. Delhi. 1975.
69. Schechtman, J.B.-The Refugees in the World, Displacement and Integration. New York, A.S. Barnes & Co., London 1963. pg. (xi).
70. Murphy, Gardner - In the Minds of Man. The study of human behaviour and social tension in India. New York (1953) (pg. 85).
71. Inkles, Alex - op cit. (pg. 90).
72. Merton, R.K. - Social Theory and Social Structure, New York, The Free Press. 1957.

2

Tibet and Tibetans:
China invasion on Tibet and Tibetan Resettlements

The people of Tibet call Tibet by the name Pō. In early Arabian works it is termed as 'Tobbat', 'Tubbat', 'Tibat' and other such variants. It is also known as the "Roof of the world" because it lies on a very high altitude.

(i) Geography

Climate : The land of snows lies within the area of 500,000 square miles which stands roughly between the 28th and 36th parallels of North latitude and the 79th and 99th of east longitude. Enclosed on three sides by mountain ranges appears like clenched right first with the whist on its north Kuen Lau (Kunlur) covers it which lies to 23000 ft. and Tangla (Tanglha) which rises to more than 18000 ft. On its southern sphere the range of Himalayas (1,500 miles) connects it to the border of 3 countries - India, Nepal and Bhutan. On its western side it is covered by Karakoram (29000 ft.) and Ladakh (19,000 ft).

On the eastern side it is connected to Chinese border. It is interesting to note here that sparsely populated country is surrounded by three most populated countries of the world India, China and earstwhile USSR. Highest Mountains which covers the land are also the source of some great rivers of Asia. In the south-west Indus and Brahamputra (Known as Tsang-po in Tibet) rise and diverts to eastward and westward in their directions. Similarly Sutlej and Karnali make their ways through Himalayas. In the north east the Yangtse, Mekong and Salween flows down the eastern borders of Tibet.

Three are several stretches of plain land and valleys where the climate is favourable for agricultural production. Whereas in Tibet the temperature ranges from 50°F to 68°F (10°C to 20°C) during summers and below 0°C i.e. freezing point in winters. Because of such climatic conditions it is severely cold and dry with very less rainfall only about 5-8 inches. Though the temperature recorded has variations according to the different places in Tibet because the country lies between 2000 ft to 29000 ft. Similarly the rainfall record also varies accordingly.

(ii) Fauna and Flora in Tibet : In Tibet very little vegetation is found except grass on the high plateau at 17,000 ft. production of good vegetation is near the rich valleys. Crops like barley, wheat, peans, beans and buckwheat are found. The yield is so high that grass can be stored for at least three years during unfavourable times.

Fruits grown in the area are peech, apple and bannana. Vegetables like mushroom, edible roots (though not all edible roots) and sweet potatoes are found. Tree like poplar, teak, pines, walnut, apricot, oaks, birches, junipers, elnus, wild rose and other thorn trees are common in Tibet In these dense forests wild bear, wild goat, leopard, tiger, langur, jackal and wild buffalo are found.

In the grass lands of Tibet deer, wild asses, yaks, forces wolves, rabbits, sheeps are common. Fishes are found in the streams and lakes in Tibet catfish, tout are common, frog, crab and tortoise are also found in Tibet. Among the ranges of domestic animals are Yak and Horse which are the means of transportation. Zo, cow (pachu) and dri are milk yielding animals. The sheep and goat gives best wool in Asia. Habitation occurs within the western region which ranges 16000 ft (m.s.l.) to 4000 ft (m.s.l.) in some parts of the southern valley.

The soil of Tibet is less fertile than that of India. So they had to depend on other sources of irrigation rather than rainfall. In India they work hard on lands and due to suitable fertile land and good rains they yield high production of crops.

(iii) Mineral Resources in Tibet : Although Tibet is rich in mineral resources but they were never used in developing the traditional society. In Tibet silver, sulphur, copper, brass, pearl, aluminium, etc. are found. Tibet is rich in gold but digging out the gold is against the religious customs of Tibetans.

The country lies between India on the south and west and China proper in the East to the North Chinese Turkistan and a narrow strip of the chinese province, Kansu seperate it from mongolia.

Tibet is one of the most remote countries cutt off from the outside world by massive mountain ranges and caves, An area of a million and a half square miles, divided into three provinces - the central province of U-Tsang (which is now Tibet Autonomous Region), Amdo (now as Qinghai); and Kham (now as Sichuan Province).

(2) Race

Ethnologists have divided the Tibetan population in two main groups one tall, long limbed, often with vaquiline features and long headed; the other shorter in stature with high cheekbones, flat noses and round heads. The former type of Tibetans are generally found in the northern and eastern parts. They are mainly nomads but also found in aristocratic families. These characteristics are traced to Mongolian and Turkic race. The second type of physique among Tibets is dominant among the valleys of central Tibet in the western parts. Modern Chinese Burmese and Thai are known to be their descendents.

The origin of Tibetan people remain obscure but as H.E. Richardson points out "they cannot with scientific accuracy be described as a "Chinese" people and indeed the chinese have for two thousand years or more looked on them as a seperate race".

(3) Language

The Tibetan script was originally borrowed from India somewhat near century. It resembles the Northern Gupta script of that time The Tibetan writing is almost different from the Chinese. There are 30 consonants and 4 vowel signs. Tibetan language has a monosyllabic basis and the world order is subject (in agentive case) : object; verb (verbal noun). It is a tonal language which is again quite different than those of Chinese.

(4) Communications

The communication means in Tibet were very remote. No proper system to send messages were prevalent in Tibet A postal service were given by the Indian borders to Lhasa and extended beyond that to the northern most parts of Tibet passing through districts headquarters on the way. There was one post office (Dha-Khang) post was taken by servants (Dhak-pa) (which are now commonly known as postmans) on horseback. The rich and aristocratic people keep their own private servants to sent their messages. Today in India they have learnt a lot about communication system and like any common Indian are very much dependent on them. Telephones, mobiles, faxes, access to computers are in common practice. They cannot think world without these systems.

Tibetan society is a traditional society and nomadic in nature. Before 1959, the population was made up of nobility, monks, traders, farmers, nomads etc. and this division is based on occupational bases and there are no "outcastes", as according to Bhuddhist religion everyone is equal.

(5) Tibetan Religion

Religion is very important for Tibetans and its imapct is very powerful even during their life in exile. The monks and nuns counted for one fourth of the population as it is a custom in Tibetans that at least one son or daughter should enter a monastic order. Some westerners feel that East is spiritual and West materialistic and Tibet is placed in the former category.

Initially Tibetans were the worshippers of Bón Religion but in the 17th century King Song Tsen gampo introduced Buddhism and recieved active encouragement from King and Kri-Srong Idebstan in the late 8th century. Monasteries being the seats of religious activities play an important role in life of Tibetans. In the shrine there are images of Bhuddha and other saints made of gold and silver. In the front of the images butter lamps burn day and night and bowls of water in small vessels are arranged in rows. In every Tibetan house one can find a private chapel and elderly people rotates their prayers wheels, at the same time turning their rosary and offer prayers.

As religion is one of the major factors in Tibetan society, so anything which goes against religion is not accepted by the society. "Tibetan religion is in fact, the mixture of Bhuddhism (its Tantric form imported from India in 700 A.D.) with the even more ancient "Shamanism" of North-East Asia a faith, according to some, of the North American Indians"[1]

The Tibetan symbols of four elements, viz., tiger, lion, eagle and dragon are used in Tibetan Bhuddhism. Prayer

Flags on the roof-top indicates the continuation of Bon practices in Tibetan Bhuddhism.

Saint Padmasambhava, a Rimpoche (Guru) was the founder of Lamaism in Tibet. A lama is a teacher, well-versed in the doctrines of Dharma, guides the pupil in the path of Dharma.

Another unique belief of Tibetan Bhuddhism is the practice of "life-cycle-rituals", which means that every human being to pass through certain stages of life prescribed by the society.

"Bhuddhists believe in the theory of re-birth and the one who choose the time and place according to their own wishes are called re-in-carnations; and those with extra-ordinary compassion, are believed to be re-in-carnations of Avlokiteshwara"[2]

Tibetans call their monasteries gompas, (secluded spot). Most of them were constructed on hill slopes, sheltered valleys facing grand plains, at picturesesque and grand spots. It was considered auspicious to face east.

Religious Beliefs and Practices

Monastery should not face a stream as for the stream would drain away the monastery. Vinicity of lake on waterfall was a sign of a good luck. Tibetans are luck addicts, good a bad omens are believed by them. "An animistic rite would be performed on the roof on the wedding morning and this is not Bhuddhism, but the pre-Bhuddhist native religion of Tibet."[3] Similarly among Tibetans it is a common belief that mole on a face made a woman deadly to her husband. Apart from mothers fatal mole another factor responsible for our step-father's death was our protest against his coming which created a bad omen[4]. It was considered a bad omen if the bridal road was blocked by snow, but if it fell when the bride was in her new home, it was a good sign[5].

Though in exile also, they have got reasonable reasons for what brought them national disaster. According to them it was thier logical and natural outcome of collective Karma. It is thus seen that Tibetans still are very superstitious and belive in theory of Karma.

Monasteries were often quite imposing buildings, several storeys in height. In the large courtyards of the monasteries lamas performed dramas. It was also used for outdoor celebrations. The walls were of rough hewn stone, plastered with mud or of stamped earth, reinforced with willow twings, flat slates being laid along the roofs to protect them from any damage from rains. The ground floor, is used as a central hall of worship. The first storey is used as a depository for the monastic neccessities like dress, utensils etc. The upper storey is used for granaries. The temple door's being protected by a Porch. Walls of this were painted effigies of the guardian deties and demons of the locality. Most of the Monasteries have large prayer wheel and 108 small prayer wheels on either side of the temple.

In the rich monasteries interior is decorated with rich silken streamer hangings. The ceitings and painted banners on silk depict Bhuddha and other saints. Even the demons or evil spirits are also depicted on them.

On the high altar there is a big life size image of Bhuddha; with two other small size images of disciplines or minor deities. Water bowls and holy butter lamps can also be seen on the alter.

On the seats of high lamas are silk cushions and silken canopies. There are no windows. The light enters the hall either from the doors or from the open top over which curtains being drawn in bad weather. Close by each monastery is atleast one large chorten (Stupa) erected sometimes as a depository of relics or sometimes in a memory of a saint or Lama.

"The Stupa originally represented the funeral mounds under which the shared relics of Sakyamuni's incinerated corpse once resposed. It soon become the chief symbolic representation of Buddhism, just as the cross become the symbol of Christianity"[6]

Later on they started containing sacred images, ashes of the deceased lama, friend or relative.

Its shape being divided into five divisions. They might represent ether, air, fire, water and earth. It can be of any size from 3 ft. to 50 ft.

Tibetan Culture

Tibetans being highly conservative by nature possesses rich and unique culture of her own which has been widely appreciated throughout the world. The Tibetan culture accquires high skills of craftsmenship and architecture. The cultural ties between India and Tibet can be seen on Tibetan art. The Nepalese artists enjoyed respect and fame in Tibet for their style. Tibetan paintings still have the imprints of there style in various regions of Tibet.

Tibetan literature which is purely religious in quite elaborative and possesses philosophical concepts of doctrines. One cannot ignore the influence of neighbouring countries on one's own country. Tibetans too is equally influenced both by Chinese civilizaiton and Indian civilization. The Chinese influence on Tibetan food, dress and organisation of the government can be seen. The Tibetan rulers wear brocade a rich fabric woven with a raised pattern a silk like the Chinese. Even the Chinese scholars were invited to Tibet from time to time to make official reports and document.

Silk worm eggs, Mulberry trees, Whisky, Barley beer and Cheese were imported from China and Chinese tea became the national drink of the Tibetans. Even the medical knowledge and treatment were also taken from China. Hence one can say that Tibet has close cultural relationship with China. Whereas Indian spiritualism, religious outlooks, moral ideas and concepts have greatly effected the Tibetan life. Exchange of religious scholars between the two countries have played significant developments in religious sphere.

POLITICAL ADMINISTRATION

Richardson in his work stated that "there was a balance between clerical and the lay bureaucracy."[7]

Political Structure

The administrative structure of the earstwhile Tibetan Govt. as presented by David Macdonald as shown in the chart.

The Tibetan government Gradation and channels of responsibility

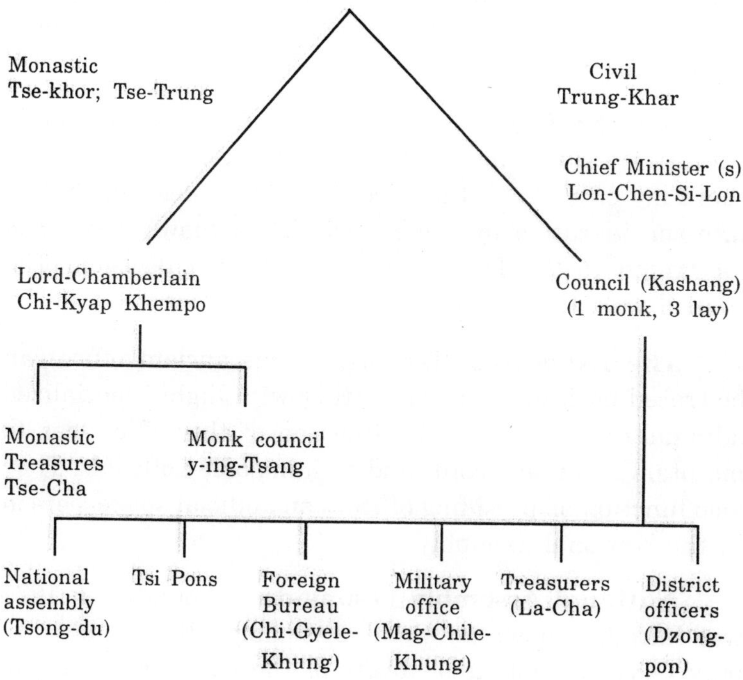

(A) Dalai Lama : On attaining the age of about 18, Dalai lama becomes the spiritual and temporal leader of Tibet. He conducts his administration through a civil service composed partly the heriditary nobles and partly of specially trained monks.

(B) Regent-(gye-Tsap) : In the absence of Dalai lama, the Regent (gye-Tsap) functions as a Deputy Dalai lama. The first person to become the Regent was De-mo-Nga-wang Jam-Pal in 1757. The Regent was chosen from one of these three lamaseries-Dre-Pung, Se-Ra and Gan-Dan.[8]

(C) Chief Minister (S) -(Lon-Chen-si-Lon) : Next in rank comes chief Minister(s) or Prime-Minister. This position was held by a senior lay official; but not a necessary part of the system. The XIIIth Dalai Lama obtain the services of the person. He functions as a bridge between him and the lay council. They did not preside over the council but passed on its recommendations to the Dalai Lama, suggesting their own opinions.

(D) The Council (Kashang) : Being the principal executive body of the government consist of one monk and there lay official. All the governmental issues were taken into consideration by the council. Their views were then forwarded to the Dalai lama for the final decision. The council was also a court of justice.

The Executive (Tsi-Pon) : This ancient office can be traced back to the eight century with highly specialized administrative offices. The function of this office was to maintain revenue records and training of lay officials. They also function as presiding officers and official spokesperson in the National assembly.

National Assembly (Tsong-du) : Founded in 1871 was initially known as "Small Assembly". It considered of only Govt. officials and abbots of the three monasteries-

Dre-Pung, Se-Ra and Gan-Dan. It was not a permanent body. Its views were reported to the council which submitted them to Dalai Lama. There is a marked change in the composition of the National Assembly during the recent times. It is known as "Great Assembly" and included the representatives of every group and occupation besides Govt. officials and abbots.

District Administration (Dzong Pon) : Most of the districts in Tibet were under the administration of two officials known as Dzong Pon. One usually a lay person and the other monk. This duplication was to put a check on the each other.

Monastic Administration of the Tibetan govt. (Tse-khor; Tse-Trung) : Of the monastic administration the highest officials was lord Chamberlain (Chi-Kyap-Pkempo). He ranked next after the council of Ministers. He was the head of the Dalai Lama's Personal household.

(a) Monk council (Yig-Tsang) : A council of four monks right under the lord chamberlain. It supervises the administration of the monasteries except for the three great Monasteries in Lhasa. They were also responsible for selection, training and discipline of the monk civil service.

(b) Monastic Treasures (Tse-Cha) : Lower than the monk council was a body of four treasures including three monks and one laymen. They acted as a watchdog of the church and often viewed with suspicion by the main body of the monks.

The monk officials Tse-deng comes from the noble families, studied at Tse-Khor the ecclesastical school, which prepares the candidate to serve in the Tibetan government. They enjoyed higher positions within the ecclesiastical court. A candidate who wished to become a monk-officer must be trained in Tse-lub-dra between the age of 10-12, which was a part of secritariat. Only through this channel a common was able to become a monk official.

Similarly, only the nobles hold high positions at Secular courts, Shar-khar. The commoner who wished to hold this position was trained in the school attached to the finance officer (Tsi-Khang). The commoner often being prepared to function holds a position of probationally officer. He could at length become a clerk but can not attain the authority of a "ruling-man" (Pōn-pō).

WOMEN STATUS IN TIBET

According to some travellers of 8th century Tibet was ruled by women and men were subordinate to them, and women enjoys an equal status and observes no purdah system. But on the contrary it is also written that Tibetan women were regarded somewhat as devils in human form; and there were many Tibetan proverbs and sayings like "Dogs, Women and Children are the roots of trouble".

Men and women were treated very differently in matters of upbringing and education. Boys and girls play different roles in society and she has no right of inheritance and cannot speak in the family matters related to property.

In pastoral areas many women remain unmarried unmarried does not mean that they were left pious and pure. They carry with them at least two or three illegitimate children and were wholly responsible in their bringing. This is one of the examples of inferior status of women. The main cause behind their this position is the entering of sons to the lamastic order. Male population kept declining and the result was polyandry and one parent (only woman) families. Woman was considered simply as a servant of the family. She was hardly given any education except few born in rich and democratic families. Even they also are not well-taught.

TIBETAN FAMILY

The traditional Tibetan family was almost like a clan especially where polyandrous system existed. The nuclear family was totally unknown to them "Individiualism and personal freedom were foreign to this system"[9].

The form of marriages prevelent in Tibet were of three types :

(1) Monogamy[10]

(2) Polyandry[11]

(3) Polygyny[12]

Though it is not mentioned anywhere, in which region these three forms of marriages were prevelant but they existed in the Tibetan Society as a whole.

Most Tibetan marriages were monogamous, but in rich families polyandrous marriages generally took place and the sole purpose for such practice was to prevent the fmaily property being divided. Polygamy was found among people of higher statuses who kept many concubines beside wives. "There are also cases of a mother and daughter sharing a husband but it is in the case when wive's husband dies leaving a daughter behind. Then the mother would remarry, taking a husband younger than herself in order to support the family, and the daughter, when she came of age, marry her stepfather[13].

Usually the marriages are arranged and intermarriages between rich and poor were restricted and as societies were divided into eight classes, people could marry with in their own class.

Another restriction on marriage was that the common serfs could not marry without the approval of their landlord, as marriage between serfs of different landlords meant that one or the other of the landlords lost a serf[14].

In Tibet, "lovers were far more down-to-earth than Romeo and Juliet. Although married couples were extremely faithful, the unmarried particularly the young people enjoyed much premarital Licence"[15].

Divorce is not so common as values are attached to the relationships, "In case of divorce women is entitled to one-fourth of the common property if she bears a son/sons, and in case of daughter she is entitled to one-sixth of the property and if no children then she claims for unspecific amount known as wages for day and night[16].

The eldest male was the ultimate authority of the family, but today in the refugedom the traditional family have undergone vast changes and the family has lost many of its tradidional functions. Within a span of decade the agrarian Tibetan family accquired the features of modern-industrial family.

In a family not only the functions and roles of individuals but the marked difference can also be observed in their costumes, ornaments, food habits etc.

The dress of both the sexes and of all classes in Tibet consists of a very full gown (Chu-pa) with a high collar and long sleeves. In the summer it is made up of Tibetan cloth (Turk) or silk. The winter gown is of sheep skin or the cloth lined with lambskin or the wadded cloth tied around the waist. The robe for laymen reaches to the knee, for priests and women to the ankle. In the central and the eastern parts of the Tibet the women wears apron, woven in varied colors and often so broad that they nearly meet at the back. The dress of priests differs from the laymen as the gown of the priests is of maroon color, underneath are a skirt and waistcoat both without sleeves. The caps are often peaked of different colours and sizes, the reformed sects wear yellow hats and the old sects wear red. Men wear hats of various kinds and are ususally fur-trimmed in winter. The national boot is of Tibetan cloth of various colours among which red is always included and is tied with gay-coloured wollen=garteus, three or four feet long with soles usually of raw yak-hide.

Similarly the head dresses of women vary in different provinces of Tibet which is also one of the chief ornaments of Tibetan women. In many parts of the country the hair is worn in a number of little plaits which descend from the crown of the head to the waist. In some parts as that in central Tibet women wear their hair divided right and left, fluffed one on each side. This increase artificiality and good look. Similarly the cheif ornament of Tibetan women is her head dress. It also varies in different parts of the country.

In central Tibet, it consists of wooden framework, ornamented with corals, turquoise and seed-pearls; In Tsang-Province, one wooden branch arises as a semi-circle above the head, another branches out behind.

The Lhasa woman favour a pattern which clings much closer to the hair. Tibetan women are fond of wearing numerous ornaments. Rings, earnings of gold and silver. Necklaces of coral and turquoise with seed-pearls, inter speused with gold on silver pendants.

In exile, they hardly wear their traditional dresses excepts on the particular occasions like marriages, functions, new year day etc.

Girls have switched over to salwar suits and other modern dresses and Tibetan boys have taken over to jeans, trousers, shirts, jackets etc. These changes do not limit themselves only to dresses but even their food habits have also changed to some extent.

The stable diet of an ordinary Tibetan is Yak's meat, barley flour, mutton, cheese and most of all tea with a butter mixed with it and barley flour dipped in the mixture, soup is also a favourite dish of Tibetans. Now living in a community with different geographical and cultural environment Tibetans have started consuming Indian food. On more reason for this particular change is that yak is not provided in India and as a refugee, butter, cheese, barley and all such things are quite costly to consume everyday. Another reason which is important in the context of above change is the changed climatic conditions, which bear some effect on their eating habits and dresses.

In relation to Tibetans the Indian saying "Jaisa Desh Vaisa Bhesh" proved true.

Traditional Economy

The word "traditional" being comparative is used here to refer the ideal type situation before the Tibetans fled their homeland. The traditional economy of tibet was based on the following types :

(a) Agriculture

(b) Pastoralism and animal husbandry

(c) Barter and trade.

Agriculture is mainly practiced in the southern and Eastern valleys. "Irrigation was primarily based on the rain water on the mountain streams which were tapped with cannals made of either narrow small ditches or of wooden pipes Fertilizer was done with animal and human waste. The major crop is barley though other crops like potatoes, cabbages, carrots, onions and peas are also grown. Their agricultural implements included the plough, iron spikes, shovels and spades."[17]

Pastoralism and Animal husbandry are closely associated with agriculture in traditional Tibetan economy. Their herds included Yaks (cross between Bison and cow) sheep and goats. The animal products were meat, butter, cheese, wool, yak-tail, animal hide etc. Animal husbandry in old Tibet was not only a source of income but also a means of control and exploitation of the tenants by estate owners. "Even the Status differentation in traditional Tibet was done on the basis of the number of animal (Particularly yaks) possessed"[18].

Barter and trade - Tibet is still in the barter stage and very little money is used. The people from the interior have butter, wool, sheep, goats and yak's tail which they exchange for cotton, sugar and cloth. But sometimes specially selling wool and butter they prefer to take money generally Indian currency.

Another interesting fact related to traditional trade is the unit of measurement and one of the common units of measurement was the length of two outstretched hands, the other being the length between the elbow and the tip of the fingers. The third unit which was generally used for imported cloths was called "Kha" or the measurement is square or the measurement is on the basis of the breadth of the cloth.

Tibetan Land - Ownership System: The man's social status and his power was based on the land ownership pattern. It was patriarchal as in any feudal society. The Tibetan society is a traditional society and is divided into two classes the aristocrats and the serfs.

The landed property was shaved by the monastery and the nobility, and nobility also possesses the private holdings besides the official. The total tax collected from the lands went to the government except those owned by monasteries.

As it is stated earlier that the Tibetan society was divided into eight classes and these were - Priestly class, Nobility, Descendants of senior lama, rich people and officials, common men (which include peasents, trader, nomad, Stone-cutter, potter, tailor etc.) craftsmen, lower castes (whch includes fisherman, ship-builder, beggars etc.) and last category includes butcher and the corpse dispatcher and they were like outcastes.

Class division was one of the open type as anyone can take any position irrespective of his family background and birth. But it was not easy for lower class person to rise high because of the absence of education among them.

Education: For the first time in Tibetan history, the Tibetans of all statuses, ranks and categories, got full opportunity for education in exile. Earlier education was the privilege of nobles, aristocratic families and lamas. Many of them joined the official school to become officials in the secular as well as acclesiastical orders. "Nobody went to a teacher unless he had specific use for education, i.e. aristocrats look education to inherit their father's places; teachers, others to help in their business maters etc., and the monks were to read only the printed form and were not allowed to learn the second form i.e., handwriting"[19].

China's Invasion on Tibet: A brief outlook

It is well known to the world that Tibet and China were under the rule of Mongolians. In 1358 Tibetans were able to drive Mongolians out of their territory, similarly in 1368 China freed themselves from Mongolians. Tibet being a peace loving country far away from violence never like any one to interfere in her territory.

In 1885, when China gave permission to British for expedition between China and India via Tibet, Tibet did not liked it Tibetan officials declared that China had no rights to give permission to the British to go through Tibet. In 1888, Tibetans and Britishers fought with each other and Tibetans could not stand long in front of large British troops.

In 1890, borders between Tibet and Sikkim was established and in 1893 Britishers established trade relations with Tibet in the beginning of 20th century trade agreement were signed in Potala giving trade facilities to Britishers in some parts of Tibet but Tibet has clearly laid down that no other country has been given right to say anything regarding her internal and political affairs Tibet has to suffer in the hands of British, slowly and steadily British concent over Chinese domination on Tibet was growing. On the other hand they would not like to trade with Tibet without any consultation with China. The changing political scene in China led Yuan to declare himself as the president by pulling out Manchus. He announced Tibet as a part of China.

The world second largest power at that time earnstwhile Russia was growing on Mongolians which China has never threatened of. As a result in 1913 tripartite conference with China, Tibet and British India took place in Simla According to the agreement (1) China holded the autonomy of outer Tibet and will not interfere in her administration and the selection of Dalai Lama. (2) China will not bring Tibet under her rule, (3) Britain and Chinese armies withdraw from Tibet. (4) Tibet will not be discussed by China or Britain with any other foreign nation.

Tibet now a full fledged sovereign state attacked on Chinese and recaptured few areas of Kham regions. China became red hot started interfering in Tibet's affairs. China growing hotter attacked Tibet and annexed major areas of Tibet. In between in 1933 itself the then Dalai Lama lost his soul and the new Reagent was installed under the headship of China.

After the independence in 1947, India recognised Tibet's independence in 1948. China could not tolerate it and attacked Tibet and India. On the eve of Chinese military invasion in 1949, Tibet was an independent state. As per the rules of international law Tibet fulfilled all the characteristics of independent statehood viz. (1) a definite territorial existence (2) a population inhabiting that territory (3) A government of its own, and (4) ability to enter into world of international relations. Chinese headed by Mao Tse-Tung captured Tibet and warned India not to interfere in her matter. Tibet was not a member of UNO and Britishers ignored help to Tibetans. India then asked the fourteenth and regining Dalai Lama - Tenzin Gyatso to communicate with China for friendly relations but the talk for peace failed. In 1952 Chinese occupied Lhasa. In 1954 India signed trade agreement with China and Panchsheel plan was the result.

As far as the status of Tibet was concerned the Indian government reffered "The Tibet region of China" of the position that Tibet forms an integral part of China. This is the biggest blunder the government of India committed which lead Tibet to her graveyard. This gave rise to moral criticsm Acharya J.B. Kriplani in lok sabha debate on 8 May 1959 stated that "Panchshil" was "born in sin" because it was enunciated to put the seal of our approval upon the destruction of an ancient nation which was associated with us spiritually and culturally". He also admired "self government" rather than "good government".

Again in 1954 China invited Dalai Lama for meeting which failed and no policy matter could be framed between the two. Then in 1956 Dalai Lama wanted to stay back in India but the then PM, Jawahar Lal Nehru advised him to go back to Tibet with four point programme, viz:

(1) Chinese troupes to be withdrawan

(2) Reinstalment of dismissed prime minister

(3) Restoration of Tibet political status as it stood at the time of the death of the thirteenth Dalai Lama

(4) To stop communism in the name of reforms in Tibet.

Chou-en-li assured that no reformations will take place in Tibet without the consent of Tibetans. In the name of introducing democratic reforms, the Chinese played oppressive games with Tibetans. The communist rule started suppressing the minority race and started digging the hole to burrow Tibet's independence and unique position of Dalai Lama.

This action of Chinese was against humanity, justice and peace they have promised, with the peace loving people of Tibet. Taking away the right of self-determination which a sovereign state enjoys, China has broken the international rules and regulations.

In 1958, Dalai Lama was invited to attend National Assembly in China. The people of Tibet never wanted Dalai Lama to visit China. Now it was the time when Dalai Lama got the news of China's attack on Potala. At ten in the midnight of 18th march 1959, Dalai Lama left Lhasa and crossed Indian border in early April of 1959.

The communists of Beijing has always misused his power and force to dominate other nations and expands his empire. The seizure of Tibet, invading Vietnam in 1978 and attack on India in 1962 are the clear examples of communists policies towards the other nations.

In 1979, again bilateral talks between Beijing and Dharamsala took place to resolve Tibetan issue. In this sequence in 1987 Dalai Lama framed five points, the basic components were :

(1) Transformation of the whole of Tibet into a zone of peace

(2) To control China's population transfer policy which threatens the very existence of the Tibetans as a people.

(3) Respect for the Tibetan people's fundamental human rights and democratic freedom.

(4) Restoration and protection of Tibet's natural environment and to check China's use of Tibet for the production of nuclear weapons and dumping of nuclear waste.

(5) Commencement of earnest negotiations on the future of Tibet and of relations between Tibetan and Chinese people.

This five point plan was not accepted by Chinese communities. India and China tied with the bonds of friendship giving slogan of *Hindi Chini-Bhai-Bhai,* cannot create situations of war by promoting the issues of Tibet and Tibetans. According to Panchsheel agreement communism and democracy are working hand in hand. But China could not stick to the Panchsheel agreement. Our leaders considers that according to it we must respect other states integrity, sovereignty and peaceful coexistence.

The Chinese assault on Tibet is a butucher's act they

have committed. It is true that India could not do anything to stop China invading and occupying Tibet but the major mistake was to recognise China's domination over Tibet.

The tragedy of the peaceful nation coannot be ignored at any cost. No doubt Tibetans have gained tremendous sympathy and support form all over the world.

India, wishes for free Tibet, because she herself has witnessed the slavery period in the hands of Britishers. She very well knows how every heart speaks out "FREE MY COUNTRY". Who will better understand Tibetans dream than any Indian. No matter what political updowns take place but one cannot ignore the fact that rule of illegal power and dictatorship does not last too long. Every Indian has a special affection for Tibet as she has more geographical, cultural and religious affinities with India.

Whatever they think of their national disaster, but the fact is that, that the China's invasion is responsible for it. "China claims that Tibet has always been a part of China derive from a period when both Tibet and China were part of the mongolion empire"[20]. "Further claims have been made to Tibet on the basis of the Emperor K'sang HSi and his intervension in Tibetan affairs in 1920"[21].

According to Dalai Lama, China attacked Tibet due to there main reasons-

(i) To accomodate China's very big population in the vast expanse of Tibet.

(ii) To exploit the rich mineral resources of Tibet, and

(iii) To dominate Tibet because that was an important step towards the domination of the rest of Asia"[22].

China is one of the major powers of the world and in U.N. with a veto Power, every nation is seeking adjustment with China. India too, claims good relations with China. "It welcomed Dalai Lama but did not give him the status of the Tibetan government in Exile"[23].

Resettlements

In the immediate years, when Dalai Lama and his followers, were forced to seek asylum in India, one of the urgent needs was a long term rehabilitation programme that would serve to bring Tibetans as one community, so that their main objective to preserve their national identity should be fulfilled.

In 1959, Dalai Lama arrived as a refugee in foreign land, in a Town Bomdia escorted with some Indian officials. After a few day rest, he travelled to Mussoorie, a small town in the Himalayan foothills. He stayed there in Kindlier's House and Birla House for one year.

Since the majority of the refugees had been either farmers or nomads, Dalai Lama requested government of India to resettle the Tibetans in agricultural based settlements. The first Tibetan settlement Lugsung Samdupling, established in 1960, was a one of the major agricultural settlement situated near mysore in Karnataka, South-India.

"Though there was not much vaccant Land, thus with assistance of government of India, Nepal and Bhutan, 52 refugee settlements have been established in India, comprising 14 major and 11 minor agricultural, 14 agro-industrial and 27 handicrafts based settlements (including 14 agro-industrial communities)"[24].

"In 1960's as many as 1500 refugees were arriving from Tibet each week."[25] As it was not an easy journey, the people got totally exhausted and suffered from psychological distress Due to warmer climate and unhygienic conditions in the transit camps, the refugees fell ill with diseases and many of them died. As they were cured, they were sent to camps in North west of India, where they could earn their livings working in road constructions. The refugees were generally farmers in Tibet, but the Indian land was totally different from the land, they were use to, but later an average of one acre was provided to them, slowly and slowly Tibetans come to learn how to farm the Indian land. They also learnt the use of modern techniques, fertilizers and yielding variety of seeds which they had never known earlier. It gave Tibetans a light of hope that life in exile will provide more than living and working in road - construction camps. "In this project 3,000 acres of land was provided by Indian Govt. to rehabilitate 3,000 refugees in six different camps."[26]

The first Tibetan settlement Lugsung Samdupling served as a model for the planning of later settlements. This settlements also has a dispensary, school, community hall, monasteries and today it accomodates 8,500 people approximately.

In 1960, Prime-Minister Jawahar Lal Nehru, personally slected Dharmasala, to be the permanent home for Dalai Lama. In 1960, Dalai Lama left for Dharamsala where the first thought was to reconstitute the Tibetan Govt. According to Nowrojee, Moutineer Hall was owned by Sarin Bashesharmath and this one storeyed building accomodated the secretariat of Tibetan government with all twenty officials at that time. It also housed the departments of religion, home, finance and foreign affairs. The other departments that of education and security were scattered aorund. Mcleodgunj wherever accomodation was available at cheap rent. As pointed out by Narkyid[27], during those early days they slept in cowsheds and sometimes two or three officials in one cowshed. They used wooden and cardboard boxes as tables and chairs in the office.

"During those early days, a minister received a monthly pay check of Rs. 75 and an office jauitor Rs. 55.50. There were two common kitchens for senior and junior officials. The monthly nictualling fee was Rs. 30"[28].

In 1963, he drew up a draft constitution for Tibet, in which is embodied a democratic form of government. It was in 1967, that the Tibetan administration shifted from

Moutimer Hall to Ganghen Kyishong purchased by them from Amarnath Sood, a leading lawyer of Dharamsala.

The two 'settlements' at Bylakuppe and Mundgod in South India are today the largest and the most settled community out of 57 Tibetan communities scattered in India.

During the year 1979, Chinese gave relaxation in the regulations at the borders of Tibet, Nepal and India so that some Tibetans could meet their relatives, then onwards Tibetans began to escape as refugees in large numbers. Though in 1979, they were few but in 1989 number increased to 689 tibetans and further the number increased to 2,066 refugees in 1990. Tibetans kept on floating to Indian terretories and in 1991 it rose to 2,725 and in 1992 the number increased to 3,374 refugees. It has been said that most of the Tibetans come from Amdo and Kham Provinces. As it was a flood of refugees in India and still Tibetans are clrossing borders, the Tibtan government have changed the policy towards new refugees. Generally, there were three categories of Tibetans seeking asylum in India:-

(i) In the first category lies monks and nuns, as they were not allowed to practice their religion in Tibet, so after reaching India, they were sent to right monastery according to the sect they belong to.

(ii) The second category includes farmers and nomads, mostly job-seekers aged from 18-30. In India, they are provided with essential weeds of food and clothes and are trained in different works and after six months they are set few to find for themselves a good job.

(iii) The third category of refugess coming to Dharamsala are children and their main reason for their escape is to get good educaiton; as in Tibet education does not go beyond primary level for them.

"But according to the new Tibetan government Policy, only genuine refugees which includes monks, nuns and children seeking education are welcomed and looked after; but people over 18 who are job-seekers were to be disappointed because of non-availability of jobs for them"[29].

There is one more reason behind the policy and it is that, that in Tibet Chinese transfer of population is increasing enormously and if Tibetans will continue to flee from Tibet, the conditions to free Tibet will be more difficult.

Tibetans in Doon valley : As been stated earlier that in 1960, when Dalai Lama reached Mussoorie, the first and the foremost objective was to look after the education and health of children coming from Tibet. So in 1960, Tibetan Refugee society school was established which now is known as (CST) (Central School for Tibetans) and in 1961 it came under CTSA Dharamsala and the present Principal of this school is Mr. Tashi Thondup. To look after these children three Homes started in 1962 whose buildings were taken on rent and in 1963 one more Tibetan Home was inaugurated. These Homes were and are financially run by foreign help. Another achievement took place in 1963 with the establishment of first Bhuddhist Temple by them in Happy Valley, Mussoorie. The Place Happy Valley also includes old age Home, Hospital, etc.

In Dehradun, there are 8 Tibetan colonies which includes the total population of 9000 (6000 males and 3000 females).

Clement Town

Dhondup Ling Tibetan settlement of Clement Town owes the credit of its establishment to Acharya Vinobha Bhave who donated 100acres of land to Tibetans in 1964. He received this piece of land for his Bhoodan Movement.[30] The Tibetan settlers of this colony were given work on contract basis by local branch of Stali Khadi Commission. The settlers started their own Khadi centre and in its governing body they included a member from stali Khadi Commission also. In 1964 the settlement was registered as

Tibetan Nehru Memorial Foundation.[31]

Basically Dhondupling is a craft community so the major activities here are the same as carpet weaving, wool spinning, tailoring, painting and carpentry sections. People over here are involved in tent making, hand made paper making and noodle making also. In 1967 a workshop was opened where motor machines, driving, carpentry, masonry and typing were taught as courses of twelve months.[32]

In the same year Nehru Memorial Foundation School was started here with10 students. In 1968 i.e., the very next year it had 100 students and the staff of school was 15. In 2002 this school had 480 students. Some of them live in hostels. There are three hostels attached to the school and out of them two are private. The school is upto class XII now and the Principal is Mr. Paljor. Major funds for its proper functioning comes from the Dharamsala government.[33]

Inside the settlement there are three monasteries. Nyingma monastery was established in 1967. with 30 months. It was renovated in 1980's Presently it has more than 400 monks. On 26th Apr. 1988. H.H. the Dalai Lama inaugurated Ngagyur Nyingma College for Higher studies. About 400 Nyingmapas are getting higher education. In year 2000 Tsering Gatsal Hospital was opened by Nyingma monastery. It has a Tibetan doctor and a lama working. They give allopathic medicines also along with the traditional Tibetan herbal medicines. There is huge 180 ft high beautiful Chorten also being contructed by the Nyingmapas. It will be inaugurated by Dalai Lama on Oct. 28, 2002. The settlement has a Kagyu monastery which was established in 1969. Presently it has 55 monks. This monastery has constructed a huge statue of Buddha, 103 feet high from land. There is a platform below. The statue itself is 80 feet in height. It was inaugunated on 21st Nov. 2001 by Dalai Lama. The Gelug monastery, has 37 monks started in 1972.

The dispensary cum infirmary was established in the settlement in 1967. There is a Community Health Worker working in it who gives allopathic medicines only.

The Old People's Home started in 1969. In May 2002 it had 10 inmates out of whom two were ladies. There is one caretaker to look after them. Whose wife manages the kitchen. Funds for the OPH comes from Dharamsala.

There is a Tibetan Children's Home in the settlement which started in 1999. It is only a hostel where 75 children are living. They go to the Nehru Foundation School of the settlement and Hilton School of Majra. The Home was funded by Madison Rotary Foundation USA and Department of Education, Dharamsala.

The Tibetan Women Association office was inaugurated by Mr. Anduk Choekyi on 10th December, 1999. Donation for it comes from Netherland and Germany. Mrs. R.D. Taring took a lot of pains for its establishment. Present Secretary of TWA at Clement Town is Pema Dolma.

Clement Town is known for its housing arrangement. There are straight roads and lanes and every houses has a lawn in front. Most of the handicraft work is done on private basis.

The population of the settlement in year 2000 was 1800 according to the office of the Welfare officer, Dekyiling and approx. 2000 according to the local L.I.U. office.

The scattered community at Rajpur had its beginning in January 1965 when an old building was taken on rent at 210 Rajpur Road. Tibetan Women's centre TWC was established in this building. It is registered under the Societies Registration Act of 1860 Uttar Pradesh.

The aim of the centre was to give work and accommodation to Tibetan women and their families. Initially the same place was used for work as well as living, so it was deplorable. The condition of the centre improved in 1973 when UNHCR (United Nations High Commission for Refugees) helped it in buying a 9 bighas land nearby.[34] The Norwegian Refugees Council helped in the construction of homes and thus 30 families were able to move to this nearby place.

Today the centre has three parts namely, carpet weaving (57 women employees), tailoring (8 women employees) and apron weaving (8 women employees).[35] The new building of TWC was constructed in 1996-97 with the help of donations by Miriam Dean Fund, UK.

Carpet weaving is a very ancient craft of Tibet. Even in exile, next to agriculture, carpet industry is the main source of income for the majority of Tibetan refugees. Tibetan culture and religion had their influence on the designs of carpets. Most of the designs have stories behind them and every single motif in the carpet has a traditional meaning. The chosen motif is first made on a graph paper and then it is woven with each knot according to the pattern. It is then beautified by embossing and leveling by a skilled trimmer. The process takes more than a month by a single worker for a 3 ft. x 6 ft carpet. The carpets are available in different sizes and colours. There are three main qualities of carpets.

6 x 8 = 48 knots in one square inch (30 count yarn)

8 x 8 = 64 knots in one square inch (6 count yarn)

10 x 8 = 80 knots in one square inch (60 count yarn)

Count is the number of yards in one pound of yarn. The carpets contain 90% woolen yarn and 10% cotton thread as warp. Most of the woolen yarn comes from Tibetan woolen Yarn centre, Panipat. There has been no change in the use of materials and methods of wearing. The same kind of material (Woolen and cotton) and the same simple tools which were used more than 200 years ago are used even today. However the present chemical dyes have made the colours fast.

The total number of salaries employees in the centre are nine who get Provident Fund. The workers however get salary to earn Rs 1500 per month. The centre in now financially independent. It manages all its expenses from its income only. The carpet weaving training centre is dependent upon donations and so sometimes it is shut down. Every worker is allowed a leave of three months for other economic activities.

Most of the carpets are made on order. Those which are available on sale are available at the show room at Rajpur Export office (New Delhi) and Tibet House (New Delhi).

The aprons are made for the married women who invariably wear it by tieing it around their waists. It has horizontal lines. The centre also produces *yarta* (Woollen material made for jackets and handicraft products). Coats' passport bags, pen cases, purses, shoulder bags, writing cases etc. All these things are available at showroom (M Block) which was made with help extended by Swedish Relief Council in 1990.

In 1971 a Kindergarten was opened with Swiss aid and its maintenance was done by French sponsorship. The previous KG which was near 210 Rajpur Road has now been shifted to new campus. The old one is used for residential purpose now. Presently the school has 12 children between the ages of three and five. The staff includes two women who are paid Rs. 800 as salary. The centre has a creach which was inaugurated in 1973. It was opened with the help of 'Save the Children Fund' UK. Here those children who are below three years are kept. Presently it has 11 childrens who are looked after by three females. There is a dispensary for allopathic medicines as well as a Tibetan medical clinic also which provides herbal medicines. Dispensary was inaugurated in 1974. There is no doctor here but only a health worker, Tashi Wangchuk who is looking after it since 1987. Earlier he was in medical core of Special Frontier Force (Chakrata).[36]

Tibetan Old Person Home was started on March 3, 1976 by purchasing a house at 208 Rajpur Road. Mrs. R.D. Taring was helped by Mrs. Dean, a British lady in its establishment. Initially it has 20 old and infirm people but now it has a capacity of accomodiating 65 people. It was expanded in 1980 (Helpage India), 1981 (Tibetan Refugee Aid Society Canada), 1979 (Dorris Biddle Home was purchased by Mrs. Mirriam K. Dean) and in 1989 (Swiss Aid). Two-to-three people share the room and there are common toilets and bathrooms. The same hall is used for puja, recreation and as dining. There are five staff members at OPH and the manager Tsering Dhumdup gets Rs. 4000 as salary from THF Mussoorie as the home is a part of THF Mussoorie. The inmates get Rs. 50 as stipend per month.[37]

A new OPH was opened in 1980 about 2 kms. ahead the old one at Rajpur inside the campus of Tibetan Homes School, with the help of 'Help the Aged India'. It has 52 inmates and it is also a part of THF Mussoorie. Previously the Homes used to get gifts from foreigners but now only monetary help is provided.

A Tibetan Homes School was opened at Rajpur in 1977 with 20 students. Today it has 561 students and 45 staff members including cooks and office workers. It is a part of THF Mussoorie. The hostel attached to the school was constructed in 1992 and here about 315 students reside. The old building of the school was demolished and the new one was inaugurated in 2000. There is another hostel few hundered meters below the school. It is called SOS Hostel and was opened on Oct. 4, 1999 by Mr. Helmut Kutin. President SOS Kinderdorf International. The hostel has 200 students all of whom attend the THF School. It has 14 family homes and each home has 15-20 children. Inside SOS hostel there is a preprimary school also. Penpa Tsering is the Director of the Hostel.

The Sakya School of Tibetan Buddhism has a temple, a school attached to it, Sakya College, a hospital and a nunnery. The temple was initially constructed in 1971 and later it was demolished and reestablished in 1995. Sakya College is a centre of Higher Tiebtan Studies. It was started in 1972 and is the a oldest school of Tibetan Buddhism in India. Main subjects taught and studied here are basic Buddhist scriptures of India and their Tibetan translations. Special emphasis is on commentorial and scholastic traditions of Sakya School of Tibetan Buddhism. The aim of the college is to keep the tradition alive and prepare Sakya teachers.

The Sakya School started in 1983 with 17 lamas. The number is now more than 200. Here the basic education is given to lamas. They learn Hindi, English, Maths and ritual part of Tantrik education. The education provided is free and normal age of entering the school by lamas is ten.

Sakya Ga-shi Hospital was inaugurated on October 11, 2000. The building was donated by Mr. Clement Del Ponte of Switzerland. The Hospital is visited by seven Indian doctors and one Tibetan doctor for Tibetan medicine. The hospital provides X-ray and blood test facilities at nominal rates.

There is a nunnery run by sakya centre at Dikyling. It started in 1996-97. At present there are 40 nuns. They are taught Hindi, English, Tibetan language and Religion. All the chores are done by the nuns themselves in rotation. Only recently the nuns are allowed to enter monasteries and perform some rituals but still there are many restrictions upon them. They do not enjoy the status which the monks enjoy.

Beside the Tibetan Women Centre, THF establishments and Sakya Centre establishments Rajpur has Morevian Institute and SOIR-IM Carpet centre.

SOIR-IM is at old Mussoorie road near Sahanshahi Ashram. It is meant for women who are living out of Women centre. It was started in 1977 by a "Swedish Organisations for Individual Relief" founded in 1938 and now working in

20 countries. It is run by Wangchuk Gyalpo in India and Nepal. Here an average worker earns about Rs. 2000 per month and they are provided free lunch, tea, medical checkup and medical expenses. Tents made here were sent to earthquake victims of Bhuj, Garhwal and Cyclone hit areas of Orissa. The ogranisation keeps contact with Indian army, Red Cross, Raffels (Mohini Road Dehra Dun), KKM (Leprosy Centre, Nalapani Road. D. Dun) and SEWA (Self Employed Women Association in Gujrat). Ved Prakash Sahoo is an Indian employed here who makes graphic designs of carpets. He is working here for last 25 years.

At Rajpur some private looms are also there where people employ 4-5 workers and make carpets independently. According to welfare officer the total population of Rajpur colony was 755 in year 2000 and according to local LIU office in 2000 the population of scattered Rajpur settlement was 1000.

Lakhanwala 1972 - Khera Camp. 1969, Manduwala 1972, Herbertpur 1977

The name of the settlement at Lakhanwala is Dhogu Yugual Ling and it was set up in 1972. The settlement at Khera is called Dhogu Ling established in 1969. Later it becamea part of Lakhanwala settlement. These settlements were established by the Rehabilitation office of Govt. of India to accommodate ex-soliders of special frontier force of establishment no. 22, as a reward for their lifelong services in the army. Besides these two settlements, this office at Lakhanwala also looks after the welfare of old Men's Home where it has 124 elderly men and other seatened Tibetan communities of Herbetpur Haripur, Barwala, Jamnapur and Selakui. This settlement is situated 32 Kms away from Dehradun on Chakrata Road. There is a settlement officer posted here by the Dharamsala administration, who works under the Welfare officer of Dekyiling.

The total area of Khera camp is 90 acres and of Lakhanwala 75 acres. Out of the 90 acres at Khera camp,

15.5 bigha for each family has been used as agricultural land which means each family has agricultural land of 3 acres and few bases. Total number of families living here are 21. They have used 1.2 Bigha land for housing.

In Lakhanwala 60 families are living and out of 75 acres of land 12 acres have been used for housing, 48 acres for agriculture, and the rest of 15 acres for construction of monastery, community hall, water pump, garden, dispensary, nursery school and officers of the settlement officer and TWA (Ttibetan Women Association).

The total population of Lakhanwala, Khera camp, Herbertpur, Haripur and Banwala is approximately 750. Herbertpur has 14 families living on rent. Haripur, Jamnapur and Banwal have 14 families all together.

There is a nursery school here which works under the management of settlement officer. There are three clinics at Lakhanwala, Khaeracamp and old Men's Home. The first two clinics have community Health workers (CHW) but no doctors. These are government clinics but the one at old Men's Home does not have any CHW. It was opened on 7 Aug. 2000 by Ms. Tsewang Dolma Shosur and it was funded by a german lady Mrs. Irmtraut Wager. The monastery at Khera camp is called Gonkar Choedey and it has 30 monks. The temple inside the Old Men,s Home is known as Geso Khang and it was opened on 2nd October 1977. There is no carpet weaving centre here. The main source of livelihood of Tibetans at Lakhanwala and Khera camp is through agriculture. Initially there was a cooperative here but it continued only till 1978. Settlers here produce rice and maize mainly. Sometimes wheat, sugarcane and Forri (sarson) is also produced.

The office of TWA was inaugurated in March 1977. There is a local Assembly of 10 members. Tibetan freedom Movement has 6 members from these settlements.[77]

The main Tibetan establishment at Herbertpur is a

Central school up to class XII. It was founded as special frontier force school (SFF) in 1977 for children whose parents were working in SFF. The school has a hostel from the very beginning. On 23 July 1994 the school was handed over to CTSA (Central Tibetan School Administration) however the hostel is still managed by SFF. Total strength of the school is 500 and like any other CST 10% seats are reserved for non Tibetans. The school does not have science and commerce streams. Only arts stream is available for senior students. The teaching staff consist of 30 teachers out of which 7 are Tibetans. Since April 1998 the principal of the school is Mr. Vinod Kumar Singh. The SFF hostel is managed by Dy. Commdt Tsewang Phusbu since December 1999.

There is another school Dawa Ringue Secondary School at Herbertpur. It is a private school of a Tibetan couple inaugurated on 12 July 1991 with 12 students. The present strength of the students is 450 and interestingly out of 450 students only 40 students are Tibetans and the rest 410 students are Indians. The principal and owner of the school is Mr. Sonam Wangdu. The school is upto class X and is affiliated to CBSE. In the beginning it had 3 teachers but slowly the number increased to 14. All of them are Indians. There is a small hostel in the school where 30 Tibetan children stay. SOS Vocational Training Centre (VTC) for Tibetans was founded by SOS Kinderdorf International Austria and is under the administration of the Tibetan Children's Villages (TCV). It is located at Selakui about 16.5 Kms from Dehradun. The first academic year was started with a batch of 132 students on 1st Aug 2000. Its aim is to provide Tibetan youth with a range of technical skills in various trades so that they can serve in industries and community centres in India and abroad, or set up their own business for self employment.

The various courses available here are computer application, architectural assistantship, motor mechanic vehicle, turner, electrician, welder, radio and television mechanic, plumber, carpentry, hotel trades (front office, housekeeping, food and beverage, cookery and bakery), service trades (secretarial, beauty culture, dress cutting and tailoring).

The total area of TVC is 65 acres, out of which only 35 acres have been used for building purposes and the rest is forest. The building has costed about 15 crores. The infrastructure has been provided by SOS Austria however the running expenses are borne by TCV. The principal of TVC is Mr. A.K. Paul and the director is Mr. Tashi Phunstok.Manduwala settlement, which was established in 1972 is called Lingtsang settlement also. The total population of Manduwala is 350 including about 100 lamas. The speciality about this settlement is that all the settlers are from Khampa province of Tibet. Most of them are relatives. This settlement has produced highly educated youth. All the houses here are private. Metal work is done here on small scale.

There are three monasteries here. The Sakya monastery is called Norpa Awon Choedon consisting of 100 lamas. One tutor from Gap UK is here to teach the lamas English. The Bonpo monasteries called Gamangelendulin. It was inaugurated in November 2000 by his Holiness the Dalai Lama and it has only one guru and one lama. The Kagyu monastery is also called Chuchaling and it has only one lama to look after it. The meditation centre Hsing Long jing ssu was inaugurated in November 2000 H.H. Dalai Lama. It has 16 lamas and one nun. The beautiful chorten at Manduwala is Holy Vijaya Stupa. It was built by Gega lama and his family in 1991.

Ling Gasen School at Manduwala is upto class Vth. It was founded in 1985 with the financial help by TNAC Taiwan and extended in 1986 with the help of TRAS Canada. Mrs. PV Pakhare is the principal of the school. There are about 50-55 students in the school. Two Britishers from Gap, UK visit here in rotation to teach students English.

Community Hall was constructed in 1998 with the financial support by Tibet Fund USA. There is allopathy dispensary in the settlement under a CHW.

Dekyiling Settlement

This is the biggest settlement of Tibetan refugees in Dehradun.. It was established in 1981. In the establishment of this settlement Uttar Pradesh government also came forward and helped in the contruction of houses. The land was purchased by Central Tibetan Relief Committee CTRC, Dharamsala from Major K.B. Raghwan. Most of the settlers are those who after migration first settled in Bhutan and later on decided to settle in India.

'Dekyiling Tibetan Handicraft cum Training Charitable Society' was established in 1982. Here 50-60 women are employed and they made woolen Yatra jackets materials, bags, traditional aprons and dress material. The raw material is sent to the Export office (Delhi) which works under the Department of Home, Dharamsala.

The payment to the workers is according to their work and an average worker is able to earn about Rs.1000 in a month. The retirement age for workers is 58 and they get stipend also afterwards. Workers get three months off during winters to try luck in business.

A creche for the children of the workers of Handicraft Centre was also opened in 1982. In fact it is a part of Handicraft Centre.

There are two schools in Dekyiling settlement. The primary school where children can study upto class III and a Secondary school which is from class I to class VIII. Those who want to study further go to Tibetan Homes or Central School.

The office of the welfare officer who is from TAS (Tibetan Administration Services) was opened in 1979 at

TWC, Rajpur. He is the representative of Dharamsala government in Dehradun. His office looks after all the settlements in D. Dun. In 1982 the office was shifted to Dekyiling settlement.

The clinic of Tibetan Herbal Medicines was opened in the settlement in 1984. With time this clinic has gained a lot of reputation and even Indians come here from far off places for treatment of asthma, blood pressure, skin diseases and arthritis. Dr. Sonam Lhamo looks after the clinic.

The Nyingmapas opened a monastery in 1982 called Lhodrak Thikchi monastery. It was renovated in 1990. 40 monks are living here right now. A public prayer hall for old men was opened here in 1992. It does not belong to any sect. The followers of the Gelug sect started their monastery in 1995 called Lhodrak Dhonneyling. There is a caretaker who looks after the building. The nunnery came up in 1997. It is run by the Sakya Centre of Rajpur. About 40 nuns study here. The settlement has a big allopathic hospital also. It was inaugurated by Dalai Lama an 6 March 1995. It was established with the financial help extended by medicines du Mondi Association, France. All the doctors here are Tibetans. There is a separate block for patients suffering from tuberculosis. It was funded by Soir-im-Sweedon.

The local peoples Assembly of the Tibetan refugees has 11 members from Dekyiling. Mussoorie, Rajpur and Manduwala settlers do not play any role in the Assembly. Members of Clement Town and Herbertpur are representatives in it.

Inside the Dekyiling Settlement elections are held every three years since 1990 and six Pradhans one being elected from the six groups, into which the entire populations of the settlement is divided. Out of the six, two are made chief pradhans.

There are few establishments outside the settlement,

which attracts attention. There is an impressive Drikung Kagyu Monastery where 200 monks take education. It was established in 1984. Besides the monastery there is Ngoenga school for handicapped Tibetan children. About 40 children live here. It was established in 2000. There is a hostel where 130 children live and they go to the schools inside the settlement. Another majestic building near the settlement belongs to The Songtsen Library. 'Centre For Tibetan and Himalayan Studies' run by the Kagyu sect , was inaugrated on March 6th 2003. It is supposed to be a secular library. But courses on Buddhism will also be conducted here.

Total population of Dekyiling settlement in the year 2000 was 2900 according the local LIU office, 2973 according to the welfare officer's office.

Tibetan Market

Any discussions on the Tibetan settlers of Dehra Dun would be incomplete unless the market in the heart of the city is not discussed.

It was started in 1970s but in 1989 it was shifted to the present location. Here the structure is permanent. The market was registered in 1987. The total number of shops here is 178 out of which 42 are owned by Rajpur settlers, 45 by Clement Town people and 91 by people of Dekyiling. There are few resident room and restaurants also in the market. In 1970s Tibetan used to get things from Delhi, Nepal, Calcutta and Darjeeling to sell here. Now most of the things are from Delhi and Ludhiana.

In the beginning the local police exploited the shopkeepers and asked them for money. Since last few years there is no such problem. The shopkeepers have to pay an income tax of Rs 1000 per annum to Indian government since last financial year 2000 - 01.

Average income of the shopkeepers is Rs 3000 per

month. In winters they are able to earn more and sometimes they earn up to Rs 4000 in winters.

The chairman of the market is welfare officer at Dekyiling. The vice chairman is elected from the shopkeepers. The shopkeepers from all the three settlements elect their pradhans after every three years. The market has a Tibetan temple also which was made permanent in 2000.

Another unique feature about Tibetan Refugees moving from one place to another is that, wherever any person decides to settle in a particular part of a country, he has to get himself registered at Tibetan Registration office run by the Indian government. At this office Tibetans are registered and given a card which after every one year is renewed at the same office whenever any person leaves the station or enters a station he has to report at this office.

In Dehradun Tibetan Refugee office was established in 1963 with the registration of 1100 refugees at that time which increased to 9000 in the year 2000.

The unexpected and sudden change from one social-set up to another is a difficut experience which Tiebtans are facing since they knocked out from a life and culture which they had refused to change for centuries.

After getting exposed to the new society, Tibetan community in India is in transitional state it is passing through various stages of change. Whatever change is studied mobility also assumes greater importance and cannot be ignored.

References

1. Gold Peter - Tibetan Reflections, Wisdom Publications, London, 1984.
2. Dalai Lama - My Land and My People, Asia

Publishing House, 1962.

3. Norbu, Dawa - Tibet the Road Ahead, Harper Collins Publishers, 1992.
4. *Ibid.*
5. *Ibid.*
6. Richardson and Snellgrove (Pg 80)
7. Richardson, H.E. - Tibet and its History. Published by Oxford University. Press, Toronto, 1962. (Pg 26)
8. Arakheri, A.V. - Tibetans in India : The uprooted people and their cultural transplantation. Reliance Publishing House. N. Delhi, 1998. (pg. 224)
9. Saklani, Girja - The Uprooted Tibetans in India - A sociological study of continuity and change; Cosmo Publications-1986.
10. Monogamy - The practice where by people marry only one spouse at a time.
11. Custom for a women to have several husbands at a time.
12. Custom for a man to have several wives at a time
13. Tibet Pictorial Book - 1989.
14. *Ibid* by Jugos Lovenska Renija Belgrade and the Shanghai People's Aut. Pub. House.
15. Norbu, Dawa - Tibet the Road Ahead. Harper Collins Publisher, India, 1997.
16. *Ibid.*
17. Tanka, B. Subba - Flight and adaptation" - Tibetan Refugees in the Darjeeling - Sikkim Himalayas (pp 81-82) Published by LTWA - 1990.
18. *Ibid* (pg. 85).
19. Arakari, A.V. - op cit. (pg. 66)
20. Tibet - the facts - A Report Prepared by the scientific Bhuddhist association for the United Nation Commission on Human Rights (pg 3)

21. *Ibid.* (pg. 5)
22. Dalai Lama; Tibet, China and the World (a compilation of interviews, Narthang Publications, Dharamsala, 1989.
23. Saklani, Girja - op cit.
24. Kumar, Anand - Tibet - A Source Book All Party Indian Parliamentary Forum for Tibet, 1994.
25. Figures taken From Deptt. of Home Records July 1992.
26. Records of Deptt. of Home 1992.
27. Narkyid - Narkyid Nawang Thondup is the official biographer of the Dalai Lama and Man credited with pioneering the Tibetan type writer and one of the few serving members of the Tibetan officials who accompanied by the Dalai Lama in his historic trip. - Tibetan Bulletin. Jan-Feb. 1998 (pg. 14).
28. Dharamsala's Tibetan Bureaucracy - The early years. Tibetan. Bulletin. Jan-Feb 1998.
29. Barker, Carol - Tibetans in Exile.
30. Tibetans in Exile op. cit. (p. 127)
31. Ibid. p. 128
32. Ibid.
33. Ibid.
34. Tibetans in Exile 1959-80. Dharamsala. p. 85. In Jan 1998 the building was taken by GRD Academy after giving a nominal compensation to Tibetans. Moreover the Tibetans were harassed to evacuate the building. It is in this building that GRD Girls Degree College has been established.
35. Ibid.
36. Tibetans in Exile, 1959-80. (p. 85).
37. Tibetans in Exile, 1959-80. (p. 87).

Plate 1. Traditional Architecture

Plate 2. Tibetan Monastery

Plate 3. Use of electric bulbs inspite of butter lamps

Plate 4. Tharchock (sacred flags)

Plate 5. Dead body resting on pyre besides river ganges at Haridwar (India)

Plate 6. Sweater-selling market dominated by women-power

Plate 7. A View of Tibetan Marriage

Plate 8. Tibetan Homes Mussoorie (Uttaranchal)

Plate 9. A View of Tibetan Parliament, Dharamsala (H.P.)

Plate 10. Tibetans with prayer wheels

Plate 11. Traditional Dance of Lamas

Plate 12. Tibetan Monastery at Manduwala, Dehradun (Uttaranchal)

Plate 13. Chorten (stupa)

Plate 14. Indian Labourers working in Tibetan Settlement, Dehradun

Plate 15. Woman Working at Carpet-Weaving Centre

Plate 16. "Yellow Hat" sect playing Rak dung

Plate 17. Shows a Lhamo Performence

Plate 18. Historical Drama depitting the Empire of Tibet

Plate 19. Damyen Dance from U-Tsang Province of Tibet

Plate 20. Small statues in a position of Cham Dance

Plate 21. Performance of dance with instruments-drum sticks, Pewang, Yangche and Damyen

Plate 22. Amdo Dance generally performed after harvest and during great festivals

Plate 23. Cham Dance by Tibetans

Plate 24. Two heads of a historic statue destroyed during the cultural revolution in Lhasa

Plate 25. Showing Gathering in a Marriage Ceremony

Plate 26. Showing Gathering in a Marriage Ceremony

Plate 27. Showing Gathering in a Marriage Ceremony

Plate 28. Various eatables offered to Deties

Plate 29. Indian Labourers in a Tibetan settlement making small prayer bells

Plate 30. Tibetans organised fete in the settlement at the time of Losar

Plate 31. Traditional Dance

Plate 32. Tibetan Performance of Music at the Birthday of H.H. Dalai Lama

3

Tibetans

Focus

The Tibet and Tibetans have escaped the serious attention of scholars interested in the comparative social and humanistic studies of diaspora in exile while it is true that number of books have been written about Tibetans in exile and there has been a little attempt to look at the interactive dynamics of the Tibetans emergent culture in their new homes. In the contexual frame of change much of literature till now focuses on the refugees and the concentration is on the description of the human conditions (such as in refugee camps and settlements), aspects of international law and political rights of the refugees.

A major theme for most of the Tibetan studies has been related to problems of adaptation and rehabilitation and the changing conditions of life in exile whether politically or economically or studies related to their socio-economic adaptation.

Most of the work done on refugees are conducted by Tibetans themselves which explains their living-conditions and socio-economic structure in Tibet which we may call as autobiographies.

These works includes "An autobiography of H.H. the Dalai Lama" and "The Daughter of Tibet". By Rinchen Dalma Tseing, "My Land and my People" by Dalai Lama etc. Then there are some studies on change conducted by various sociologists. One of them is study by Girija Saklani "The uprooted - Tibetans in India" which studies the cross-cultural interaction among the Tibetan refugees and the host country.

But the Present work is quite different from all the studies done till now. It is a sociological study of social change and social mobility among the Tibetan refugees. The changes have been taken up due to the migration of Tibetans and their effect on the socio-economic mobility of Tibetans. As the prsent study is based on Dharamsala and Dehradun the change in economic, political and social condition of the two places have been taken up seperately; which shows the difference among the Tibetan refugees of Dharamsala and Dehradun if any.

Scope and Objectives

It is clear that all societies are characterised by continuity and change there are various factors responsible for this process. In order to study specifically about social change occuring in a particular community it is necessary as well as important to study certain aspects of changes which include what it is that has changed? How and at what rate it is changing? Why the changes have taken place? what are the factors responsible for change? and, what is the direction of change in which it is taking place? An atempt has been made to include all such questions in the present study in relation to Tibetan refugees. The study does not restrict itself to any particular aspect of problem but it is a comprehensive study with the focus on the following thematic concerns :

(a) Social change in traditional social structure and institutions which includes family and marriage, religion, economic and political structure and various other changes related to women and Education which will make up the future society.

(b) Problems of adjustment between the first and second generations of the refugees.

(c) Attitude of the refugees facing new change.

The study besides being an attempt to analyse social change also lays emphasis on the nature of social mobility in a traditional-cum-pastoral society and in this respect study deals with

(a) Different mobility rates and its implications in various groups and individuals of a community.

(b) To investigate inter-generational mobility among Tibetan refugees.

(c) The channels of social circulation which provide the individual to move up and down from stratum to stratum.

(d) To analyse both the positive and the negative attitude of tibetans towards change.

To retain their cultural identity persistance to change is accepted as the main aim in their refugee existance.

Conceptual Framework

Social Change : Social change is a word used to describe variations in or modifications of any aspect of social processess, social patterns, social interactions or social organisation.

Social change studies cover wide areas. Family organisations, community structure, economic and political structure all have been analysed in respect of their changning roles and status principles, functions, variations in forms and its implications to the social system as a whole. These type of studies are sometimes conducted independently and sometimes as a part of the study of social mobility of occupations, groups or categories. In the conceptual framework of the study both of these analytical approaches have been treated together.

"Social change means the transformation of major aspects of a culture and society change in beliefs, values, customes, behaviour, social relations, material culture, stratification and anything else of importance."[1] Social change takes place everywhere and at all times. "The sense of time and the perception of change are inextircably lined with human experiences".[2]

But it is also time that some aspects change more rapidly than the others.

Changes take place on two levels, the individual or microlevel and the social or macro level (Laucer 1977 P.5.).

Changes that take place on the individual level show changes. Among the individuals attitudes, behaviour, interacting pattern. These are all micro-level changes. On the other hand changes which include the whole society like changes in institution, economy, political system and other structures of the society are macro level changes.

Social change is the most complex phenomenon and a result of various factors for e.g. Social conflicts, technological innovations education, natural catastrophes etc. but no single cause beings a major social change, all the factors are inter connected with each other. Change in one aspect of society leads to change in another aspect.

The changes may be immanent, preserving the existing framework, altering only some features of the system or the entire order may undergo a complete transformation from one type of social stratification to a different type of stratification is the result of changes in society. The sociological attack on the problem of the stratification seeks to answer a series of questions. The first is the structure of stratification in any given society or group. Second is the basis of the measure of stratification.

The work related to the first category tries to decide how many classes are there in a particular society, what are their characteristics in terms of income occupation and prestige, and where the members of a particular class are located in physical and social space. Related to the second category, there are two approaches adopted in placing people in social strata. The first is "objective" measures stressing on the amount of income, possessions, education or power a man has.

The second is "Subjective" or psychological measures stress on the feelings a man has about the class he belongs to.

The stratification system can be divided into two societies. The "open" and "closed".

Social Mobility: "By social mobility is understood any transition of an individual or social object or value - anything that has been created or modified by human activity from one social position to another".[3]

The closed system does not allow an individual to change his status according to his wish, all statuses are ascribed. Contrary to it "open" stratification system allows the individual to move up and down from one social stratum to another according to his capabilities and opportunities. This movement of individuals between different levels of helrarchy, usually defined in terms of broad occupational or social class categories is referred to as social mobility.

"The amount of social mobility is often used as an indicator of the degree of openess and fluidity of a society"[4].

Geographical Mobility or Migration

The respondents of the present study are refugees and have migrated from Tibet to India and various other parts of the world. In this context it is important to know what Migration means? what are the causes and effects of migration?

There are number of cases of population movement from one geographic area to another and these movements primitively took place for better opportunities of hunting and food gathering, but it was at much a later stage that the population movements began to have different set of causative factors, which give rise to new culture and civilization.

The movement of people from one geographic area to another is termed as "migration". There are various factors responsible for the geographical mobility which can be studied as follows :

(i) Physical migration is the cause of war or natural calamities like earthquakes, drought, famine, flood, etc.

(ii) Unemployment, low living standards, absence of social security and search for better economic opportunities are the main causes which leads to economic migration.

(iii) Family trouble, housing and occupational facilities, future of children, motivation from relatives and friends already migrated is the cause of social migration.

(iv) Psychological migration is the result of personal conflict, escapism, restlessness, difficulties of adjustment in existing society and sense of adventure.

(v) Religious migration is the cause of religious intolerance and desire for religious freedom.

(vi) Political migration is the result of discrimination, political ambition.

(vii) Proffessional migration is due to inadequate renumeration or return, inadequate research facilities, etc.

The effects of migration differs from person to person as international migrants have often been individuals while the internal migrants tend to move as whole families. Tibetans are migrants from Tibet, as after the invasion of China on Tibet, Dalai Lama and his followers seek a asylum in India. Thus the political and cultural insccurity was the most prominent cause which force the Tibetans to become refugees.

Refugee?

To study about Refugees it is imortant to know who is a Refugee? "A refugee is any person who under the stress of force majeure has left his home and becomes dependent on the hospitality of others"[5]

Tibetans are refugees as the constitution defines refugee as "those persons who are outside their country and had valid objections to returning to their country and had not accquired a new nationality".

Tibetans are not only international migrants but after taking asylum in India, they have been moving to camps and settlements within the boundaries of India, either for better living or for better occupational opportunities. This can be reffered as "internal migration" of the refugees.

As it is stated earlier that the internal migrants tend to move as whole families, but in the case of Tibetan refugees it is not true, for better educational facilities and more opportunities for jobs, Tibetans move from one place to another within the territory of the refugedom and its it is also not necessary that they should shift their families all the time from here to there.

In relation to the concept of migration two basic set of factors are involved, "The Push and the Pull" factors.

"Push factors are those that push people out of an area or a country, those that make it more difficult to live in a given place". In the present conditions of Tibetan refugees the Push factors is China who invaded Tibet, making the life of Tibetans miserable.

"Pull factors is contrast are those, that pull people into a region or country and make desirable to live in". This pull factors here signifies India, which gave asylum to Tibetan refugees where they could practice their religion and maintain their cultural identity thus making the area desirable to live in. Most migration involves "Push" and "Pull" factors in combination.

Since the Tibetans have migrated from Tibet various changes can be observed in them, whether they are related to socio-economic conditions or whether socio-religious sphere. Thus to study and analyse these changes it is important to study about their traditional pattern of living life in Tibet and this has already been mentioned is the previous chapter.

Types of Social Mobility

Geographical mobility is movement in physical space, whereas social mobility is movement of a person; group or category from one social stratum to another. Wherever "direction" of change is studied, social mobility is classified into horizontal mobility and vertical mobility.

Horizontal Mobility

It means "movement back and forth on the same social level from one similar social group or situation to another".[6] The permanent movement of an individual from on set to another is horizontal social mobility.

Vertical Mobility

It is defined as the movement of people from one social status to another, from one class to another. Vertical social mobility can be either upward or downward that is person may shift to a higher status or he may slip to a lower status. For the proper functioning of vertical social mobility there are various "channels" which allow the individuals to make up and down from one social stratum to another and these channels are various social institutions like schools, political organisations, economic oragnisations and proffessional organisations. Whenever we deal with mobility we cannot ignore its effect on Human behaviour and psychology. According to Sorokin "Mobility diminishes intimacy and increases psycho-social isolation and loneliness of individuals."[7]

The past 10 years have shown tremendous change in various stratas of Tibetan society due to Tibetans taking to western education, modernisation and democratization. Thus it will be a discriptive study dealing with social change and social mobility in various spheres of Tibetan Society.

Methodology

Methodology is concerned with the study of research methods, with the nature and quality of data produced by various methods and the logic rationale behind the use to which those data are put in sociological research.

The study being baed on diachronic approach, the data for the study was collected by various methods of data collection.

For the purpose of study considerable amount of literature available on Tibetan society was studied which covers not only the traditional cum-pastoral society but also its hidden truth and historical background. The literature was also supplemented through oral data and for the secondary sources the following literature was consulted.

(a) Historical documents and written literature on Tibetan Society.

(b) Rcords and necessary information on Tibetan Refugees from the Tibetan administration available at different refugee settlements, as well as in the police records and registration offices.

(c) Records of the Central Relief Committee.

(d) Literature on problems dealing with the refugees.

(e) Literature on social change and mobility was also consulted.

Sample and administration of schedule

A sample survey of Tibetans was conducted, a survey which involves the collection of standardized information from a sample selected as being representative of a particular group or population. It is essential that sample should be representative and this is often accompolished by "random sampling". Random sampling is one in which each person or item has an equal chance of being chosen. Thus through the process of random sampling sample of 200 Tibetans were collected. To study the opinions and the attitudes on various aspects of social change and structure of their future society, interview schedule was used on the sample collected.

Interview is one of the most widely used methods of gathering data in sociology. They consists of a researcher asking the interviewee or respondent, a series of questions and he has the freedom to phrase questions as he like. In relation to the present study the interview schedule was partly structured and partly unstructured, allowing the respondents to express themselves, freely one various items of information.

The data consolidation, tabulation involved a great deal of coding and categorization.

Focused interviews were also conducted with a large number of Indian officials dealing with the Tibetan matters, with those persons who are employed in the Tibetan goverment in exile or serving in the Tibetan administration.

Focussed interview is generally used to study the social and psychological affects of mass communication and tries to know his experiences, attitudes and emotional responses regarding the present situation under the study.

Informal conversations were held at different places like coffee shops, restaurants, offices, library (LTWA), schools, monasteries etc. Appointments and meetings were engaged with the Tibetan leaders in Dharamsala (where the Tibetan government in exile functions) as well as in Dehradun, this worked for the purpose of data generation on the traditional pattern as well as the structural processes at work of the community in exile. On contacting men, women, children during the occassions such as Losur (New Year Day of Tibetans) and Kalachakra Puja[8]. This provides the information about thier traditional celebrations and how they have now changed the way of celebrating various festivals where relatives are scattered and economy is weak.

Problem during interview

It is found that the Tibetans are unwilling to express their opinions to an outsider and expecially the lay men who know not much about political matters and changing conditions of life.

The effort is made up to bridge the communication gap by the co-operation of interpreters, leaders and few Tibetans in general who know either English or Hindi.

The study is a broad-vision survey of the processes of change and mobility rather than investigation of any special feature of the society and study attempts towards a comprehensive explaination of the topic.

After the data has been collected full attention is paid to their analysis and interpretation as the purpose of the former is to summarize the completed observations in such a manner that they yield answers to the research questions and that of the latter to search for the broader meaning to these answers by linking them to other available knowledge. The procedure used in analysis and interpretation will cover the following topics the establishment of categories, the application of the categories to the raw data through coding, the tabulation of responses, statistical analysis of the data, drawing inferences about causal relations and the use of non quantified data.

Presentation

The description of the study design is one of the major steps in social research. A research design is the arrangement of conditions for collection and analysis of data in a manner that aims to combine relevance to the research purpose with economy in procedure.

The research has been concerned with describing the characteristics of communities who hold certain views or attitudes and behave in certain ways.

Thus for the purpose of the study to be fulfilled descriptive and analytic design methods have been used with the help of statistical and diagramatical presentation.

The Book runs into ten chapters. The first chapter is based on theortical perspective explaining social mobility and social change.

The second chapter is concerned with China's invasion on Tibet resulting in their migration and settlements in different parts of the country.

The third chapter describes the methodology and universe.

The fourth chapter is related to the abrupt changes among Tibetans after their settlement in exile in the institution of family and marriage.

In chapter fifth the changes and the process of mobility in women society with the changing status and role of women is dealt with. It also emphasis on the emerging consiousness among the women refugees.

Chapter sixth explains the functional views of religion raising a question of rationality, turning from "sacred" outlook to "Secular" perspective.

The liberal perspective of education which as compared to the past is most modern and is one of the major factors of chaning the socio economic status of the Tibetans and a staircase to their upward mobility is studied in seventh chapter.

The chapters eighth and ninth chapters is related to the economy and polity of the refugees respectively and their changing patterns from traditional-cum- pastoral society to modern industrial and democratic society.

The last or the tenth chapter is a comparative analysis of Tibetans of the two areas on the basis of which the conclusions are drawn.

Universe

Drawing mainly from the field work and data collected by the author, is primarily based on two places i.e. Dehra Dun and Dharamsala. On the basis of these two places sample of two hundred Tibetan refugees are drawn.

Dharamsala is in Kangra district of Himachal Pradesh and Dehradun a district of Uttaranchal. It should be made clear that not of whole Dehradun district is under the study area but only Dehradun city is taken under study. These two places consists of refugees in various settlements and scattered colonies.

In Dharamsala, Mcleod Ganj is studied and in Dehradun mainly three colonies namely "Deikyling" at Sashtradhara Road, "Dhondupling" at clement town and Manduwala and one scattered colony at Rajpur covers the field area.

The respondents drawn are from different age-groups as also shown in Table No.-3.1. In the age group of below 20, (1.81%) are males and (8.88%) are females. in the age group between 21-30 (50.90%) are males and (52.22%) are females. In between 31-40, 15.45% are males and 20% females, from 41-50, (18.18%) are males and (12.22%) females, in the next group of 51-60, (8.18%) are males and (3.33%), females, in the second last age-group of 51-70, (4.54%), are males and (3.33%) are females and in the age-group of above 70 only (90%) are males and no females.

Therefore 110 are males and 90 are females which makes the sample of study.

Table 3.1. : Tibetan refugee respondents on the basis of age group

Age group	%of males	% of females
Below 20	1.81	8.88
21-30	50.90	52.22
31-40	15.45	20
41-50	18.18	12.22
51-60	8.18	3.33
61-70	4.54	3.33
Above 70	0.90	—
Total	**110**	**90**

Source : Field-work.

It has been kept in mind that the respondents from every strata of the society are selected so that they constitute a concrete universe to the study "The Social Mobility and Change among the Tibetan refugees." Classification based on sex is not sufficient therefore distribution done on the basis of Marital status and place of birth as shown in Table

No. 3.2. and Table No. 3.3. are also taken into consideration. Out of 200 respondents 55(21.5%) are born in Tibet, 127 respondents i.e. (63.5%) in India, 5 respondents i.e. (2.5%) in Nepal and 13 respondents i.e.(6.5%) in Bhutan. Those born in Nepal and Bhutan migrated to India mainly due to non-available of freedom of religious practice.

Table 3.2. : Respondents related to their place of birth

Place of Birth	No. of Respondents	% of Responses
Tibet	55	21.5
India	127	63.5
Nepal	5	2.5
Bhutan	13	6.5
Total	**200**	**100**

Source : Field-work.

Table 3.3. : Represents the marital status of the respondents

Marital status	No. of male respondents	% of Responses	No. of female respondents	% of Responses
Married	59	53.63	45	50
Unmarried	50	45.45	39	43.34
Widow/ Widower	—		5	5.55
Divorcee	1	0.92	1	1.11
Total	**110**	**100**	**90**	**100**

Source : Field-work.

The "universe " of the study is composed of heterogeneous group with different socio-economic conditions and different regional backgrounds. The primary source of data i.e. the informants are basically from different regions of Tibet like Kham, Amdo, U-Tsang and Lhasa.

Tibetan refugee respondents on the basic of region of origin is represented in table No. 3.4. It is found that the majority of Tibetan refugee informants are from Lhasa, the capital of Tibet. The next highest percentage of refugees belonged to U-Tsang part of Tibet is 29.5%. Refugees from Amdo region are 16.5% of the total 200 respondents and the refugees from Kham region of Tibet are only 15%.

Table 3.4. : Representing the place of origin of the respondents

Region of origin	No. of respondents	% of Responses
U-Tsang	59	29.5
Kham	30	15
Amdo	33	16.5
Lhasa	78	39
Total	**200**	**100**

Source : Field-work.

It was in 1960, when Dharamsala became the temperary headquarter of The Dalai Lama, it has written to International repute as "The little Lhasa" covering 28.81 sq. km. (2881 acres). Dharamsala's altitude varies between 1250 mt (4400 ft.) and 2000 mt (6,560 ft). Dharamsala is evocative of imperial days in places like Mcleod Ganj and Farsythe Ganj. Headquarter of the Kangra district, it became the capital in 1852 and is 125 years old. Dharamsala divided into upper and lower towns with a scenic background of snow capped, mountains, forests of giant conifers meets at carefully cultivated tea gardens at a beautiful resort of Dharamsala which stands on the spur of Dhauladhare range.

The mountains enfold three sides of the town and the valey stretches beyond the south. The high altitude and cool weather have contributed towards the creation of environment favourable for Tibetans. Most of the Tibetans have made Dharamsala their temporary home living mostly in Mcleod Ganj.

Mcleod Ganj or the upper Dharamsala is 9.5 km from Dharamsala lower with famous Tibetan institutions, some being "reincarnations" as it were centuries old institutions in Tibet. The famous Buddha temple is situated opposite to the present abode of H.H. The Dalai Lama and around it are situated Tibetan Monastery and numely.

The Tibetan Institute of Performing Arts (TIPA) is just a kilometer walk from Mcleod Ganj and Preserves a number of musical dance and theotrical traditions of Tibet. There is also a Tibetan Handicraft Centre situated at Mcleod Ganj. Between Mcleod Ganj and Dharamsala lies the Library of Tibetan Works and Archives (LTWA) where Buddhist works from distant Tibetan refugee camps and settlements come to read the ancient manuscripts preserved here. One cannot miss the Tibetan Buddhist atmosphere in visible symbols, rituals and in the presence of groups of lamas everywhere. It is an attractive place for the spiritually inclined and some are getting into Buddhism and meditation including a few western monks and nuns. Library faclities and study courses make it an ideal place to learn about Tibetan and Mahayana Buddism.

Dun, Doon on Dhoon, in the Sanskrit and Hindi languages means "Valley" which has not been mode by river erosion but is formed by Tectonic activity with in the earth. The Oxford dictionary defines it as "Valley in Shivalik Hills". Dehradun covers the total area of 3088 sq. km. and is situated 1200 mt. above sea level and is now the capital of Uttaranchal newly formed in November. 2000 and was formely a district of Uttar Pradesh. To the East of Dehradun is Tehri garhwal, to the North Uttarkashi, in west lies Himachal Pradesh and to the South west is Saharanpur.

The word Dehra means "Abode" and "Dun" is named after Dronacharya, as he was in search of a lonely place where he could perform his devotions and he came to the village of Dwara in the Deadar Parbat below the Himalayan Mountains, situated a few kilometers East of Dehradun. Hence the whole valley of Doon was called

Drona Ashram, "The Abode of Drona". Another historical account tells us the nomenclature of Dehradun is totally different. The Dehra Dun is composed of two words that is "Dehra" and "Doon". Dehra is derived from the world "Dera" which means to camp and history reveals that the Guru Ram Rai arrived here in 1676 and camped with his wife and followers. And Doon is the distorted word of "Droni" Droni is the Sanskrit word, describing the place situated between the two hills. The climate being moist and not so liable to extremes of heat and cold as other districts in the North-West, the cold weather commences earlier and lasts longer than in the plains while the rains of the summer monsoon are much heavier and more continous.

Dehradun has a long history of producing and exporting Tea and the first tea garden in India was laid out in Doon valley by the East India Company; but it has been suffering from innumerable problems over several decades like Tea, Basmati rice is the gift of Dehradun soil to the world as it can be produced only in Dehradun due to its special natural conditions. Till the end of 1970, Doon was pride of place in the orchards held by the Leechi trees but today due to changing climatic conditions and increasing urbanization Leechi orchards have converted into residential plots or other commercial activities.

As Dehradun is a colder place as already discussed, the climate is also favourable for Tibetans, hence it is in 1960 that the Tibetan refugees started settling in Doon valley. In Doon there are various settlements at various places like Rajpur, Clement Town, Sashtradhara Road, Manduwala, Harbatpur, Haripur, Lakhanwala Dakpathar and Vikasnagar.

Socio-Economic Conditions of Refugees in Exile

The community of refugees in India contained members of every social and ethnic group inhabiting Tibet. Three stages of socio-economic adaptation as given by Methfessel.

Decades	1959-69	70-80	81-91
Dominant economic business activity	Road work and coolie	Agriculture and handicraft	Private service sector
Dominant type of housing construction	Temporory camps	Permanent settlements	New enlargements
Dominant type of income	Food rations and daily wages	regular wage and agricultural	Profits from private business

Sources : By the Methfessel[9]

New Economy

Intially Tibetans were engaged in road-construction work and handicraft work but living a long period in exile the Tibetans have adopted a high occupational adaptability making a very rational choice of occupations as shown in Table No. 3.5. Today, Tibetans have adopted new occupations. They are engaged in business, they are employees and professionals. Out of 200 respondents, 163 are working in various areas of employment and out of which 40.49% are employees in Tibetan govt. Services, 32.55% are doing their own business mostly shopkeepers i.e. 19.63% and rest 26.99% are profesionals for e.g. doctors, engineers, teachers etc.

It is clear that in both the places Tibetans are not labouress or road workers as they were initially engaged to it.

Table 3.5. : Occupation of the Tibetan respondents

Working	**No. of Respondents**	**% of Responses**
Independent business	53	32.55
Employee	66	40.49
Proffesionals	44	26.99
Total	**163**	**100**

Source : Field-work.

Whatever they earn, is not a question because refugee government is unable to provide them higher amount of income as it is clear from the Table no. 3.6.

Table 3.6. : Representing Income of the respondents

Income	No. of Respondents	% of Responses
Not fix	34	20.86
1000 and below	19	11.66
1000 - 2000	26	15.95
2001 - 3000	22	13.50
3001 - 4000	34	20.86
4001 - 5000	13	7.97
5001 - 6000	5	3.07
6001 - 7000	3	1.84
7001 - 8000	4	2.45
Above 8000	0	0
Voluntary workers	3	1.84
Total	**163**	**100**

Source : Field-work.

In refugee conditions, Tibetans are not able to earn much but whatever government in exile provides them, they are satisfied with that a important fact about the community is that all its members are engaged in some or other type of work and every kind of work is accepted by them.

Another important feature of Tibetan society is, person who is capable of doing work hardly remain unemployed.

In the urban market place Tibetans in ovated new market strategies which proved successful to the economic conditions of Tibetans. Successful entry into the occupation system of the host country is generally considered to be a major factor in the adjustment and integration. However the refugee influx may still cause conflicts at the local level, but it is true that taking up of different occupations is one of the principal causes of mobility among the Tibetan refugees.

Not only the economic conditions but changes in the sphere of education, religion and polity have also contributed to the mobility of Tibetan refugees.

Education

Education is playing a vital role as a tool of social mobility. There was no practical liberal education in Tibet, whatever little educational opportunities existed were controlled and dispensed with the religious establishments i.e. the monasteries.

Now a higher value is being attached to modern secular education than to sacred education. This development has resulted in a much higher amount of social mobility with increase in a number of young people qualified for jobs. This has further led to equal opportunities for women.

It is important to know the educational level of the respondents constituting a sample out of 200 respondents (10.5%) respondents are totally illeterate, (6.5%) respondents completed their education till primary level, (8%) respondents have done their J.H.S., (20%) respondents have studied till high school, another (29%) respondents are graduates, (7%) respondents are post graduate and (4.5%) respondents have specialized in various areas of education as shown in Table No. 3.7.

Tibetan women association in its report to the furth world conference on women (at Bejing) admits that "traditionally girls in Tibet had fewer educational opportunities". But in exile girls are equally educated to men as compared to the Past.

Table 3.7. : Representing Education of the respondents

Education	% of Respondents	% of Males	% of Females
Nill	10.5	8.63	10
Primary	6.5	10	11.11
J.H.S.*	8	7.2	8.88
H.S.	20	18.18	22.22
XII	14.5	14.54	14.44
Graduate	29	33.63	23.33
P.G.	7	7.27	6.66
Specialization	4.5	5.45	3.33
Total	**200**	**110**	**90**

Source : Field-work.

*JHS Junior High School H.S-High school graduate

It is found that the younger generation is more keen to study Modern secular education. The elderly people points out that they had less opportunities to study in the past but now they cannot afford to loose education.

It is therefore important to know the relation between education and age group of the respondents as shown in Table No. 3.8.

Religion

The central part of the Tibetan Society is Religion and the whole national life revolved around religion which attracted and absorbed the best human talent. But in the refugedom changes in the core sphere have also forced many changes into the ideological perceptions especially in

Table 3.8. : Relation Between Education and Age of the Respondents

Education	Below 20	21-30	%	31-40	%	41-50	%	51-60	%	61-70	%	Above 70	%	Total
Nil	—	3	2.91	7	20	1	3.22	3	25	6	75	1	—	21
P	—	3	2.91	1	2.85	7	22.58	2	16.66	0	—	—	—	13
J.H.S.	1	8	7.76	3	8.57	4	12.90	0	—	0	—	—	—	16
H.S.	3	17	16.50	7	20	9	29.03	3	25	1	12.5	—	—	40
XII	3	18	17.47	5	14.28	1	3.22	1	8.33	1	12.5	—	—	29
G	3	42	40.77	6	17.14	5	16.12	2	16.66	0	—	—	—	58
P.G.	—	11	10.67	2	5.71	1	3.22	0	—	0	—	—	—	14
SP	—	1	0.97	4	2.85	3	9.67	1	8.33	0	—	—	—	9
Total	**10**	**103**	—	**35**	—	**31**	—	**12**	—	**8**	—	**1**	—	

Source : Field-work.

the younger generation born and brought up in India, perceptively, the old religious order is also under the process of reformation in many ways.

The impact of western culture on the monks depends on their ability to read and write English. Many monks raised in India are oriented towards west, the majority of those from Tibet (the "new-comers" as they are usually called) are oriented towards Tibet whereas some for personal and political reasons intend to remain in India.

On raising the question whether their religious ceremonies have been simplified as compared to the past 64.5% responses were in "Yes" and reasons were as follows:

(a) Economic Factor - As they are refugees they do not have enough money to continue with long prayers for many days and could not spent much on their festivals and Pujas.

(b) Time Factor - Tibetans are hard working and as already mentioned that mostly all members of the community are working to earn their livelihood, so if they spent their time in festivals and poojas, that will result in a loss of business or other works they do.

(c) The third reason is the change in social environment, now as they are more educated, more rational they consider religious ceremonies as a waste of time and money, the ceremonies which are really important and necessary and have no other alternative than to perform, them.

(d) Political changes - There have been some radical changes in the Political values and attitudes of Tibetan refugees who have undergone a quick process of "Politicization". Even the Dalai Lama administration could not be left untouched. Change is also occuring in the Tibetan Political system and it is hoped by Dalai Lama himself that these changes will allow the people of Tibet in determining the future of their country. "The "democratization" has reached out to

> Tibetans all over the world. I believe that future generations of Tibetans will consider these changes among the most important achievements of our experiences in exile".[10]

Even the institution of Dalai Lama has also came to question. on asleing whether the Dalai Lama should be elected?

The majority of respondents that replied in Negative are 49%. They are satisfied with his mode of selection. The respondents who replied positively are 20.5% They are also satisfied with his mode of selection but in near future they watn that this selection should involve a voting pattern as the world is moving towards democratization and the people should get the right to choose their candidate. On the other hand 29.5% respondents gave no response to it because some have never thought of it, some never wanted to involve in such questions as shown in Table No. 3.9.

Table 3.9. : Representing the opinion of the respondents on election of Dalai Lama

Sl. No.	Category of Responses	No. of Respondents	% of Responses
1.	Yes	41	20.5
2.	No	98	49.0
3.	Uncertain	2	1.0
4.	No response	59	29.5
Total		**200**	**100**

Source : Field-work.

Traditional Hierachial Pattern versus Modern Stratification

The traditional pattern of social stratification was formely based on ascriptive status has now become achievement oriented. Tibetan society was organised upon the medieval feudalistic pattern and "Property" the criterion to decide the stratification pattern. The traditional social structure normally had two broad section the mobility and the commoners. The traditional system of social ranking based on property (mainly landed estates) become totally irrelevant in their new existence. Similarly on system which was based on religious beliefs has lost its importance in exile. Even the pre-eminent Position of Dalai Lama as the "living Buddha" and the "God-King" has been to some extent injured and it is now evaluated in terms of new values of rationality rather than the traditional values. These changes in the Tibetan mode of thinking have brought about significant changes in their institutions, attitudes and values. The new - Land holding pattern has brought considerable changes and mobility in the refugee's social life. Now in the settlements they are provided with equal amount of land on individual bases. Everybody is a land owner and the land has to be returned to the settlement corporation after the owner's death; it cannot be inherited by children's automatically though few rich refugees have owned thier houses in the settlement.

Most of the discussion of social structure of a highly stratified society and the social mobility has been focussed on ascriptive and achievement principles so far as modern-industrial socities are concerned. From the point of view of democratic societies ascriptive systems are considered as obstacles which should be removed as soon as possible.

There is yet another dimension to the problem namely time, while analysing the structural conditions for the change which the Tibetans refugee community is undergoing. It is necessary to highlight the role of new generation that has grown up outside the Tibet.

It reveals emerging inter-generational differences among Tibetans. Have intergenerational mobility rates changed with time and to what extent the members of one decade achieved greater upward mobility than the members of the previous decqde It has been known that in each decade variation in levels of technology, fertility rate and net inter-generational migration contribute towards differential mobility rates.

References

1. Goode, Erich - Sociology (pg 532).
2. Moore, W.E. - Social Change - Prentice Hall of India (Pvt.) Ltd. New Delhi, 1965. (pg. 22).
3. Sorokin, P.A. - 'Social & Cultural Mobility' 1959. (pg. 133).
4. Nicholas, Stephen and Byran - Dictionary of Sociology - By Published by Penguin group. 1984, 88, 94. (Pg. 386).
5. Carlile A. Macarthey- "Refugess: ercy. of the social sueaces (Volume 13 pg 200).
6. Fichter, Joseph H. - Sociology, published by University of Chicago 1957. (pg. 319).
7. Hallen and Prasad - Sorokin and Sociology. By Arvind Vivek Prakashan, 1982.
8. The word "Kalachakra" means "Cycle of time" the Kalachakra tantra is the prefound bhuddhist system or teaching and practice. The Mandala is the residence of Kalachakra deity. This Mandala is actually three dimensional being a five storyed "devine mansion" at the centre of which Kalachakra deity stands. Festivals of Tibet - By TYC, March 2000 (pg. 4).
9. Tibetan Culture in the Diaspora - Papers presented at a panel of the 7th Seminar of the International Assignment for the Tibetan Studies GRAZ-1995.
10. Tibetans in Exile - An article by H.H. Dalai Lama at House of Commons All-party Parliamentary group, London 20th March 1991.

4

Family and Marriage

Family as described by George Peter Murdock decades ago is a "social group characterized by common residence, economic cooperation and reproduction"[1] This definition covers polygamous and monogamous unions as well as conjugal and extended ones.

Family is an institution and universal. It assigns, responsibility for the physical survival, up-bringing and socialization of children. It ensures its own continuity by teaching socially sanctioned norms from generation to generation

Changing composition and size of the family - Joint V/s Conjugal

While fleeing from Tibet some of the people migrated alone leaving their families behind. After coming to India they established new families with new members.

It was found necessary to know the types of family that existed in Tibetan society prior to refugehood and after refugehood. The information was collected on the basis of two types of family as shown in Table No. 4.1.

(i) **Conjugal type :** A family unit that is made up of parents and their children is called nuclear family.

(ii) **Joint type :** A family unit made up of more than parents and their children.

The information collected by the respondents indicate that prior to refugeehood only 3 families (1.5%, were conjugal type and the rest 197 families (98.5%) were joint families.

At present conditions have changed. Today there are 185 conjugal type (92.5%) and only 15 joint families (7.5%).

Table 4.1. : Type of Family

Sl. No.	Type of family	No of families prior to refugeehood		After refugeehood	
		no.	%	no.	%
1.	Conjugal	03	1.5	185	92.5
2.	Joint	197	98.5	15	7.5
	Total	**200**	**100**	**200**	**100**

Source : Field-work.

Size of the Tibetan Family

The size of the family was studied on the basis of the total number of the members. It was divided into three categories :

(1) Family consisting of 1-4 members,

(2) Family consisting of 5-8 members, and

(3) Family consisting of 9 and above members.

During the study it was found that prior to refugeehood there were only 3 Jamilies families of the size of 1-4 members i.e. (1.5%). After seeking refugehood the number of such families increased to 57 i.e. (28.5%) in these (28.5%) families most of the members were born and brought up in India.

There were 185 families constituting of 5-8 persons i.e. (92.5%) prior to refugeehood. Now the number has decreased to 138 families i.e. (81.5%).

There were 12, families where the number of members were 9 and above i.e. (6%) prior to refugeehood. Now there are only 5 families i.e. (2.5%). The data is represented in Table No. 4.2.

Table 4.2. : Size of the family

Sl. No.	Size of family	Prior		After	
		no.	%	no.	%
1.	1-4	3	1.5	57	29.5
2.	5-8	185	92.5	138	81.5
3.	9 and above	12	6	5	2.5
	Total	**200**	**100**	**200**	**100**

Source : Field-work.

The change from joint families to conjugal families may be due to the following reasons :

(i) In Tibet for economic cooperation and pattern of land holdings, joint families were more advantageous and therefore in practice.

(ii) Tibetans are moving from polyandrous tradition to monogamous from of marriage,

(iii) Modern education made Tibetans know about the importance of small families.

(iv) Circumstances of living has also affected the family patterns of the Tibetans.

It shows that now the large size of the families is not liked by the people. They are shifting from large families to small families.

Composition and size of the family seperately studied were unable to provide the information required to know more about the changing pattern of Tibet family so, both the composition and size of the family were jointly studied as indicated in Table No. 4.3.

(i) Out of 185 conjugal families, 54 families i.e. (29.18%) are included in the family size of 1-4 and 131 conjugal families i.e. (70.82%) are included in the family size of 5-8. It indicates that in this category the members included in the family are parents and their offsprings.

(ii) On the other hand, out of 15 joint families, 03 families i.e. (20%) falls in the category of the family size of 1-4, The other 7 families i.e. (46.67%) fall in the category of the family size of 5-8, and the rest 5 families i.e. (33.33a) fall in the category of family size of 9 and above.

Table 4.3. : Representing the family size and family type

Sl. No.	Family size	Family type			
		Conjugal		Joint	
		no.	%	no.	%
1.	1-4	54	29.18	03	20.0
2.	5-8	131	70.82	07	46.67
3.	9 and above	—	—	05	33.33
	Total	**185**	**100**	**15**	**100**

Source : Field-work.

Findings indicate that composition of new families is towards nuclear type. In joint families the members included in the family apart from spouses and their offsprings are in-laws, distant relatives and kins, servants, are generally not found in refugee families.

It is clear from Table No. 4.3. that family size of 5-8 members was dominant not prior to refugeehood but also after refugehood. The difference lies in the composition. Previously these families were joint janiilies but now they lies under the category of nuclear type of jarivlies.

Traditional System of Authority

Tibetan households were generally patrilineal in nature. Father or elder brother were considered as the senior member of the family who has right to take decisions on behalf of other members of the family.

At present the situation is very different. The traditional values have lost their importance. The youngsters with new perpectives and values are moving away from the main family.

It was tried to collect the opinions of the respondents about the change in the family authority structure.

The responses collected and tabulated according to their age-group and educational status as represented in Table No. 4.4. and 4.5.

(i) Change in perception with regard to age-group the age-group of the respondents have been categorised as follows :

Age group		No. of respondents
(i)	Below 30	113
(ii)	31-40	35
(iii)	41-50	31
(iv)	51-60	12
(v)	Above 60	9

Source : Field-work.

In the age group of below 30, 77 respondents i.e. (78.58%) express their opinion in positive direction while 36 respondents i.e. (35.30%) express themselves negatively.

In the next age group between 31-40, 07 respondents i.e. (7.14%) replied positively and the rest 28 respondents i.e. (27.46%) replied in negative towards the change in the authority structure.

In the third category of age-group between 41-50, there are 08 respondents i.e. (8.16%) who seem to agree with the change whereas 23 respondents i.e. (22.54%) disagree with the statement.

In the fourth category of age-group between 51-60, there are 5 repsondents i.e. (5.10%) who agree towards the perception of change. The remaining 07 respondents i.e. (6.86%) disagree to it.

The last age-group categorised as above 60, only 1 respondent (1.02%) feel that traditional authority structure has changed. The rest 8 respondents (7.84%) feel that it is not true. Family authority structure remains the same as it was prior to refugehood.

Table 4.4. : Opinion towards change in the authority structure of the family with regard to age-group

Sl. No.	Age group	Preception of respondents Yes	%	No	%	Total no.	%
1.	Below 30	77	78.58	36	35.30	113	56.5
2.	31-40	7	7.14	28	27.46	35	17.5
3.	41-50	8	8.16	23	22.54	31	15.5
4.	51-60	5	5.10	7	6.86	12	6
5.	Above 60	1	1.02	8	7.84	9	4.5
	Total	**98**	**49**	**102**	**51**	**200**	**100**

Source : Field-work.

The responses collected as shown in Table No. 4.4. 49% resondents were of the opinion that there has been a change in the traditional authority structure. Another 51% respondents were of the opinion that there has been no change. According to them male member of the family i.e. father is the head of the family. If father is absent the next head of the family is the elder brother or son.

The responses found are somewhat mixed.

The next important variable taken to study the change in the traditional authority structure is educational status of the respondents. In this context three categproes of educational level were formed :

(1) Illiterate - Those respondents who never had even little education.

(2) Less-educated - Those respondents who completed their education till intermediate level.

(3) Highly educated - Those repsondents who have completed their graduation, who are still studying or those respondents who have done their specialization.

In the first category there are 21 respondents, out of which 10 respondents (10.20%) agree with change and 11 respondents (10.78%) disagree with the change in the traditional authority structure. In the second category there are 40 respondents (40.82%) who agree with the change and 58 respondents i.e. (56.86%) disagree with the statement. In the third category of highly educated respondents, 48 respondents (48.98%) express possitively towards perception of change. The rest 3 respondents (32.36%) express their views negatively towards change in the traditional authority structure.

Table 4.5. : Perception of change in the authority structure with regard to educational status.

Sl. No.	Educational status	Opinion of respondents Yes	%	No	%	Total no.	%
1.	Illiterate	10	10.20	11	10.78	21	10.5
2.	Less-educated	40	40.82	58	56.86	98	49
3.	Highly educated	48	48.98	33	32.36	81	40.5
	Total	**98**	**100**	**102**	**100**	**200**	**100**

Source : Field-work.

The responses given by the respondents of various educational levels are also somewhat mixed.

Change in the Kin Relationship

In traditional Tibetan family kinship relations were strong and siblings were closely attached to each others.

In the refugehood while analysing the changes in the authority structure two variables i.e. age group and educational status were taken into consideration similarly both these variables are also important to study the changes in the kinship structure. When the respondents were asked about the changes in the kin-ship relations, 161 respondents i.e. (80.5%) were of the opinion that nowadays old traditions have lost their importance. They feel that now siblings are less affectionate and less attached to each others.

Another 27 respondents i.e. (13.5%) feel that now the siblings are more attached to each other as shown in Table No. 4.6. According to them many Tibetans have lost their family members during flight. Those remained they do not want to loose one another . The remaining 12 respondents i.e (6%) feel that there is no change in the kindship pattern. Kins are affectionate and attached closely in Tibet and here in India too, the attitude has not changed.

Table 4.6. : Representing change in the kinship structure

Sl. No.	Change of attitude	No. of respondents	% of respondents
1.	Less affectionate	161	80.5
2.	More affectionate	27	13.5
3.	No change	12	6
	Total	**200**	**100**

Source : Field-work.

Change in the perception of respondents in the kinship structure with relation to age-group :

To study the changes in the kinship structure with relation to age of the respondents, the respondents are categorised into the following age-groups.

(i) Below 30

(ii) 31-40

(iii) 41-50

(iv) 51-60

(v) Above 60

There are 161 respondents (80.5%) of the opinion that today siblings are less attached and less affectionate with each other. Out of these 97 respondents (60.24%) falls under the category of the age group of below 30, 28 respondents (17.4%) fall under the age-group of 31-40, 22 respondents (13.67%) are under the age-group of 41-50, 8 respondents (4.97%) are from the age-group of 51-60 and the rest 6 respondents (3.72%) fall under the category of the age-group of above 60.

Those respondents who feel that in the present condition of exile the siblings are more attached and more affectionate are 27 i.e. (13.5%) of these 7 respondents (25.93%) are from the age-group of below 30, another 7 respondents (25.93%) are from the age group of 31-40. 9 respondents (33.33%) are from the age-group of 41-50 and 4 respondents (14.81%) are from the age group of 51-60. There is no one in the age-group of above 60.

The remaining 12 respondents (6%) are those who feel that there is no change in the Kinship structure. Out of these 9 respondents (75%) are from the age-group of below 30 and the remaining 3 respondents (25%) are from the age-group of above 60.

The position as shown in Table No. 4.7. of this category seems to be extreme. There is no respondent between the age-group of 31-40, 41-50 and 51-60 who feels that there is no change in the Kinship structure.

Table 4.7. : Change in Kinship relationship with relation to age-group

Sl. No.	Age-group	Change in perception of the respondents					
		Less attached		More attached		Same as before	
		No. of respondents	%	No. of respondents	%	No. of respondents	%
1.	Below 30	97	60.24	7	25.93	9	75
2.	31-40	28	17.4	7	25.93	—	—
3.	41-50	22	13.67	9	33.33	—	—
4.	51-60	8	4.97	4	14.81	—	—
5.	Above 60	6	3.72	—	—	3	25
	Total	**161**	**100**	**27**	**100**	**12**	**100**

Source : Field-work.

Table No. 4.7. indicates that older generation seems to be more positive towards change in the Kinship structure than the younger generation.

The change in the kin-structure is also analysed with regard to the educational status of the respondents. It will show the attitude of the illiterate, less educated and more educated respondents in regard to their perception toward changing kinship pattern as shown in Table No. 4.8.

Table 4.8. : Change in perception towards kinship structure with regard to education

Sl. No.	Education	Change in preception					
		Less affectionate		More affectionate		Same as below	
		No. of respondents	%	No. of respondents	%	No. of respondents	%
1.	Illiterate	20	12.43	—	—	1	8.33
2.	Less-educated	62	38.51	25	92.6	11	91.67
3.	Highly-educated	79	49.06	2	7.40	—	—
	Total	**161**	**100**	**27**	**100**	**12**	**100**

Source : Field-work.

Finding indicates that 161 respondents who feel that siblings in the present conditions are less affectionate, 20 respondents (12.43%) are from the category of illiterate, and 62 respondents (38.51%) are from the category of less-educated respondents and 79 respondents (49.06%) are from the category of highly-educated respondents. Those respondents who feel that today kins are more attached with each other are 27 out of them 25 respondents (92.6) are from the category of less-educated and 2 respondents (7.40%) are from the category of highly-educated respondents.

The last category of respondents who think that there is no change in the kinship structure are 12 respondents. of these 1 respondent (8.33%) is from the category of illiterates and 11 respondents (91.67%) are from the category of highly educated respondents.

It is clear from Table No. 4.8. that there is no illiterate respondents who feels that affection among the kins have grown in recent times. On the contrary there is no respondent highly-educated who feels that there is no change in the kinship structure. Majority of the respondents who feel that relationships among the siblings have weekend are educated.

Husband-Wife Relationship

The husband-wife relations are considered as an indicator of change in the family. Traditionally women's status was inferior to men's. Today women are playing an important role in all the aspects of the family life.

During interviews it was observed that wives accompany their husbands in replying most of the questions. They sometimes even restrict their husbands from giving some comments. Husbands were also observed consulting their wives not only on the matters of the household but also on the matters related to the economy and polity. Awareness among the women in Tibetan society has contributed towards the change in the family structure, changes related to the socio-economic aspects of the society and the political structure of the society.

The role of old people is rather limited. They take part in discussions, and give opinions. The youngsters hardly listens to them. The old people do not oppose the changes occurring in the community. They know well the causes of the changes and necessity of the change in the Tibetan community. The only regret is that traditional values should not be lost.

Importance of son in a Tibetan family

While studying the changes of the family structure among Tibetans one must not forget the importance of son in a Tibetan family.

Traditionally son has to play an important role as a member of family in the Tibetan society. It was customary to send the elder son in the monastic life. He was the, one, who holds authoritative position in the family.

It was therefore necessary to find the attitude of the respondents towards the importance of son in the family.

In this context respondents were asked about the necessity of son in the family.

Out of 200 respondents 139 respondents (69.5%) feel that girls and boys are equal. They did not feel that son being necessary in the family. Remaining 61 respondents (30.5%) feel that it is necessary to have a son in the family.

Table 4.9. : The perspective of the respondents

Sl. No.	Importance of son in family	No. of respondents	% of responses
1.	Yes	61	30.5
2.	No.	139	69.5
	Total	**200**	**100**

Source : Field-work.

There were various reasons given by the respondents on the importance of son in the family :

(i) To continue the family name from one generation to another.

(ii) Girls get married and parents are left alone with nobody to look after them. Son after marriage will bring the wife and she will take care of the old parents and the youngsters.

(iii) If there is a boy in the family, in odd situations he can run here and there even during nights. Girls are generally useless during odd situation and emergency.

The opinion of the respondents in relation to the importance of son in the family was cross-tabulated with the variables of age-and education.

Table 4.10. : Opinion of the respondents in matter of importance of son related to the age-group

Sl. No.	Age group	Opinion of the respondents			
		Yes	%	No	%
1.	Below 20	4	6.56	6	4.31
2.	21-30	28	45.90	75	54
3.	31-40	9	14.76	26	18.70
4.	41-50	8	13.11	23	16.53
5.	51-60	6	9.83	6	4.31
6.	61-70	5	8.21	3	2.15
7.	Above 70	1	1.63	—	—
	Total	**61**	**100**	**139**	**100**

Source : Field-work.

From the findings it is clear that the opinion of the respondents who are old in age seems to be positive. They feel it is important to have a son in the family. The young and the middle aged people do not feel the same.

The opinion of the respondents on importance of son with relation to their educational status is indicated in Table No. 4.11.

Table 4.11. : Opinion of the respondents on the matter of importance of son in relation to educational status

Sl. No.	Education of the respondents	Opinion of the respondents Yes	%	No	%
1.	Illiterate	11	18.03	10	7.20
2.	Less educated	36	59.01	62	44.60
3.	Highly educated	14	22.96	67	48.20
	Total	**61**	**100**	**139**	**100**

Source : Field-work.

From the findings it is clear that the opinion of the respondents who are illiterate and less-educated are mixed. The respondents who are highly educated do not find that son is necessary for the family. It shows that education has played an important role in changing the attitude and perception of the respondents.

Another important information regarding the change in the family is related to the various restrictions imposed on the family members.

Type of restrictions on the family members

When the respondents were asked about the restrictions imposed upon them by their family or the community, It was found that there were number of such restrictions, which are not imposed equally on all the members of family.

The restrictions are categorised as follows:

(1) Related to education

(2) Related to occupation

(3) Related to relation with opposite sex

(4) Related to marriage

(5) Related to food, drink and smoke

(6) Related to wearing certain type of clothes

(7) Related to late night outings

(8) Any other :

The responses received were cross-tabulated with the age-group as shown in Table No. 4.12.

(i) Respondents below the age-group of 30, generally have restrictions on choice of occupation, relation with opposite sex and late night outings.

(ii) Respondents between the age-group of 31-41, have two types of restrictions on them viz. relation with the opposite sex and late night outings. The respondents in the age group of 61 above 70, are considered to be the elderly people of the community. They have restrictions on food habits though not on drinking and smoking. One can see elderly people smoking Bidis and roaming in streets. The second type of restrictions is on their late-night outings.

In the age-group between 41-60 respondents, say that their is no restrictions imposed on them. They are free to do things in their own way.

From the Table No. 4.12. it is found that Tibetans have restriction with relation to the opposite sex. But in practice it has been observed that in Tibetan Community men and women mix freely with each other.

Pre-marital sex relations are resported in some cases. Where in some other cases the lovers have even children before marriage.

Table 4.12. : Restrictions imposed on the respondents with relation to age

Sl. No.	Age Group	Restrictions imposed on the respondents (i)	(ii)	(iii)	(iv)	(v)	(vi)	(vii)
1.	Below 20	—	+	+	—	—	—	+
2.	21-30	—	+	+	—	—	—	+
3.	31-40	—	—	+	—	—	—	+
4.	41-50	—	—	—	—	—	—	—
5.	51-60	—	—	—	—	—	—	—
6.	61-70	—	—	—	—	+	—	+
7.	Above 70	—	—	—	—	+	—	+

Source : Field-work.

Life of the Tibetans is not very restricted. Males and females both have right to choose their own way of life.

Various reasons behind the changes in a Tibetan Family

(i) The impact of modern education have contributed in the change of relationships. Tibetans are now aware of their status and role in the family organization.

(ii) Many kinds of technological innovations have had adverse effect on the relationships. Improving transport and communication technology has in some measure weakened the bonds of family life. Transport and communication has played the role in lessening the isolation of the family unit. On the contrary it had enlarged the individual S world.

(iii) Another important factor responsible for the adverse effect on the relationship is opportunity for job. Men, young and old, tended to be away from their homes to earn their livelihood.

Marriages among Tibetans

In Tibet three forms of marriages were prevalent in the community-

(i) Monogamy - The practice whereby people marry only one spouse at a time.

(ii) Polygyny - Custom for a man to have several wives at the same time.

(iii) Polyandry - Custom for a woman to have several husbands at the same time.

Polygyny being mainly practiced among noble and aristocratic classes and polyandry being mainly found both among the nobility and the commoners.

Monogamy

Today monogamous marriages are in practice. Many changes have taken place in the ideal form of Monogamy. There was only one case reported in the sample of non-fraternal polyandry.

The openness of Tibetan regarding marital relations is further proved by an incident when a husband belonging to a noble family married his third wife to another man realising that she was well educated, younger to him in age and deserve a better husband. The lady Rinchen Dolma Taring (earlier Tsarong), whose second marriage was with Jigme, the eldest son of Raja of Sikkim. Her younger sister Chandgehup married the younger brother of Jigme.[2]

At another instance, the father wished his eldest son to marry the youngest of his wives that is the fifth wife. (perhaps actually during his life time).[3] In exile elder brother does not have any authority over younger brother's wife. All brothers have their seperate families with wife & children. Thus, polyandrous marriages are not reported.

Buddhist values are also at stake in exile. The monks who were considered to stay in monastic life are reported to have left their monastries and entered the materialistic world by marrying and settling their families with in the colonies.

Changing Pattern of Marriage

Traditional marriages were mostly arranged Parents choose life-partners for their children and children regard their decision willingly. In the new-setting love-marriages have taken place of arrange marriages. Now love-marriages are becoming the norm.

In the present sample out of 111 married respondents, 74 respondents (69.66%) reported love-marriages, where 37 respondents (33.34%) reported arrange-marriages. The data also represented in Table No. 4.13.

Table 4.13. : Type of marriages reported by the respondents

Sl. No.	Type of marriage	No. of respondents	% of respondents
1.	Arrange marriage	37	33.34
2.	Love marriage	74	69.66
	Total	**111**	**100**

Source : Field-work.

Age at Marriage

The age at marriages in Tibetan society rests on three factors :

(i) economic condition of a person

(ii) social status of a person

(iii) perfect match.

For girls the age at puberty is taken as a suitable age for marriage. Today even girls are getting married late. The reason is that the person who is getting married should be aware of the responsibility of a marriage. Table No. 4.14. shows the age of the respondents in which they got married. Out 60 married males and 51 married females, 32 males (53.33%) and 40 females (78.43%) belong to the age-group of 18-25.

Another 25 male respondents (41.66%) and 11 female respondents (21.56%) belong to the age-group between 26-35 years. In the age-group of 36-45 yrs. there only 2 male respondents (3.34%) and no female respondent is included. In the last age-group of 46-50 there is only 1 male respondent (1.66%) and no female respondent is found.

Table 4.14. : Age of the respondents at which they got married

Sl. No.	Age of the respondents	No.of male respondents no.	%	No. of female responents no.	%
1.	18-20	7	11.67	11	21.56
2.	21-25	25	41.67	29	56.87
3.	26-30	20	33.33	9	17.65
4.	31-35	5	8.34	2	3.92
5.	36-40	2	3.34	—	—
6.	41-45	—	—	—	—
7.	46-50	1	1.66	—	—
	Total	**60**	**100**	**51**	**100**

Source : Field-work.

The lowest age at marriage recorded among girls were 18 years and among boys 20 years. It is found that girls get married early.

Child marriages are not in practice and late marriages are considered to be more stable.

In few cases it was found that in Tibetan society man marrying a women older than himself is not uncommon. Table No. 4.15. represents the cases where wives are younger, equal and older in age than the husband.

Out of 60 married male respondents 32 respondents (53.34%) say that their wives are younger to them. 21 respondents (35%) say that their wives are equal in age. Very few respondents 7 males (11.66%) say that their wives are older to them.

Table 4.15. : Showing Difference of age between husband and wife

Sl. No.		No. of male respondnets	% of respondnets
1.	Wife younger than husband	32	53.34
2.	Wife older than husband	7	11.66
3.	Wife equal to age of husband	21	35
	Total	**60**	**100**

Source : Field-work.

In cases, where wives are older than the husband is firstly because many persons have lost their spouses during flight. So, after coming in India they got settled at various camps. In these camps due to various circumstances, they had to accept the person without considering the age of the person.

Secondly, these persons who lost their spouses during their flight were also eager to marry. They married the person they come across.

Thirdly and lastly, the persons due to various attractions fall in love with each other and married. Age and status did not matter at all in such cases.

Rules of Marriage

Tibetans are strictly endogamous in nature. Marital alliances rests on various factors- economic status, ritual status, ethnic groups, tribal groups and occupational status.

In the new social environment many people violate the rules of marriage.

Today Tibetans are scattered all over the country. Here everyone is more Tibetan than a Kham or an Amdo. The traditional rules of marriage are weakening day by day.

During the study it was found that Tibetans are breaking the rules of marriage as couples are married from different places of their origin.

In the present study 19 married respondents (17.11%) are from Amdo, 21 respondents (18.92%) are from Kham, 33 respondents (29.73%) from U-Tsang and 38 respondents (34.24%) from Lhasa.

Table No. 4.16 shows that out of 19 respondents from Amdo, 10 respondents (52.63%) are married to Amdo, 3 respondents (15.8%) married in Kham, 2 respondents (10.52%) married to U-Tsang and 4 respondents (21.05%) are married to Lhasas.

Out of 21 respondents from Kham, 2 respondents (9.52%) are married to Amdos, 9 respondents (42.86%) are married to Kham, 5 respondents (23.81%) to U-Tsang and another 5 respondents (23.81%) are married to lhasas. Married respondents from U-Tsang are 33, out of these 4 respondents (12.12%) are married to Amdos, 19 respondents (57.58%) are married to U-Tsang and 10 respondents (30.30%) are married to Lhasas.

Out of 38 Lhasa respondents, 26 respondents (68.42%) are married to Lhasa only, 11 respondents (28.95%) are married to U-Tsang and only 1 respondent (2.63%) are married to Amdos.

Table 4.16. : Representing the place of origin of the married respondents to the place of origin of their spouses

Sl. No.	Place of origin of married respondents	Total	Place of origin of the spouses Amdo	Kham	U-T	Lhasa
1.	Amdo	19	10	3	2	4
	(%)	(17.11)	(52.63)	(15.8)	(10.52)	(21.05)
2.	Kham	21	2	9	5	5
	(%)	(18.92)	(9.52)	(42.86)	(23.81)	(23.81)
3.	U-Tsang	33	4	—	19	10
	(%)	(29.73)	(12.12)		(57.58)	(30.30)
4.	Lhasa	38	1	—	11	26
	(%)	(34.24)	(2.63)		(28.95)	(68.42)
Total	**111**	**17**	**12**	**37**	**45**	
	(%)	**(100)**	**(15.31)**	**(10.82)**	**(33.33)**	**(40.54)**

Source : Field-work.

In aggregate 17 respondents (15.31%) are married to Amdos, 12 respondents (10.82%) are married to Khams, 37 respondents (33.33%) are married to U-Tsang and 45 respondents (40.54) are married to Lhasas.

It is clear that Tibetans still follow the rules of ethnic and geographical locations It is not strictly observed as it was in Tibet. Those who have married outsider their place of origin are respondents between the age-group of 20-35 years. Such marriages are generally love marriages.

Marriage Ceremony

Weddings are usually arranged during the months of December and February. There are no legal documents or religious implications in a Tibetan marriage. Tibetans being luck addicts performs animistic rite, on the wedding morning. Usually the groom's family members approaches the bride's family to ask the girl in marriage. But it is not always the case. It is not a rule. The auspicious day and time for marriage is fixed after consulting a Lama. Marriage celebrations is considered auspicious during dawn.

The people of U-Tsang presents ornaments, clothes, etc. to their bride. As a custom these gifts are presented by groom's father's brother. Then it is also custom that the mother's brother and groom reaches the brides residence one day earlier to the marriage to bring the bride to the groom's family. Generally 3, 5, 7 or 9 people can go to the bride's residence. Males entertain the men from groom's side and females prepares the bride for marriage ceremonies. Exchange of Kha-ta and good wishes takes place. A sacred divine dagger and five coloured sticks (red, yellow, blue, green and white) with silk ribbons is put around the neck of the bride to bring her good luck.

At the time of party the bride's family members are suppose to weep more loudly.

At the door of groom's residence his mother and sisters welcome the bride with Kettles full of Tibetan Tea and Chang. Now, the bride dips her fourth finger of right hand in the Chang and sprinkles it three times up towards the sky. This is like her offering to the family deity she enters in the house placing her right leg first inside. She is suppose to sit at the left of the groom.

Then the bride's mother's brother sit in a line, to the right of the bridal couple and the groom's mother's brothers sit in a line to the left. At first the groom's parents offer Khata and then the bride' relatives. At this time all the relatives and friends presents Kha-ta, cash and gifts to the newly wed, and sometimes to all the members sitting in the line. The invities are then served with sweet rice (De-see), Chang, Beer, Coke, Tibetan Tea, Indian Tea. lunch is also served to the guesto. Ceremonial songs are sung and music system is a part of entertainment.

Tibetan marriages last for three days. Today Tibetans finish all the Situals within a day or two and only necessary things are brought.

It was found that Tibetans still follow the rules of marriage regarding class and religion. When the respondents were asked whether they will prefer to marry a Tibetan of any class or status' or a Tibetan of different place of origin than their; and any person who is not a Tibetan. Table No. 4.17. shows that out 89 unmarried repsondents 63 respondents (70.79%) can marry a person irrespective of class and Status. 78 respondnets (87.64%) said that marrying a person from a different province does not matter at all. Only 4 respondents (4.5% were of the opinion that they can marry a person irrespective of his/her religion).

Table 4.17. : Preference of the respondents to various options in case of marriage

Sl. No.	Do you prefer to marry	No. of respondents Yes	%	No	%
1.	A Tibetan of any class/status	63	70.79	26	29.21
2.	Tibetan from a different province	78	87.64	11	12.36
3.	A non-Tibetan	04	4.5	85	95.50

Source : Field-work.

It is clear that class/status or province is no barrier for the Tibetan to marry. Religion still play an important role in case of marriages. Tibetans themselves do not prefer to marry outside their community.

Inspite of being the rigid attitude of Tibetans towards religion few cases were reported in the settlement where Tibetan boy is married to Indian girl and Tibetan girl married to Indian boys. Only one case was reported in the sample where a Tibetan lady (widow) was married to the Indian Brahamin boy. After the death of her husband her in-laws did not allow her and her children to live with them. She brought her children back in the Tibetan community. After asking her neighbours it was found that many people do not have respect for her as she is the wife of an Indian.

Today everyone's personal values are more important than any traditional rules and custom.

Some woman may value a man's sense of humor than any other feature. Similarly a man might wish to have an educated wife than to have a beautiful or wealthy one.

On asking the unmarried respondents seperately from boys and girls as to what qualities they prefer to be present in their husband or wife.

The repsondents ranked the qualities which according to them were most essential, less essential and not at all essential. Out of 39 unmarried female respondents the first preference was given to the loyalty of the husband, 28 respondents (71.79%) say that he should be honest and faithful towards the responsibilities. The second preference was given to the economic status of the husband. According to 22 respondents (56.41%), say he should be capable enough to fulfil the demands of the family.

The third preference was given to education. According to 21 females (53.84%), he should be highly educated. They feel that education makes the person move understanding towards the family. The last or the fourth preference was given to the personality. 18 females (46.15%) prefer that husband should be smart and good looking.

Not only females, males also prefer to have wives of their choice. Out of 50 unmarried males, the first preference was given to the nature of the girl. 48 male respondents (96%) feel that girl who is polite can lead a better life.

The second preference was given to personality of the girl 46 respondents (92%) think that wife should be beautiful. The last or third preference was given to Education. 39 respondents (78%) feel that if the wife is educated she will help in the family's economy. Educated wife will be more understanding in odd situations than an un-educated wife.

Widowhood

Widowhood is considered to be the natural breaking of a marriage. Traditionally widows were not allowed to remarry or participate in any rituals and ceremonies. However, this custom is not strictly observed.

There are 5 widow respondnets (2.5%) in the present sample. When the respondents were asked about their present residence whether they are living in their parental house or in their in-laws house. Table No. 4.18. shows that out of 5 respondents, 3 respondents (60%) reply that they are staying in their husband's house, 1 respondents (20.%) is staying at her parent's house and another 1 respondent is staying neither at her husband's house nor at her parents house she owns her own house in the settlement.

Table 4.18. : Repoesending the residence of the widows

Sl. No.	Respondents residence	No. of respondents	% of responses
1.	Parent house	1	20
2.	In-laws house	3	60
3.	Neither parents house nor in-laws house	1	20·
	Total	**5**	**100**

Source : Field-work.

In Tibet widows were not allowed to remarry. If she wishes to remarry again than only after one year and forty nine days she could do so. such remarriages are not viewed favourable by the people. The food cooked by her was considered impure and was not taken by other members of the family. Some of the widows even get their head shaved off she was not allowed to attend any ceremonies as she was considered to bring illuck and misfortune.

However, things are changing in exile. Widows today are allowed to remarry any person they like. Even the respondents when asked about the restrictions imposed on widows all replied in negative. They say that now widows attend all ceremonies and religious activities performed in the family. They are free to drink, dance and enjoy all the ceremonies. They are even allowed to remarry.

On further asking the respondents about their economic conditions, as how they run their family. Out of 5 responses received, 4 respondents (80%) say that their children (son or daughter) are earning well in business and they themselves are engaged in petty business. 1 respondent (20% who is staying at her parents house say that she is dependent on her parents she has no children.

Divorce

Divorces are a threat to the institution of marriage.

In the present sample 2 case of divorce are reported. Out of which one is of male and another of female. When they were asked as for how long did their marriage survive? The male respondent replied his marriage survived for one and a half year. The female respondent replied that after three years she got separated from her husband.

The reason for the separation given by the male respondent was daily quarrels. The reason given by the female respondents was the extra-matrital sexual relations of their husband.

In a Tibetan society there is no written document signed by the partners for the divorce procedure. They don't have to go to the courts for the matter. They simply leave each other if decided by them that they cannot continue to live together.

In the sample case, the spouses had no children therefore they planned to remarry.

In older days elder people of the community involved themselves in such disputes. They tried to unite the couple instead of seperating them.

Lack of such authoritative persons in the present family organisation lead to deviant behaviour of the individuals. As a result high rate of divorces in the society among younger generation is reported. Divorces have become common in the society.

One of the main reasons behind the high rate of

divorces in the Tibetan community today is the changing role of women.

Majority of girls are now educated and working better than the boys. The working wives are also expected to look after the children and house properly. These expectations lead, to conflict of roles. They also suffer from ego problems. All these little conflicts and minor contradictions lead to marital breakdown. This story is not confined to Tibetans only but in every community people have experienced the same problem.

Rituals and Ceremonies is a part of Marriage

The ways of performing ceremonies mirrors the socio-economic status of the family. Ceremonies and rituals performed in a Tibetan marriage cannot be an exception.

It is true that Tibetan society is moving from traditional to modern life-styles. Even the style of celebrating the marriage ceremonies have changed. The young generation is more inclined towards western modes.

One can observe the people dancing in western style, playing western music, serving cakes and pasteries etc. This is not much liked by the older generation but they could not afford to speak against it.

Traditionally all the rituals and ceremonies continued for days together. People use to spend money according to their economic status. It is perhaps difficult now for the Tibetans refugees to spend too much time on these rituals. Usually such activities need much more time than the individual can give. Even the role of relatives have also weekend in marital ceremonies.

Marriage: A Channel of Social Mobility

Tibetan society in the past, as already discussed was divided into several divisions namely high and low sections. One of the basis of which was economic status of the family.

In case of marital alliances class endogamy was strictly in practice. It is now observed that contrary to the old tradition the low status man marries a high status woman and high status man marries a low status women.

A woman's status can change in either direction as she shares her husband's status. Here marriage serves as a channel of social mobility. It can be upward social mobility or downward social mobility.

It is seen that male generally does not gain in status. If he marries a woman of high status, it might help him in elevating his status indirectly. Valuable contacts and influential family background is considered more important for males to establish their own economic status.

One cannot deny the fact that Tibetans have undergone rapid changes. They are moving from traditional values to secular values. Change in family structure and institution of marriage as explained on the basis of two variables age and eduction, can be due to the changed conditions. It is true that Tibetan refugees have accepted and adjusted to the ways of the modern world.

References

1. Murdock, George Peter, - Social Structure, Macmillan, New York. 1949.
2. Taring, R.D. - Daughter of Tibet. (pg. 102-103).
3. Stein, R.A. - Tibetan Civilization. Fabes & Faber Ltd., London, 1972 (pg. 101).

5

Women and Society

Original sin in the Garden of Eden was woman's. She tasted the forbidden fruit, tempted Adam and has been paying for it ever since. M. Haralambos in his book 'sociology-Themes and perspectives' quoted that, In Genesis the Lord said, "I will greatly multiply the sorrow and thy conception; in sorrow thou shalt bring forth children and thy desire shall be to thy husband and he shall rule over thee."[1]

Sociologist might consider the above definition as one of the reason for the status of women in the society since times immemorial.

The women is in general considered to have inferior status to that of the men. They are in subordination to the male authority and this gradation is maintained in all the aspects of life. They are largely excluded from positions of Power. The roles accorded to women in the every known human society are that of taking care of children, cooking, washing mending and to look after the benefits of the family members. Formely, Tibetan women were regarded somewhat as devils in human form and they were hardly treated as human beings. Tibetan women lived under the four-fold oppression of the state, the clan, religion and the society and were subservient in their own families. The old Tibetan legal code included the following stipulations. "Do not let women have the right to discuss the affairs of the state. She would not be allowed to participate in military and political affairs".

These were many Tibetan proverbs and sayings like "Dogs, women and children are the roots of trouble" or "if you believe what a woman says the roots of your house will soon be overgrown with weeds" or "a woman's talk is like a galloping of a mare".

"From ancient times the belief prevailed in Tibet that the male was innately superior to the female and the humiliating description "Kyemei", meaning low and degrading persons was applied to women"[2]

But there are another category of scholars who write that, "men and women treat each other as equals" and noted the high status accorded to the Tibetan women.

In terms of populaiton the ratio of men and women was roughly equal and this trend is prevelant even in exile. "A survey conducted by the Planning Council in 1992 in 34 Tibetan settlements and 58 scattered communities in India shows that the male and female ratio is roughly equal 51 : 49"[3].

In the present study also the data collected with 200 persons, the ratio of male and female is 110 : 90. The composition of the Tibetan Population also reveals the socio-cultural status of the Tibetan women.

The sexual division of labour and inequality between the two sexes is determined to some degree by biologically or genetically based differences between men and women. This position is opposed to those who argue that gender roles are actually determined and inequality between the two sexes results from socially structured power relationships.

Role of Women

Parson characterises the role of women in the family as "expressive" which means she produces warmth, security and emotional support.

Similarly the Tibetan woman, have certain roles to perform in the society. On asking women: as what work society expects from a woman. Child rearing, taking care of household work, working outside, to take care of household work plus work outside.

Out of 200 respondents, 52.22% gave their first preference to the fourth option. It means woman should not only take care of household activities but she should also work outside to contribute in the economy of the family.

The second prefrence given by 37.77% respondents was to the second option. According to them society expects women to look after her house only.

The third prefrence was given to first option by 28.88% respondents. They say that the major role of women in the society is to take care of her children. The minimum response was given to the third option by 16.66% respondents as shown in Table No. 5.1. According to them women should work outside. It is necessary for a woman to earn independently.

Table 5.1. : Respondents expriesing their views on the role of women

Role expected from a woman	No of respondents	% of responses
1. Child rearing	57	28.88
2. Household work	75	37.77
3. Working outside	33	16.66
4. Household work + working outside	105	52.22

Source : Field-work.

Due to progress and upliftment of women it is felt necessary that besides working at home, women should also engage themselves working in different jobs and business outside according to their capability.

A reason for such a dramatic change in the perspective of Tibetans may be because of education provided to girls of the community. Besides it Tibetan needs more hands to earn their livelihood respectfully and do not like to be parasite on the host country.

Before 1949, Tibetan population was engaged in a mixed economy consisting of agriculture, pastoralisim and trade. As such both male and female were engaged in all the three activities but there was a sexual division of labor in the society.

Women in the Economic Activities

Based on traditional ways and livelihood patterns, Tibetans were divided into five main classes viz. monks, traders, farmers, nobles and herders. Among the farmers and the nomads, women did almost every type of work, maid servants were engaged to do the household work in the aristocratic families of Tibet. In the exile conditions nobody employ servants in the houses. On asking the respondents whether they employ servants in the family, all the responses were negative. The reason given by them is that they do not have enough money to keep servants for their work.

Women of the middle class of a Tibetan family did all sorts of household work. Both the sexes were engaged in cutting down firewood and collecting fuel. The men generally prefer to remain themselves idle (quite similar to the trend in males among the hilly regions of Garhwal). Tibetans are businessmen and even in the changed conditions of exile business seems to be more in the hands of women. In Dehradun as well as in Dharamsala, one can see wide spread Tibetan markets and these markets are fully controlled by women power.

About one-third of the total population of the Tibetans are engaged in sweater-selling which are machine-made and bought from Ludhiana. Apart from this they also sell other summer garments, electronics and cosmetic items.

In fact the customers for these shops are those who are tourists and come in the summer season to visit hills. Local people rarely go there as they sell items at very high rate, which are easily available in local Indian markets at low price.

The next important occupation followed by Tibetans in exile is farming but it is hardly practiced in the hilly regions of Dehradun and Dharamsala.

The total working population of Tibetans under the present study is 163, out of which 75 are females and 88 are males. Out of these 75 working females, 29 females i.e. 38.66% are from Dehradun and the remaining 46 females i.e. 61.33% are from Dharamsala. It means that women in Dharamsala are more actively working as comapred to the women in Dehradun. It is also important to know in which field of occupation, women of the two places are generally engaged. Out of 75 working women, 49 respondents (65-33%) are engaged in government jobs of which 17 respondents (58.62%) are from Dehradun and 32 respondents (69-56%) are from Dharamsala as represented in Table No. 5.2.

Another 9 respondents (12%) are working in Private jobs. Out of which 4 respondents (13-8%) are from Dehradun and 5 respondents (10.88%) are from Dharamsala. The rest 17 respondents (22.67%) are engaged in different business. 8 respondents (27.58%) are from Dehradun and 9 respondents (19.56%) are from Dharamsala.

Table 5.2

Working female respondents engaged in different fields of work in Dehradun and Dharamsala

Type of work		No. of respondents			Total		
		D. Dun	%	D. Sala	%	No.	%
1.	Govt. job	17	58.62	32	69.56	49	65.33
2.	Pvt. Job	4	13.8	5	10.88	9	12
3.	Business	8	27.58	9	19.56	17	22.67
	Total	**29**	**100**	**46**	**100**	**200**	**100**

Source : Field-work.

It is clear from Table No. 5.2. that women in Dharamsala are mostly engaged in government job Women in business activities and Private jobs are mixed in both the places.

The next important means of Tibetans to earn their livelihood is running resturants providing Tibetan food. Carpet weaving and handicraft shops which are totally run by women and quite a large number of educated women are engaged in teaching jobs in schools for Tibetans and government offices of Tibetans.

There are number of houses which are run with the single woman's income and this does not bring any shame to the family or to the husband. The income is always "Collective". Men therefore engage themselves in the hosue-hold activities including washing, dishing, taking care of children etc. and they do not feel bad about it rather they are proud of their roles they perform in the family.

When important matters concerning the family are discussed, women's opinion too is considered. With the advance of age a Tibetan woman accquires a higher status in the society. Tibetans address any elderly woman with respectful term "A-ma" meaning mother. If she is of equal age she is referred to as "A-Cha-la" meaning respectful sister and the younger girls are referred to as "Pu-mp" meaning daughter.

A Tibetan woman is physically strong and undeniably intelligent and brought up in the free environment with boys and men; but girls do not, as a custom, had the right to select the boy of her own choice for marriage, thus the choisce rests with her parents. In case of marriages, "a son is consulted by her father as to the bride proposed for him but the parents consult their daughter hardly at all."[4]

However in exile, there is no such restriction and girls are free to marry whomsoever they like. There are number of cases of love marriages today as compared to those in the past. Table No. 5.3. represents the total number of cases of love marriages as well as arrange marriages in a present Tibetan community.

Out of 111 married couples, 33.33% are those who married according to the wishes of thier parents i.e. the arrange marriage and the rest 69.66% couples married according to their own choice i.e. love marriage. One can therefore observe the changes among both the sexes in relation to the choice of their partners. It also indicates that now Tibetans are free to marry who so ever they like, but chosen mate should be a Tibetan.

Table 5.3. : Respondents and the type of marriage

Type of marriage	No of responses	% of responses
Arrange	37	33.33
Love	74	69.66
Total	**111**	**100**

Source : Field-work.

Cases were also found where Tibetan females, are married to Indian, but yet, have not given up their religious practices and perform the Hindu rituals also.

There are two major aspects in whcih the Tibetan woman refugees have retained their uniqueness, viz : the dressing style and their religious faith and practice. The majority of Tibetan women are not willing to marry outside their religion because they feel that if they marry outside their religion they have to come across tremendous adjustment problems.

In the changing conditions of exile women are free to do things at their own, though there are certain restrictions imposed on them but moreover they do what they feel correct for them.

On asking the respondents if they are society free to do whatever they like? Out of 90 responses recieved 87.77% say that they do according to their will as shown in Table No. 5.4. Parents hardly, refuses their wishes. But another 12.23% say that they still lead their life under many restrictions and are bound either by their spouses or their family memebrs. The restrictions impsoed on them are - restrictions on illegal sex, coming late at night, smoking (not drinking). These restrictions are imposed generally on all the young girls of the Tibetan community.

Table 5.4. : Representing the opinion of the respondents on their freedom to express their wishes.

Opinion of the respondents	No of respondents	% of responses
No restrictions imposed	79	87.77
Restrictions on many things	11	12.23
Total	**90**	**100**

Source : Field-work.

They have not become so western and modern as to leave their traditions and culture behind. The restrictions are not maintained on wearing the clothes of their choice, type of food they would like to eat, in relation to their education and choice of occupation.

Almost all the working women are members of Tibetan women's Association (TWA). It is the only women's organisation that has been set up to channelize the resources and energy of Tibetan women. It was reactivated in 1984. It works for the preservation of Tibetan relation, culture and identity. Its purview includes political, relations, cultural educational, social welfare and ecological activities.

They demonstrate against the chinese for the humiliation they are giving to Tibetans, but they hardly go on strikes.

Tibetan working women are not aware fully about strikes and unions generally operated in factories and industries. They are hard working and belive "work is worship".

Even the laws made by the government for working ladies are not well-known to them. Out of 90 females, (both working and non-working) only 41 females (i.e. 45.55%) are aware of maternity leaves, only 1 female i.e. 1.11% knew about the law of relaxation in working hours given to women, 21 females i.e. 23.33% agree that government has made the law that no night duties and no field work will be done by women and rest 12 females i.e. 13.33% were aware about various harassement laws made by the Govt. for their protection. On the other hand 15 females i.e. 16.66% were totally unknown about any of these laws mentioned here.

Table 5.5. : Representing the awareness of women towards the laws made by the Govt.

Opinion of the respondents	No of respondents	% of responses
Relaxation in working hours	1	1.11
Maternity leaves	41	45.55
Harresment	12	13.33
No night duties	21	23.33
No field work	21	23.33
Unknown	15	16.66

Source : Field-work.

Women's Education

Traditonally women had fewer educational opportunities. According to a survey conducted by the planning council in exile more than 90% of girls between the age group of 6 and 17 years attended schools.

Education being the most important factor of change had influenced the lives of women by opening new opportunities for them, so that they could make considerable progress in every sphere of life.

In Tibet men and women were treated very differently in matters of upbringing and education. As it has already been mentioned that the education system was fully under the control of monasteries thus, when the boy child attains the age of eight, every family despite of rich or poor would try to get the boy into a lamasery only the girls from the aristocratic families were given the minimum education which was too exceptional.

Even the report to the fourth world conference on women at Bejing admits that "Traditionally girls had fewer education than boys."

In exile, being exposed to the modern society, the establishements of the Tibetans central schools (by the Government of India) and the Tibetans eagerness of learning have produced a dramatic change. The totally illiterate community turned to almost literate society including higher education among both men and women.

The educations is compulsory among Tibetans because they feel that it is only through education they could lead a better life and strengthen their society for the liberation of their chinese's occupied land. There are several women's association running throughout the world and the main purpose behind the formation of such associations is to fight against the male torture and molesting.

But in case of "TWA", the purpose is very different from the one mentioned above. They do not have to fight for the tortures and molestations as it does not exist in Tibetan society. On the other hand they try to strengthen themselves for the liberation of Tibet occupied by the Chinese.

The aim of "TWA" is to talk of tortures and pains given to them by the Chinese which is entirely different to the torture and pain given to girls by their in-laws and other relations in Indian society.

No case of rape was found within the community, but at the level of friendship girls are free to live their life as they like. For them sex is fair pleasure therefore, voluntary and consensual.

The dreaded dowry system and tightening of women's feet which is inseperable part of Indian culture is not the domain of Tibetan society. In simpler words, it is a dowryless society. It is also not necessary that the girl after her marriage move's to her husband's house. If she is the only daughter of her parents it is quite possible that the husband joins the wife's family. In the Indian society, are call it "Ghar Jamai" which is not worth appreciable among Indians. The Tibetan family and the Tibetan husband do not feel anything bad about it.

When the question was put up before male respondents on their wish to live with their in-laws. Out of 110 male respondents (which included both married and unmarried) Maximum males i.e. 65 males (59.09%) feel nothing bad about staying with wife's family. But another 45 males i.e. 40.91% feel that it is not appreciable to live with the family of in-laws as shown in Table No. 5.6. Out of these 40.91% respondents, few of them do agree that if circumstances leave no choice for them except to live with wife's family to lead their life, they can think over it for a while.

Table 5.6. : Male respondents on their opinion to stay with their in-laws

Opinions of the males	No. of responses	% of responses
Yes	65	59.09
No	45	40.91
Total	**110**	**100**

Source : Field-work.

Women in the Family

She also plays an important role in the Tibetan socio-religious ceremonies too. During festivals and occasions they sing and dance with male members of their groups. They visit all their relatives and exchange gifts. They yield considerable respect as Wives and Mothers.

In remote pastoral areas of Tibet women bear their children outside the family as it was considered a bad deed. In backward agricultural areas child birth use to take place in the cowsheds or sheep pens. This system was somewhat similar to the system of child-birth in Garhwal region, which was pradiced long back.

But now more and more women move to clinics or maternity homes or are assisted by midwives at their home. The names chosen for the child are often derived from the vocabulary of Buddhism-Trashi meaning "Good luck" Tsetun "long life", Dikyi "happiness", Phuntso "satisfaction" and so on. Though some parents have their own ideas about names such as Gaukkajai "born to my need", Samde, "My dream come true," Bukbi "a son to come". Abscence of surnames and gender specific names indicate the absence of strict and clear-cut division on the basis of sex, caste and family identity.

Tibetans in exile have discarded gender-unequal practices of Polygomy and Polyandry and other archaic social formulations immediately upon leaving the country. Divorce as well as extra-marital relations are thoroughly discouraged but no taboos or censuring are imposed.

On asking the respondents whether they know someone who have extra-marital relations? Out of 200 respondetns only 49 respondents (24.5%) were those who have come across such cases, while the rest 151 respondents (75.5%) were totally ignorant about such relations.

When they were further asked whether such relations are tolerated in the society? Only 19% respondents say that society has nothing to do about it, it means that these respondents have no objections on extra-marital relations but the majority of respondents i.e. 81% discouraged and raise objections to such type of relations, as shown in Table No. 5.7.

Table 5.7. : Opinion of respondents about extra Marital relations in the society

Are such relations tolerated	No. of responses	% of responses
Yes	38	19
No	162	81
Total	**200**	**100**

Source : Field-work.

The divorced woman does not become the object of gossips and the childless woman is never looked down upon or deserted.

In ancient Tibet when a woman prostated herself before Buddha in worship the first word she might say something like "Pray Buddha, show mercy on me, let me give birth to a son", and if a woman gives birth to a son, there would be ceremonies to celebrate. The incarnation of a male would be held on the third day after the child's birth. But if a girl be born in the family, the ceremonies would be postponed to the fifth day because it was believed that a girl bare too much hard luck with her. Therefore, it would not be proper to hold the ceremonies too early.

There are still few families who feel necessary to have a son in the family. Though they are satisfied with the girl child also but son is preferred.

Despite of many constraints education has also helped in changing existing gender roles. Today Tibean women are more informed and educated. They increasingly realise their prospects and roles other than housewives.

On asking whether working women are more expressive to represent themselves than the non-working women, out of 75 working women respondents 70 women i.e. 93.33% feel that women who are working in some job or doing some pvt. business is more aware of the changing world. She better knows how to handle a problem or to react in particular situation. she is more confident and therefore more able to express her views than a housewife. But there are 5 respondents from the same working category i.e. 6.66% who think that it is not always the case as shown in Table No. 5.8.

Table 5.8. : Working Women Respondents on their opinion about the expressive nature of working and the non-working women

Opinion of the respondents	No. of responses	% of responses
Yes	70	93.33
No	5	6.66
Total	**75**	**100**

Source : Field-work.

Here, it is important to know that what the rest non-working women have to say about this opinion. Out of 15 non-working women respondents 10 respondents i.e. 66.66% agree that working women can express themselves more nicely as compared to those who are just housewives. The reason being the same as given by the working women. But on the contrary, 5 female respondents i.e. 33.34% do not agree with it as represented in Table No. 5.9.

Table 5.9. : Respondents who are not working on their opinion about the expressive naturc of working and the non-working females

Opinion of the respondents	No. of responses	% of responses
Yes	10	66.66
No	5	33.34
Total	**15**	**100**

Source : Field-work.

In the case of up-bringing of children when they were asked whether the child of a working women has some different personality development as compared to that child whose mother is simply a housewife. What do they think about it? The responses received are as follows : out of 90 female respondents, 30 women i.e. 33.33% are in favour of the role played by house-wife in matters of child-up-bringing. She remains in house and can look-after the activities of child very closely and every minute. The working women cannot afford time for the child and it can happen that the child feel himself neglected. She cannot become an effectionate mother and thus child can develop a habit to share things outside instead of telling her mother as shwon in Table No. 5.10.

Table 5.10. : Respondents who are not working on their opinion about the expressive nature of working and the non-working females

Opinion of the respondents	No. of responses	% of responses
favourourable	30	33.33
Unfavourable	44	48.44
Uncertain	16	17.77
Total	**90**	**100**

Source : Field-work.

But 48.44% female respondents i.e. 44 females are in favour of the view that mothers who are working women had better knowledge of the modern society, changing environment and educational pattern and thus can guide a child in a more proper way. The child of such women are able to adjust themselves with the changing environment easily. The rest of females i.e. 17.77% respondents feel that one cannot be very sure about the statement. Both the working and the non-working women teach their children good lessons and high morals. But the way to teach their children may be different in one or the other way.

Among the Tibetans, the participation rate of women in the public sphere is growing day by day. They are now participating in all the activities of the society.

Women in Tibet prior to 1949, never participated in political activities and played no official role. After the democratic set-up of the Tibetan government-in-exile women's participation in the political field is encouraged. It was in 1975, the seats for women were reserved in Tibetan parliament. This was mainly to give equal opportunity to women to compete with men.

In 1990, for the first time in Tibetan history, a Tibetan women was elected to the office of minister (in Tibetan Kalon). In the twelth ATPD, the minister for department of Health and Education were women and also in the thirteenth ATPD, women are given due representation. They are selected but it cannot be make-out from the list of names how many women are elected and what are their portfolios. The various official workers and secretaries appointed by the Tibetan government are women.

Role of Nuns

Talking of Tibetan women, the role of nuns cannot be ignored; as they have been neglected in most of the Tibetan studies. Though smaller in number than the monks, they play a significant role in Tibetan religious life.

In 1977, "Out of 5143 monks in exile, 392 are nuns out of which 191 are Nyingmapa"[5] . In 1993, there were total 402 nuns in India but today in the year 2000 there numbere has increased to 549.

Mostly nunneries are headed by a male lama though there were few exceptions[6] Dorje Phagmo is believed to be the be incarnation of Tara, the mother of all Buddhas.

"Nunnery is like a lotus flower resting calmly on the troubled water of worldly life, with its roots firmly enchored in the ground beneath the swamps of cycle existence, may it also be a source of strength and inspiration for many lay persons"[67] While studying the changes brought among Tibetan women society, it was found that the "migration" has proved advantageous for them than adversely affecting the migrants. The refugedom has given them whatever is necessary for their upliftment and progress. The society is unexpectedly devoid of any gender inequality.

According to the publication from UNHCR, titled "International migration policies and the status of female migrants", migrant women more than men are important agents of change.

It is found that there are two obstacles which block the progress of Tibetan women. The first is less education provided to them and second their orthodox and conservative nature.

Both these factors combindly make their talents and potentialities submissive.

References

1. Haralambos, M. - Sociology: Themes and Perpectives published by Neil O' Brien, Oxford University Press, N. Delhi 1980 (Pg 369).
2. Renija, Jugoslovenska -Tibet Pictorial book - by Belgrade. Shanghai people's Art. Publication House, Gallery Book, New York 10016 (1989).

3. Women and Society - Tibetan Bulletin. (Pg. 6) May - June 1994.
4 Bell, Charies - People of Tibet by Published by Book Faith, India - 1998 (Pg. 145).
5. Norbu, Dawa - Tibet - The Road Abead. Harper Collins Publishers, India 1977. (Pg 266)
6. Samdhing monastry head Lama was a woman. She was probably the only Female incarnate in the Tibetan religious heirarchy.
7. Bouquet, A.C. - Sacred Books of the World. Cassel, London, 1998.

6

Religion

Over thousand of years Tibet has developed a culture that is uniquely its own and rich in both variety and form. Any change brought in the religious framework of the Tibetans is of great sociological importance.

Religion is the most important aspect of the cultural system of a society. Religion is acquired by a man as a member of his society through socialization. The essential function of religion lies in the regulation, maintenance and transmission of sentiments on which the society depends. Emile Durkheim defines religion as "a system of belief and practices pertaining to the sacred".[1] Lobsung Lalungpa views religion specially Buddhism as "a belief in Psychological realignment with sets of principles and practices which leads to the realization of the ultimate truth".[2]

The present study deals with all the changes that have taken place in a Tibetan refugee community and this includes religious changes also, and this has been done by acquiring the in depth knowledge of the Tibetan religion "The Tibetan genesis framed and developed all the necessary political, legal, economic and social institutions which were sophisticated by her own religious tradition and are independent of others".[3] The earliest form cf worship in Tibet was known as Bōn. The Bōn religion was shaministic, include devil worship and was pure and simple[4]. Even today the pre-Buddhist customs and their symbolism have remained in Tibetan society.

Padmasambhava was a great tantric guru living in Udayana, in North-west India. He visited Tibet in 747 A.D. It was his association with King Deutsen that led to spread of Buddhism in Tibet.

Padmasambhava (The "Lotus born one") was a founder of Lamaism is usually called by the Tibetans as Guru Rim-Po-Che. After Padmasambhava several Buddhist scholars visited Tibet and thus right from the begining of script to the development of grammer Poetry, Drama, ethics and logic, astrology and medicine, Tibetans were constantly helped by the collective efforts of Indian Pundits and Tibetan translators.

The Tibetan Buddhism is a combination of two major Buddhist Systems Mahayana and Vajrayana.

Mahayana and Vajrayana

Mahayana evolved during the first century A.D. and depicts the theoritical aspects of Buddhism. Mahayanists have two choices - the Sutra, the exoteric course; and the other Sutra, the esoteric course both the courses are contained in the Tripitaka, which in Tibet, is classified into two collections, the words of Buddha (Kan Gyur) and the commentaries of others (Ten Gyur). Tibetans who follow the Mahayanism path follows the esoteric course rather than the exoteric course.

Vajrayana or Tantricism evolved in the second century A.D. depicts Buddhism as adopted by commoners in daily life.

After Buddhism was introduced the Lama dominated people became magic loving and Lamas controlled all the authorities of the state. "The Tibetans literally put down weapons at the lotus feet of the lamas and followed the white path of peace as pointed out by the Buddha".[5]

There are four main sects in Tibet[6]

1. Sa-Skya-Pa = named after a place, 1034A.D.
2. Bka-bag-yud-pa = Black Hat Sect, Hat Sect, 10/2 A.D.
3. Rnying-ma-pa = Red Hat sect, 810A.D.
4. Dge-lugs-pa = Yellow Hat Sect, 1357A.D.

There are certain facts which proves that in traditional Tibetan Society there were acute rivalries among the four sects. But in exile there is a landmark change among the relations of four sects and now all the four sects are heading towards ending sectarianism and promotes joint efforts towards maintaining ther religious structure. A number of monks belonging to Sakya, Kagyu, Nyingma and Gelug Sects have been resettled with their followers in various parts of India.

Four Sects:

(i) **Nyingma Sect :** It is the old school sect founded in 8th century by Saint Padmasambhava. They say that there are nine Paths to enlightment; the first three through Sutras and the last six by tantras[7]

Nyingma monks have freedom to marry and live in chapels. These monks are long haired and perform occult services. In Tibet the important monasteries of this sect were Mindroling and Dorjee Duak on the banks of Tsangpo[8] "Terma" are their main religious text. In India the supreme centre of this sect is in P.O. Chandragiri, Distt. Ganjam, Orrisa.

The teaching of this sect were compiled into 61 volumes. The Principal monastic institutions of the Nyingma tradition established in exile are in

Karnataka, Dehradun, Simla and Dharamsala. The Nyingma tradition is Headed by H.H. Penar Rimpoche.

They favour the deeper practices of yoga and believe that yoga and meditation lead to the Purity of man.

(ii) **Sakya Sect :** This school is named after the great Sakya monastery founded by Khan-Konchok Gyelpo (1034-1102). Its teachings were founded by Indian Tantric Birupa and Drokmi Lotsawa (a translatar at Hevojra tantra). Hevojra Tantra is the main text of Sakya. Gyelpa has built a monastery in the Tsang Province of central Tibet and named it Sakya or Grey Earth monastery. Their notable feature is that its abbotship (Sakya Trinzin) is hereditary passing from uncle to nephew rather a continous line of reincarnation. This sect also believes in power of Tantra and Sutra. The main centre in India is Sakya Centre, Rajpur Road, Dehra Dun.

(iii) **Kagyu Sect :** Kagyu means (orally transmitted Percepts) i.e. the teacher transfer its knowledge orally to his pupil. The lineage was started by the Indian master Naropa. In Tibet its main monasteries were Tsusphu, Driguntil, Tauklung and Ralung.

This school does not demand celibacy as essential. This sect was founded by MARPA in the middle of the 11th century. This tradition is also known as "Black Hat" and has remained strong and successful due to an unbroken time of Karmapas, reincarnation of the foundation. The present head of the karma kagyu tradition is H.H. XVIII Drodul Trinley Droje, duly recognised by the XIV Dalai Lama. In India the biggest Kagyu Centre is Rumtek monastery, Gangtok, Sikkim.

Kadam - Atisa founded this school and asked its students to follow four rules very strictly - celibacy, abstinence from intoxicants, prohibition of travel and money lending. The central practice was "Purification of mind". Its major centres were Retsing, Laugtsang and Sangphu. But the Gelupas absorbed the Kadampas in 15th century.

(iv) **Gelupa sect :** It is a reformed sect founded by Tsong Khapa (1337-1419) who after trying all other sects found Kadam better and continued its teachings Tsong Khapa stressed on strong and tough monastic life where monks were supposed to study and meditate. He also stressed the thorough learning of sutras before graduating to tantras.

An Examination system was also introduced at this time where the highest degree was Ghese. In 1409 Garden monastery was founded by him His chief disciples were Dalai Lama, Considered to be the reincarnation of Buddha. These are also known as "Yellow Hat" Sect. In India its main centre is Geluk centre, Garden Lachi, Mundgod, Karnataka.

Concerning the above four sects, scholars use to say, "The Nyingma has played the road for the Dharma teaching in Tibet. The Kadampas were the source of a hundred thousand upholdness of the teachings. The Sakyapas expanded the complete teachings of the Dharma. The Kagyupas offered a special path for the incomparable master meditators. To Tsong Khapa was the sum of the expandness of excellent docrtine (eleminating the darkness about the teachings of Buddhichilta, Sunyata and tantra[9]"

Despite many differences on the point of doctrine, all Tibetans follows the low of Buddha and describe themselves as Nangpa, those who are all with in the laws of Buddha. Tibetans have been able to retain their most traditional religion with its own traditional fundamental concepts, laws, beliefs and practices.

TIBETAN RELIGION

Tibetans in religion have remarkably maintained their religious and cultural identity through setting up their religions institutions in India. As the monastic establishment has been the most essential need of the religion various monasteries were established since they took asylum in the country.

Monasteries, Monks and Nuns

Today, the monasteries are made of concrete. The basic structure of walls sloping inwards have been retained in many buildings. Rectangular windows are edged to give a traditional feeting. One can see the decorated Pillars, walls and doors in all the monasteries. It is clear that the traditional Mandala Plan survived in the exile community also. In constructing the buildings local architects, buildings and masons are involved, as, participation of Tibetans in construction work has been ceased. The gilded roofs which covered the monasteries earlier has been replaced by the new concrete linter[10].

Tibet was dolted with some 3688 monestries before 1959 and some of the well-known monasteries of Tibet and the number of monks in each before 1959:

Monastery	No. of monks
Derge (Nyingma)	600
Sakya (Sakya)	500
Dagla (Kagyu)	100
Drepung (Geluk)	8300
Sera (Geluk)	6500
Gaden (Geluk)	4000
Lithang (Geluk)	7000
Tashi lunpo (Geluk)	4000
Amdo Tashi Kyel (Geluk)	4000
Amdo Kumbum (Geluk)	3000

Most monasteries were supported by the state in the form of land grant as well as essential items such as barley, cheese, butter, vegetables and tea, pilgrims also contributed towards a considerbale part of income of these monasteries.

EDUCATION SYSTEM IN MONASTERIES

"Tibetan monasteries represents one of human history's most ambitious and radical social and Psychological experiments precisely because they were attempting to achieve on a massive scale, the creation and perpetuation of a sub-culture which institutionalised the basic Buddhist Principles of non attachment, material lubrication, celibacy and transcendental wisdom".[11]

It was in 749 A.D. that first Tibetan monastery "Sanye" came into being with the joint efforts of King Trisong Detsun and Acharya Padmasambava. Acharya Santarakshita who was then the Principal of Nalanda University became its first abbot and then seven distinguished young Tibetans were trained there. First Tibetan abbot of this monastery was Walpal rang".[12]

In 1408 Tsang Khapa established Gaden monastery and his two. disciples founded Drepung and Sera monasteries. They had influence all over the Buddhist world. All the monk officials were selected in democratic way according to the person's knowledge.

In monasteries students does not have to pay any fee, nor the staff gets any salary. The only thing enjoyed by them were food and accomodation. Thus it was a great help for poor families who sent their children in monasteries as they had a chance to be properly fed and educated.

Though entering into a monastic life was a decision of a boy and his family but it is well-known that almost every family in Tibet had at least one son as monk. This tradition restricted the growth of population in Tibet.

The discipline in the monastery was not very strict and young monks were told not to accept whatever is written in the text without analysing that. Though spiritual knowledge was the ultimate goal of monastic life but beliefs are also not forced upon them. Initially the monks take the vows of getsul, the first state of monkhood and the later stage of fully oriented monk is called gelong.[13] The monastic universities had a intensive course of education. For twenty years students studied the following subjects.

1. Prajnaparamita - The Perfection of wisdom.
2. Madhyamika - The middle Path
3. Vinaya - The canon of monastic discipline
4. Abhidaeuna - Phenomenology
5. Metaphysics
6. Logic and dialectics.

To examine student, teachers take oral recitation test and group discussions are held. Higher exams were always in congregational debates. "The highest monastic degree are dge-bshes, Lharam, dge-bshes ling-se, dge-bshes Daram, dge-bshes Tsoram[14]. Dge-bshes (Geshe) is equivalent to doctrate degree of philosophy.

No paper degree was awarded in Tibet. One could be geshe only in Gaden, Drepeing and Sera monasteries.

In Tibet there were two tantric colleges also where acceptionally talented gelongs used to go to achieve the highest monastic degree of "Thripa" after getting which a person was elligible to become abbot of either of these three monasteries.

As far as education is concerned pupil learn U-Chen Script which is used for printing as well as U-med script which is ordinary written form. They consisted of loose leaves, held between two flat wooden pieces tied with yellow or red cloth.

At present, monasteries are a seen as a combination of monk, study, prayers and meditation. The government of India, has alloted some lands to the large monasteries to cultivate. Though monasteries are supported by state in the form of land grant and even funds are given to these monasteries from various parts of the world but still it is difficult for the Lamas to live dependent on the community, therefore they are adopting new occupation to earn thier livelihood. The monks are also sent out to perform prayers and rituals in the lay community, this also provides some income. Since it is difficult for the Tibetan population to catch to the demands of monks it proved as one of the reasons that today in exile it is not necessary for family to send a boy to monastery to become monk.

"It is very similar to the catholic monastic life of the west which is the largest monastic system of christianity[15]".

MONASTERIES IN DHARAMSALA

In 1960, when Dalai Lama shifted his headquarters to Dharamsala, Tibetan refugees since then visit the place as a Pilgrimage. It is transformed into a symbol of deep religious faith of the Tibetans. The town itself has come to be known as "Little Lhasa". The residence of Dalai Lama "Theckchen Cholina" is the Indian Potala which includes his personal residence, office and personal monastery.

In front of Dalai Lama's residence is a Buddhist temple Tsuglag khang (Central cathedral) constructed in 1969. It is one of the fine specimen of Tibetan architecture. The temple enshrines three images :

1. Guru Padmasambhava
2. Avlokiteshwara, and
3. Sakyani Buddha

Namgyal Monastery: The monastery is situated next to the central cathedral and the monastery has around 200 monks at present, of which the younger monks study the major texts of Buddhist Sutra and Tantra.

Namgyama Stupa: This Buddhist Stupa is located in the shop-lined centre of Mcleod Ganj surrounded by prayer wheels in the memorail of the Tibetans who lost their lives fighting for a free Tibet.

The statue of Sakyamuni Buddha enshrined in a small chamber. The Stupa is built in the tradition of the Indian Emperor Ashoka (3rd Century B.C.) and represents peace and progress.

Dip-tse Chokling Monastery: The idyllic, golden roofed dip-tse-Chokling monastery can be seen below Mcleod Ganj. It also has a small number of foreign Buddhist students apart from Tibetan monks.

Nechung Monastery: It is situated just below the Tibetan Library in Gangchen Kyishong. It is the seat of Nechung, the state oracle and Protector deity of Tibet. About 70 monks study here and carry on the secret and the sacred rituals.

Gadong Monastery: It is also located in Gangchen Kyishong and is the seat of Tibetan governments second oracle known as Gadong. Today it has 15 monks and supported by its restaurant and guest house.

MONASTERIES IN DEHRADUN

The biggest settlement in Doon valley Diekyling established in 1981 has two monasteries :

1. Lhoduak - Dhonney - ling containing five monks in all.
2. Thikchi monastery also known as Tse-Chu-Gompa.

There is also one public prayer hall with the capacity of 90 people where normally aged people do prayers four times in a month.

Then there is another settlement Dhondupling established in 1983 has three monasteries.

1. Nyingma Monastery with 350 monks.
2. Gelug monastery with 47 monks, and

3. Kagyu monastery with 55 monks.

They are given religious education and religious prayers are performed.

The third settlement Lingtsang in Manduwala also has three monasteries known as Ngou monastery with 355 monks. Then there is one meditation centre recently established in 1999 with a capacity of 50 monks and one Bon (Pre-Buddhist) Monastery.

At Rajpur, there is a sakya college where young monks are given higher religious education up to doctrate level. The capacity of the college is 200 students so far. Then there is a Sakya centre where young monks are given normal religious education and the present monk population is 220.

Nunneries at Dharamsala

1. Gaden choeting nunnery : established in 1973 initially had 12 nuns but the present strength of the nunnery is over 100.
2. Shugseb and daluma ling nunneries : are founded in the early 1990's to house and educate nuns escaping religious repression in Tibet. The total population of the nuns in both the nunneries is 142.

Nunneries at Dehra Dun

1. There is one nunnery at Dickyling settlement housing 120 nuns and is under the administration of Sakya Centre Rajpur.
2. There is one small nunnery at Dhondupling settlement housing 10-15 nuns.

In Tibet nuns were not permitted to join the great festival of moulam[16], and were ordered to sit behind the monks during great Prayers no matter how learned they were. But in exile far the first time in Dharamsala, H.H. Dalai Lama allow the nuns to join the moulam and take the confessions during the days of soljong. The first great Prayer in India was held at Bodha Gaya Bihar in 1961. The head of the monastery is known as Abbot and of nunneries are abbess.

At present there are 181 monasteries and 8 nunneries established in India, Nepal and Bhutan. The Chart below represents the total no. of monks and nuns in all the monasteries and nunneries and to which sect they belong[17].

Tradition	No. of monasteries and nunnries	No. of monks/ nuns
Nyingma	55	3962
Sakya	20	1135
Kagyu	36	2056
Gelup	65	9924
Bon	5	299
Nuns/nunnries	8	549

In this way Tibetans in exile are trying their level best to maintain thier religious and cultural heritage.

In 1959, two tantric colleges were established in Dalhousie (H.P.) and in 1961 home-cum-school was founded and was given the name of Mahayana monastic house. Temple at Happy valley, Mussoorie is one of the first Buddhist temple established by them in 1963. The very same year, the Tibetan council for cultural and religious affairs called the meeting headed by H.H. Dalai Lama with members including all the four sects and the purpose was to strength the religious unity and to lay emphasis on the role of the religious leaders in the political field too.

This council is in contact with all the Tibetan Buddhists residing in India as well as other countries.

Each Tibetan Buddhist sect has its own representatives in the Tibetan administration, in order to look after the neccessities properly in the exile conditions.

At present Mr. Tashi Wangal is the minister of department of religion and culture. The other deputies of the four different sects are -

Nyingma deputies	(a) Tsering Phunts or
	(b) Kalsang Tsewang gyari
Kagyu deputies	(a) Lodeo Tharchin
	(b) Sheuals Tauchin
Sakya deputies	(a) Pema Jungbey
	(b) Guru gyaltsen
Gelug deputies	(a) Youtsen phuntsok
	(b) Tashi gyaltsen
Bōn deputies	(a) Sonam Sangpo Jadur
	(b) Thokme Thuley Dorje

The establishement of Tibetan music, drama and dance society (Bho kie Dhoegar) in 1960, also contributed in keeping the traditional alive.

To preserve the religious and cultural heritage of Tibet, the Library of Tibet works and Archives (-LTWA) was established in 1971. It aims to preserve Tibetan books, rare manuscripts brought by the refugees from time to time from monasteries of Tibet. It also maintains Tibetan Buddhist Philosophy and their unique system of meditation.

Another achievement towards maintaining the cultural continuity is establishement of Buddhist School of Dialectics in 1973 at Dharamsala. In 1977, Central institute of higher studies at Sarnath, Varanasi was registered.

Recently in the year 2000 the Tibetan government has given the permission for the construction of library of Tibetan works in Dehra Dun.

The monastic establishment on the other hand had to struggle with the reality.

In the refugedom, they are not able to maintain large number of monks in the monasteries, so it is found necessary that the monks should get involved with some professional work to keep themselves economically self sufficient. It is also seen that there is a wild competition among the different sects to develop their monasteries for which they had to earn money through various mediums like leasing in of lands, giving loans on interest etc. "It was, also observed that the few monks have taken land on lease individually, from the local Indian farmers and have earned additional money. They also lend money to needy Tibetans and Indians, on interest which helped them to increase their capital[18]. Though there are various foreign donars who step forward to help monasteries but could not reach up to the needs of the monasteries. It is worth mentioning here that in Tibet, it was customary to send one son of the family, more often the younger one to join the monastic life, but this tradition has been largely effected in exile which results in weakening the strength of monastic order.

In India lamas are not given any special place to live which is aloof from rest of the colonies but they had to adjust themselves with in the community. Even the rules and code of conduct are not strictly followed.

Now one can see lamas playing cards and badminton with ordinary people and chatting in the streets. The student monks are drawn more towards the worldly matters and one can see them purchasing luxury items such as radios, gazetts, watches, bicycles, motorbikes etc. and they even go to cinemas for recreation. They have adopted new idas and customs and do not follow the rules of monasteries strictly. Even the attending lamas of the colleges do not have full knowledge of the religion and prayers. Today, Lamas are forced to dress like ordinary Tibetans except of the Tongas (robes) which specifies the sect to which they belong.

The loss of economic power by the religious institutions has nullified the option of joining the monastic order as a means of achieving upward social mobility. Before 1959, they monastic community constituted 20% of the total refugee population whereas in exile it is only 7.20%[19] when the respondents were asked to express their views on the diminishing influence of religion in all the spheras of social life, views of the respondents are shown in Table No. 6.1.

Out of 200 respondents, 101 respondents i.e. 50.5% agree that as compared to the past, nowadays religion has lost its value and the influence of religion is diminishing day by day. Though 99 respondents i.e. 49.5% disagree with the statement. Religion according to them is still playing a key importance in life of Tibetans Table No. 6.1.

Table 6.1. : Diminishing influence of religion now a days

Views about diminishing influence of religion	No. of respondents	% of responses
Yes	101	50.5
No	99	49.5
TOTAL	**200**	**100**

Source : Field-work.

When the respondents were asked to put forward the causes behind the diminishing influence of religion, following reasons came in the limelight.

(i) **Education :** One of the main reasons given by the respondents is modern[19] education. In Tibet education was totally under the control of monasteries and all Tibetans were not lucky enough to get education. But in exile they have come close to the outside world and felt the need for liberal and technical education for their betterment.

Education unhiddens many truths which were till now unknown to them. Therefore the first prefrence was given to education as the main factor of Change in the religious values and ideas.

(ii) **Lack of time and less money:** The second prefrence was given to less time and limited money they have in exile. According to the respondents, in Tibet, they had enough time and money to continue the celebrations of festivals for many days. In order to fulfill the basic needs of the family, they had to work hard, and their absence for a day or two would adversely effect their financial condition. They are also not in a position to spend much money, therefore few important festivals and occasion are celebrated and that too in a limit.

(iii) **Impact of Media:** The younger generation nowadays, is more oriented towards media. Their growing love for music and films had adversely effected their religious ideas and values. Instead of attending Pujas or Prayers they would like to watch movies and serials. In Dehra Dun one can see Lamas going to movie halls. Another factor according to Tibetans which is responsible in making religious beliefs less effective, is media.

(iv) **Science and Technology:** Science and technology is considered as one of the factors responsible for the diminishing influence of religion. Few Tibetans feel that science and religion are contrary to each other. Science and technology has made man more materialistic and man searches logical meanings behind every event. They don't trust religion blindly, as it was before exile. Tibetans have became "rationale" in their modes of ideas. They themselves agree that "Religion has kept them backward and they were unable to see beyond it". It is true that new inventions in science and technology is a big obstacle in the way of religious beliefs and ideas but it had also proved the beneficial aspects for Tibetans.

(v) **Western influence:** Another reasons which could be extracted from the opinions of Tibetans on the diminishing influence of religion is effect of western world. As it has been stated earlier also that "East is spiritual and West materialistic, thus people living in India are quite close to these western societies. Indians have adopted western culture to some extent and therefore, Tibetans too, cannot remain untouched. Tibetans have now become more individualistic and materialistic. In Dharamsala as well as in Dehra Dun one can easily come across Tibetans wearing western dresses, listening to western music etc.

The whole life style of the up-coming generation in Dehradun has undergone a dramatic change which differs to the life-style adopted by Tibetans in Dharamsala.

The Tibetans residing at Dehradun are enjoying practically the western style of life whereas, it is not possible for the residents of Dharamsala to enjoy the same life-style.

Though the Process of change is occurring in both the places but there is a difference between the speed of change between them. This is because firstly on account of rigrous discipline of the government in exile at Dharamsala and secondly because of the healthy strength of Lamas residing at Dharamsala than the ordinary lay Tibetans.

The reasons mentioned for the diminishing influence of relition in Tibetan community are justified. The Table No. 6.2. clearly explains the responses given to each cause mentioned. As Dharamsala is the temporary head quarter of H.H. The Dalai Lama many Tibetans from all over the world visit the place as the Piligrimage. It is thus of a interest to know about the comparative percentage of respondents of Dehra Dun and Dharamsala on the question of diminishing influence of religion.

Table 6.2. : Factors responsible for the diminishing influence of religion

Factors responsible	No. of respondents	% of responses
Education	178	89.1
lack of time and less money	138	69.3
Impact of Media	74	36.63
Role of Science and technology	55	27.72
Western influence	53	26.73

Source : Field-work.

Out of 100 respondents from Dharamsala 44% respondents feel that it is true that religions ideas and beliefs are nowadays vanishing from the society whereas, the majority of respondents i.e. 56%. feel that it is not true. People are still religious and cannot disregard its teachings and morals.

On the other hand the majority of Tibetans i.e. 57% from Dehra dun agree with the statement and only 43% disagree with it. Therefore, it is clear from Table No. 6.3. that people residing at Dharamsala are more religious in their act than Tibetans residing at Dehra Dun.

Table 6.3. : View of the respondents with regard to the place of their residence

Place of residence of the respondents Dharamsala	No. of respondents	% of responses
Dharansala	Yes - 44 No - 46	44 56
Total	100	100
Dehradun	Yes - 57	57
	No - 43	43
Total	100	100

Source : Field-work.

The differences can be due to the facts already mentioned and in addition to it one can see the mix community at Dehradun which is the adaptar of western life-style.

When the respondents were asked about the commercialization of religion, all Tibetans responded in negative. The lamas are not greedy and they never ask for money by themselves. When they are called on Particular occassions to perform ritual ceremonies, they do not demand for anything and neither the monasteries. Whatever Tibetans help them, they do it at their own wish, not by any compulsion on force. It has been already mentioned about the views of Tibetans on the diminishing influence of religion but one fact which cannot be ignored is that, they celebrate their festivals and occassions. The question which arises here is what is difference (if any) in celebration of religiois caremonies as they use to be performed in the past. On asking whether the religious caremonies have been simplified or not as compared to the past? The responses recieved as represented in (Table No. 6.4.) shows that majority of respondents i.e. 64.5% believe that in exile religious ceremonies have been simplified. They believe that the main reason behind the simplification of religious ceremonies is lack of time and limited economic resources. They even do not feel anything wrong in it. According to them more time and money should be spent on the development of their people in exile to improve their standard of living. There is no use to show off. Religion lies within their heart and simplification of ceremonies should not be mistaken.

The remaining 35.5% respondents disagree with the statement. According to them it is the prime purpose of Tibetans in exile to maintain their religion and culture because they had to transfer it to the next generation. Therefore, all ceremonies are celebrated with great enthusiam and nothing important is left to be done during those ceremonies.

In the new social environment and changing socio-economic conditions one of the major change that disturbs the community is the declining religious characteristics of the younger generation; which has turned towards "materialism" and "individualism".

Table 6.4. : Views of the respondents about simplification of the religious ceremonies

Religious caremonies have been simplified	No. of respondents	% of responses
Yes	129	64.5
No.	71	35.5
Total	**200**	**100**

Source : Field-work.

"As strategy of limited acculturation has developed over time to allow the Tibetans living outside their home-land to continue practicing their own cultural traditions, while stimultaneously adjusting to social life styles. Sociological study of Tibetans living abroad suggest that some refugees are having difficulties in negotiating their multiple identities and that pure Tibetan culture has sufferred as a result[21].

The religious head of the Tibetans is Dalai Lama. It is found that the Dalai Lamas are always a male personality since times inmemorial. When the question was raised in concerned to the male authority, nobody was able to tell why are Dalai lamas males only.

Though they worship Dalai Lama and considers "Him" as the reincarnation of Buddha but they have never thought of it. May be because Buddha was male therefore Buddha's reincarnation will also be a male personality not a female.

Further they were asked about the functions of their religious and temporal and political head.

According to the Tibetan refugees the main function of Dalai Lama is to provide moral support to refugees that one day they will definately return to free Tibet. He is also a political head of the Tibetan government-in-exile situated at Dharamsala. He also tries to take care of the benefits of the refugees all over the world which could help the Tibetan refugees to lead a better life in exile.

The devaluation of the Tibetan religious faith in the changed conditions has forced them to realise that Religion should not interfere in state matters and state should not interfere in religious freedom of the individuals.

This means that Tibetans are now able to evaluate incidents apart from religious angle and has become secularized. It can be said that Tibetan society is undergoing a process of "desacrilization".

Death Rituals

Tibetans believes in the theory of re-birth. It is believed those who die with desires will take a rebirth and his soul rotates through the cycle of birth and death the "Wheel of life".[22] Tibetans believe that human body is made up of four elements : fire, water, earth and wind and therefore they follow four means to dispose the body - cremation, floating in water, burial and expose to wind.

In Tibet there were 4 methods to dispose their dead:

Funeral Rites

(1) Celestial Burial is general funeral rites for common and lay people The body is wrapped in white cloth and kept in a corner of a room for atleast five days. In these five days monks and lamas are consulted as to when the soul is to be released from the body. The members friends and relatives offer a silk Khata to the desceased. They also bring barley beer, butter, incense sticks and money to give to the family members of the desceased as "Condolences". Fami'y members are not allowed to comb their hair, neither wash their faces or laugh not do they speak loudly till the dead body is in the house. Even the neighbours express their grief by avoiding laughing, singing or dancing around the house.

The monks consulting their sacred books chose a propitious day for the funeral. The ceremony starts before dawn. Then the body is stripped and climbs are bound and body is wrapped in a blanket (Phula) which the hair takes to the door of the house, where the undertaker of the celestial burial (Tam-den) is waiting to take the body away on his back. A corpse is then kept on the high rock near to this they lit a fire on which they sprinkle some tsampa. The smoke brings sacred vultures to the corpse. Now the undertakers cut the body into pieces. Bones are crushed, mixes them with tsampa and small balls are made out of its vultures are first fed by these balls made of bones and then the corpse pieces are offered to them. It is believed that no piece should be left as to set the soul free. After the ceremony is over these caretakers are served with barley beer and family produced food as a fee to their service.

2. Water Burial: Another method to dispose their dead is water burial. This method is often used for poor people, beggars, widows and widowers. It is quite simple than the celestial burial. Here the corpse wrapped in white cloth is taken to the river bank, and thrown in.

3. Burial in the ground: It is also one of the techniques to dispose their dead but this technique is used if the person is suffering from some disease like leprosy or small pox. This method is also applied to criminals where law deprived them the above type of burials.

Feeding of corpse to fishes has a religious significance. This deed is considered as gift to lord Buddha. Fishes were known as "Gods of the river" and eating them was against Buddhism.

4. Cremation : The method of cremation is used for the high lamas and highly placed persons. The body of the deceased is washed with salt water and left to dry. Then special and precious ointments and spices are applied on the body. After the body is burnt the remains of the body are stored in stupas or chortens. The stupas are plated with gold and silver in which ashes of Dalai Lama and Panchen Lama are preserved. In the halls of the monastries stupas of bronze, wooden and clay stupas are placed according to the status of the lamas.

This tradition is somewhat 2000 years old. It was started by King Drigum Tsenpo who adopted the method of burial in the tomb. When Buddhism was introduced in Tibet, other rites came into use, such as cremation of learned lamas to release their soul in accordance with the Buddhist scriptures.

After death various worships take place to relieve the soul from the worldly attachments.

After death the body is covered with sheet of white and Lama only can tell as from which part of the body the soul has released. The Lamas recite number of prayers and mantras for the full day and night till the corpse is carried for disposal. After consulting astrological book (Tsi-pi) by a Lama, it is clear as to how, where when and by whom the corpse should be disposed off. In Tibet it took three to four days to decide a particular day but today it is a matter of only one day. Now immediately after the death the body is loaded in a truck or bus and taken to Haridwar for cremation. There a bed of woods is made and body is placed over it. On the corpse, Khata (offered by friends and relatives of the deceived), some packets of Ghee, kerosene oil, etc. are sprinkled so that it can burn easily. After the body is burnt, the ashes are thrown in the holy river Ganga.

After coming in India Tibetans came across the problem in disposing their dead in the traditional way. Indians did not allow them to cut the corpse into pieces or just throw them away.

Now the Tibetans cremate their dead and this is the only way to dispose the dead body.

Even after disposal the food is offered to the dead, three times a day. This continues for forty nine days.

Going to Pilgrimage on holy places were most common among Tibetans. These are number of sacred places in Tibet but today Tibetans are unfortunate as they can not go to Tibet and visit their holy places. When they were asked, to which place or places they go for piligrimage. Tibetans say that they are lucky enough that they can go to Buddha Gaya for prayers.

Many Tibetans named Lumbini, Dharamsala, Sarnath and Nalanda as pilgrimige places. The dying faith in Tibetans religion in the purely different conditions may be considered from other angles also.

Tibetans are luck addicts and the concept of superstition has a strong belief among them when the respondents were asked about their belief in superstitions. Out of 200 respondents 43 respondents (21.5%) hold a strong belief in superstition 67 respondents i.e. (33.5%) show moderate remaining 90 respondents (45%) do not believe much in superstition.

Table 6.5. : Opinion of the respondents about superstition

Your belief in Superstition	No. of respondents	% of responses
Weak	90	45
Moderate	67	33.5
Strong	43	21.5
Total	**200**	**100**

Source : Field-work.

Further it is important to know which age-group is more consious towards superstitious beliefs. The relation between the two when studied shows that the Tibetans below the age group 20, 50% have a moderate outlook, 30% have a weak attitude and 20% strongly believe towards superstitions.

The next age group between 21-30 includes 103 respondents, out of which 56.31% respondents feel that superstitions are nothing.

According to them what they do in life good and bad is more important and the results of their work is their luck. Another 38.83% respondents of this age group show moderate feeling towards it. They feel that if a person succeeds in life, they consider it their effort and if a person fails to gain something the blaim goes to such superstitions. The rest 4.85% respondents, still consider superstitious saying in their deeds and actions. According to them superusitions are not new but age-old and there must be some logic behind it, which they don't know but, yet holds full faith in superstition.

In the next age-group of 31-40 there are 35 respondents and the respondents between the age-group of 41-50 are 31 as represented in Table No. 6.6. They all show mix attitude towards superstition. Those who believe strongly in superstition have the same reasons as others have that superstitions are age-old and they should believe in them otherwise some bad will happens to them.

But those respondents who have a weak attitude are more rational and practical towards every event of society. One of the respondents during the study put forward his own example which was very interesting:

> He said, "one day I had to leave the office early and after eating my breakfast I took out my motarcycle from the garage. I tried to start it but unable to start. At the same time my old mother

> around 70 years of age came out of the house and said some prayers which was like this "O" God please forgive him and help him to start his motorcycle". I asked what is going on in her mind she replied very simply, "Son! you forgot to light the butter lamp and it is not a good sign therefore, you have to face a problem". I called the mechanic to know what was wrong and he said that the wire has loosened, immediately he made some connections in the wire and the bike started at once. My mother also asked me to light "Butter lamp and she believed that doing so his motorbike will start. but without the right connections of wire no butter lamp could have started it".

Coming back to the explaination, the respondents between the age-group of 51-60 are 12, out of which 66.66% respondents hold a strong belief towards superstition and 33.33% respondents did not believe at all. This age group of respondents are generally those who were born and brought up in Tibet, though few in India also. These people do not want to escape from their old religious beliefs, what so ever they have heard about them.

The next age-group 61-70 comprising of 8 respondents and almsot all the respondents i.e. 87.5% hold a strong belief towards superstitions and the rest 12.5% show moderate attitude towards religions superstition. According to these strong beliefs that one should work according to omens which are both good and bad in nature.

The last age-group i.e. above 70 are staunch believers of superstition. The ladies are generally seen on roads having prayer wheels and rosaries in their hands. According to them everything in the world is made by God and the given certain indications to men to do their work in a particular time and in a particular way. These indications given by God are called superstitions.

Table 6.6. : Respondents views on of superstitions belief with relation to the age-group

Age group	Total no. of responds	Weak		Moderate		Sttong	
		No.	%	No.	%	No.	%
Below 20	10	3	30	5	50	2	20
21-30	103	58	56.31	40	38.83	5	4.85
31-40	35	14	40	10	28.5	11	31.4
41-50	31	11	35.48	11	35.48	9	29.03
51-60	12	4	33.33	—	—	8	66.66
61-70	8	—	—	1	12.5	7	87.5
Above 70	1	—	—	—	—	1	100
TOTAL	**200**	**90**		**67**		**43**	

Source : Field-work.

On the whole, those respondents who show moderate attitude towards superstition are among those people who sometimes for their profits believe in superstition and they also don't believe in superstition things if they are gaining something doing so.

As it has been stated earlier that today Tibetans are more oriented towards liberal education rather than traditional religious education, and this has made them more rational and logical.

It was important to know whether education in anyway has an effect on their superstition beliefs. Is there any relation between education and belief in superstition. The responses categorised are shown in (Table No. 6.7.). Those respondents who are illiterate and less educated have either moderate attitude or strong belief towards superstitution.

Respondents who are highly educated represents weak attitude towards superstitions.

Table 6.7. : Respondents showing the relation between education and belief in supersition

Education		Belief in superstition					
		No.	%	No.	%	No.	%
Nil	21	5	23.8	—	—	16	76.19
Primary	13	4	30.7	5	38.46	4	30.7
J.H.S.	16	6	37.5	2	12.5	8	50
H.S.	40	13	32.5	20	50	7	17.5
Intermediate	29	20	68.9	6	20.68	3	10.34
Graduation	58	27	46.55	29	50	2	3.44
P-G	14	8	57.14	5	35.71	1	7.14
Specialization	9	7	77.8	—	—	2	22.22
TOTAL	**200**	**90**		**67**		**43**	

Source : Field-work.

Table No. 6.7. shows that liberal and modern education has played a vital role in eliminating superstitious belief which were age old and has no scientific proof for their actions.There is a feeling somewhere hidden among many Tibetan refugees that the Tibetan religion needed "reforms" which are essential for the proper development of the community. Religion should not be considered as an obstacle for the progress of the Tibetan community.

Education will help the people to understand both the religion and practical realities of life.

Another very peculiar characteristic of the Tibetan religion is ther belief in astrology. Generally while fixing the marriages Tibetans consult horoscopes and other astrological predictions made by the lamas.

When the respondents were asked about their belief in astrology/numerology, 95.03% respondents say that they believe in astrology and especially for marriage fixations.

Even the science has given similar results as predicted by astrologists. Therefore, they had no objection on astrology or numerology. But on the other hand, 4.89% respondents say that when they got married they neither consulted horoscopes nor astrological beliefs because they believe that they loved each other and living in on another's company was more important and till today everything is going fine. So they don't believe in any astrological or numerological predictions. Even when the unmarried girls and boys were asked whether they will marry according to astrological belief and predictions made by lamas. The answer was a mix attitude but choice of mate comes first and not astrology. Therefore, the declining attitude of young generation towards astrology/numerology can be easily make-out.

In Tibetan religion it is said that there is life after death and by doing good deeds people will go to heaven and if bad deeds are done by a person, he/she will go to hell. Asking respondents, 88% Tibetans agree that there is life after death and whatever they have done good or evil they have to pay in the "next birth". They believe in theory of "Karma". But 10% Tibetans out of these 88% do not agree with the existence of hell and heaven. According to them nobody has seen what happens after death therefore they don't believe in hell or heaven.

On the contrary 12% Tibetans say that they don't believe in continuation of life after death and neither they believe hell or heaven as some place. They are of the same opinion that "nobody has seen what comes after death". All these respondents are between the age group of 18 to 30 and their education standard is from intermediate to Post-graduation out of which few are still studying.

It cannot be said that all the Tibetans who are young are not at all religious or they do not believe in "Karma" or "Dharma". Even the youngsters have religious faith. They are also strong believers of Buddhists teachings but their perspective is more different than those of the older-generation.

Infact Tibetans have suffered a lot in the past due to blind devotion towards religion and religious activities. Thus keeping themselves aloof from the rest of the world. Since ages now their close minds have open to more wider aspects of life. Their minds have open to "desacrilizaiton", "Secularization" and "democratization".

If it is possible to go back to free Tibet, it is a fact that they could not afford to leave the security of their country in the hands of "religion", "superstitions" and "miracles". It is also true that new scientific innovations, technologies and modern education has overtaken religious ideas and values. There will be a revolutionary change even in the monastic order which is prevailing in Tibet since centuries.

References

1. Durkheim, Emile - The elementary form of religious life (Pg. 62).
2. The Tibetan Journal Vol. I, No. : 3 and 4 By dobsong lalungpa - 1976. (pp. 9-16).
3. Tibetan Review Vol. VIII, March 1973.
4. Macdonald, David - Cultural Heritage of Tibet.
5. Norbu, Dawa - Red star over Tibet, Callins, St. James Place London, 1974
6. Arakheri, A.V. - Tibetans in India, The uprooted people and their cultural transplantation Reliance Publishing House, New Delhi 1998 (Pg. 252).
7. Ganjang Khantse Rimpoche - The Diversity and Unity of Four Sects. Tibetan Review 1976.
8. Chan, Victor - Tibet.
9. Tanyang Khautse Rimpoche - The Diversity and Unity of Four Sects - Tibetan Review. Sept. 1976.
10. Tibetan Review - Sept. 1976. (pg. 23).
11. Monastic education system of Tibet - By Pema Chhliyor - Tibetan Review. Dec. 1984
12. Silhau, Kunchock op. cit.

13. Chhlujar, Pema op. cit.
14. *Ibid.*
16. The paradox of Tibetan education in exile - By Christiane Labiesse. Tibetan Review. Aug. 1995.
16. Moulam - (Moulam chenmo) the great Prayer, the most significant of Tibetan religious festivals is held annually in the First Tibetan Month, a few days after the onset of the Tibetan new year. These days are dedicated to the peace ane prosperity of land and also commenorate the miracles performed by the Lord Buddha. The highlight of the great Prayer is the holding of the annual examination in geshe degree. (Doctrate degree in psycho-ethic philosophy)
17. Integrated development Plan-II. May 1994. (pg. 90).
18. Arakheri, A.V. - Op. cit. (pg. 255).
19. Saklani, Girja-The Uprooted Tibetans in India. Cosmo Publications, New Delhi 1984.
20. Modern education is used in the sense of liberal and secular education.
21. Tibetan Culture in the Diaspora - 7th international seminar
22. Arakheri, A.V. - Op. cit. (pg. 283).

7

Education

Child in the society after getting his primary socialization has to move from the particularistic standards and ascribed status of the family to the universalistic standards and achieved status of the adult society. Thus education prepares young people for this transmission.

Initiation and learning are declared as the second birth which is more important than the physical birth. Father and mother produces the body only, while the teacher causes the pupil to born a second time by imparting to him sacred learning, therefore this second birth is the best. It is real exempt from age and death.

From the functionalist perspective, the functions of education are :

(i) Transmission of societies norms and values.

(ii) To prepare young people for adult roles

(iii) The provision of knowledge, skills and training necessary for effective participation in the jobs for which they are best suited.

Education functions as a bridge between the family and the society, preparing the child for his future roles which he has to perform in a particular society.

The main purpose of the Tibetan educational system is to remove ignorance and generate wisdom and knowledge combined with compassion.

On coming to exile, one of the top priorities of H.H. The Dalai Lama was, education for hundreds of children. He believed that only a successful educational system would maintain Tibetan identity, culture and heritage. It will also enable the Tibetan children to adjust with new ideas and technology.

When Dalai Lama talked Mr. Nehru on the matter of education of Tibetan children, Mr. Nehru assured him that all the children will be provided good education in various public schools at the expense of Indian government. The ideas was not acceptable to Dalai Lama. He said, it is true, that public schools will provide the Tibetan Children modern and scientific education but these schools will not provide them the opportunity to learn and know their culture. This purpose could only be fulfilled by starting separate schools for Tibetan children.

At the request of Dalai Lama the government of India agreed to his proposal.

Tibetan Refugee Schools

At present there are eighty five Tibetan schools in India, Nepal and Bhutan with the total enrollement of 27,220 students.

Twenty three of the eighty five schools are residential and the remaining sixty two are day schools. In addition to it there are sixty two pre-primary school with 1997 children.

Total Tibetan Refugee Schools in India

The total number of Tibetan Refugee schools in India are sixty-seven with the total enrollement of 22,392 students as represented in Table No. 7.1.

Table 7.1. : Details on data of schools

Administration schools	Residential students	No. of school	Day student	No. of schools
CTSA, N Delhi	6	3814	22	5973
Sambhota TSA Dharamsala	4	869	11	1191
TCV Dharamsala	8	7286	10	1173
THF Mussoorie	2	1316	—	—
Other schools in [illegible]	1	432	3	338
Total	[illegible]	**13717**	**46**	**8675**

Source : Field-work.

Schools in Dehradun

The total number of Tibetan refugee schools in Dehradun are 5 viz : CST Herbetpur (538 students), Deikyling Day school (295 students), THF Rajpur (462 students), Tibetan Nehru Memorial Foundation, Clement Town (480 students) and Ling Tsang School (53 students).

Schools in Dharamsala

The total number of Tibetan refugee schools in Dharamsala are 4 viz : TCV, upper Dharamsala (2409 students), TCV lower Dharamsala (713 students) TCV, Mcleod Day school (175 students) and Gankyi Day school (78 students).

Teaching and Curriculum

The teaching and cirriculum in Tibetan schools is similar to that of Indian schools. The medium of instruction is English. One of the major difference between the Tibetan schools and Indian schools is that in Tibetan schools learning Tibetan language and culture is an integral part of the cirriculum.

Tibetan folk dance and music are taught in addition to other subjects. In 1973, proceedings of the second central conference of Tibetan Youth held in Delhi on Nov. 25, stressed on putting greater efforts in providing higher education to Tibetan Youth. It also laid stress on providing scholarships to poor and helpless children by means of an open competition for all classes. The aim is to make the Tibetan society literate so that they could cope with the modern world.

The educational goals of Tibetan schools are:

(i) To get modern, scientific education,

(ii) To preserve their culture and religion, and

(iii) Fostering a streng sense of nationalism.

The Tibetan schools are the mixture of tradition and modernity. They not only give modern, education but also impart the knowledge of Tibetan culture. Here the responsibility of the teachers is more than those of the officers in the administration. If the settlement officers or administrators make some mistake it might entail some financial loss wich can be recovered; However, if teachers fail to impart proper education to the Tibetan children the damage can not be remedied.

Dalai lama in his speeches repeatedly said that they have the opportunity to receive education and if they forgo this opportunity voluntarily, it will really be very sad.

Today, education has been widely accepted by all. Almost every Tibetan child is getting education in exile. It is found that the respondents of the younger generation are more educated as compared to respondents of older generation which is evident from Table No. 7.2.

Table 7.2. : Representing relation between age group and education: Education Age-group

		Below 20	21-30	31-40	41-50	51-60	61-70	Above 70
Nill	21	—	3	7	1	3	6	1
Primary	13	—	3	1	7	2	—	—
J.H.S.	16	1	8	3	4	—	—	—
H.S.	40	3	17	7	9	3	1	—
XII	29	3	18	5	1	1	1	—
Gra.	58	3	42	6	5	2	—	—
P. Gra.	14	—	11	2	1	—	—	—
Spec.	9	—	—	—	—	—	—	—
		—	1	4	3	1	—	—
Total	**200**	**10**	**103**	**35**	**31**	**12**	**8**	**1**

Source : Field-work.

In this way education has been permanently elevating the humble born to the upper ranks or barring down those born in the highest strata.

Educationists has increasingly come to realise the vital role played by the parents in the complex process of education. They can guide, encourage and motivate their children to learn more and more. But it is unfortunate on the part of Tibetans that most of them do not have educated parents who could give them proper guidance.

When the respondents were asked about their parents education, out of 200 respondents the majority of 159 respondents (79.5%) say that their parents were not educated. As their parents were born and brought up in Tibet where there was no formal education. Earlier education has been forbidden to the poor and lower classes and controlled by the monasteries. Only 31 respondents (15.5%) say that their parents are/were educated because when they came to India they got the opportunity to get proper education. 8 respondents (4%) say that only their father's are/were educated and mother's illeterate, suprisingly only 2 respondents (1%) as shown in Table No. 7.3. say that only their mothers' are/were educated and that too after coming to India but fathers' were/are illiterate.

Table 7.3. : Represents the educational status of the respondent's parents

Educational status of parents	No. of respondents	% of responses
1. Both parents educated	31	15.5
2. Both parents uneducated	159	79.5
3. Only father educated	8	4
4. Only mother educated	2	1
Total	**200**	**100**

It is evident that in the present Tibetan society education represents one of the most important channels of social vertical circulation.

Further respondents were asked on the problems and difficulties faced by then because of their parents being uneducated, out of 169, 85.21% respondents agree that they came across number of difficulties because of the uneducated parents. Though 14.79% respondents say that they were always encouraged by their parents. Their parents imparted them spiritual teachings of Buddha which enlighten their path.

It is found correct that children whose parents are uneducated face few difficulties in their study. They are not able to solve the problems related to the subject and child has to move from one place to another to solve the problem and sometimes children ditch their parents.

This can be one of the reasons why good schools interview both the students and the parents, and this can be a reason why the children of educated parents tend to be high achievers.

There are some Tibetan who drop out without completing their education even when they have reached a certain level of education in the schools. This is something very unfortunate.

There are four categories of respondents in the educational level :

(i) In the less ecucated category are those respondents who have studied only till Junior High School.

(ii) In the educated category are those respondents who have completed their intermediate level.

(iii) In the highly educated category are those respondents who continued their study to the level of graduation, post graduation or specialization.

(iv) Those who have not studied even primary are under the category of illiterate respondents.

In the age-group of below 20 there are 10 respondents and nobody is illiterate whereas there is 1 respondent in the age-group of above 70 and is uneducated in the age-group of 21-30, the total number of respondents are 103 out of which only 3 respondents i.e. (2.91%) are uneducated as represented in Table No. 7.4.

In the next category of 31-40, there are 35 respondents out of which 7 respondents i.e. (20%) are illiterate.

In the age-group between 41-50 there are 31 respondents out of which only (3.22%) are uneducated.

In the age-group between 51-60, there are 12 respondents and out of which 3 respondents i.e. (25%) are illiterate.

In the second last category of age-group which is between 61-70 there are 8 respondents, out of whcih 6 respondents i.e. (75%) are illiterate.

Table 7.4. : Representing the uneducated respondents with relation to age-group

Age group	Total no. of respondents	No. of illiterate respondents	% of responses
Below 20	10	—	—
21-30	103	3	2.91
31-40	35	7	20
41-50	31	1	3.22
51-60	12	3	25
61-70	8	6	75
Above 70	1	1	100
Total	**200**	**21**	

Source : Field-work.

It shows that illiteracy declines as we move towards younger generation.

Less educated respondents in relation with age-group

Those respondents who are less-educated i.e. those who studied till primary and junior high school are 29 in number. Out of these 29 respondents only 1 respondent i.e. (10%) is under the age-group of below 20. 11 respondents i.e. (10.67%) are under the category of the age group varying between 21-30 comprising of 103 respondents. In the next category of age-group 31-40 there are 35 respondents out of which 4 respondents i.e. (11.42%) are less-educated under the age-group of 41-50, there are 31 respondents out of which 11 respondents i.e. (35.48%) are less educated under the next category 51-60 age-group there are 12 respondents out of which 2 respondents i.e.

(16.66%) are less educated there is no respondent in less educated category in the age-group of above 70, as shown in Table No. 7.5.

Table 7.5. : Representing the lesseducated respondents with relation to their age-group

Age group	Total no of respondents	Education Nil	Primary	J.H.S.	No. of respondents	% of responses
Below 20	10	—	—	1	1	10
21-30	103	3	3	8	14	13.59
31-40	35	7	1	3	11	31.42
41-50	31	1	7	4	12	38.70
51-60	12	3	2	—	5	41.66
61-70	8	6	—	—	6	75
Above 70	1	1	—	—	1	100
	Total	**200**	**21**	**13**	**16**	**50**

Source : Field-work.

It is evident from the Table No. 7.5. that even in the category of younger generation one can see less-education. All the 50 respondents gave one or the other reason for their less-educational status as shown in Table 7.6.

(1) 10 respondents i.e. (20%) say that they were not interested at all in the studies.

(2) 6 respondents i.e. (12%) say that nobody studied in their family at that time because they did not belong to aristocratic families.

(3) Another 22 respondents i.e. (44%) say that their financial conditions were not good. They had to work in the fields or roads. They had never thought to continue the studies.

(4) 10 respondents i.e. (20%) say that they had problems in the family which were personal and therefore could not study.

(5) The most different reasons was given by 2 respondents i.e. (4%) they say that they had fallen in love with the opposite sex. They were unable to concentrate on studies and therefore had to drop their studies in the middle.

Table 7.6. : Representing the reasons given by the male and female respondents seperately on their having less or no education

Reasons for less or no education		No. of respondents Male	Female	No. of respon-dents	% of respon-ses
1.	Not interested	6	4	10	20
2.	Nobody studied in the family	1	5	6	12
3.	Financial crises	12	10	22	44
4.	Family problem	3	7	10	20
5.	Love-affair	1	1	12	4
	Total	**23**	**27**	**50**	**100**

Source : Field-work.

On asking the respondents if they feel bad about not studying or droping their education in the middle. 34 respondents (68%) replied positively. The rest 16 respondents i.e. (32%) replied negatively. They do not have, any regrets about it. They feel that whatever happened was due to circumstances. Family needed them more so it was their priority to help their family.

The respondents were further asked if they had completed their studies they could have led a better life. Out of 50 respondents 33 respondents i.e. (66%) say that it is true. They could have led a better life if they were educated as it effected their economic status as well as social status.

The rest 17 respondents i.e. (34%) responded in uncertainity as represented in Table 7.6. according to them they might or might not have led a better life.

Table 7.6. : representing the opinion of the respondents who could have led a better life if educated

Opinion of the respondents	No. of respondents	% of responses
Yes they could have led a better life	33	66
No it is not so	—	—
Uncertain about it	17	34
Total	**50**	**100**

Source : Field-work.

All the 17 respondents i.e. (34%) who were uncertain as shown in Table No. 7.6. were luck, addicts. According to them whatever they earn and how they spend their life would depend on fate. Education has nothing to do with it. The uneducated person can lead a happy and satisfied life than the one who is educated.

The respondents were then asked, if opportunity is provided to them, would they like to study? out of 50 respondents 82% respondents rejected the idea of studying while the rest 18% feel that they will be fortunate to continue their studies.

All the 50 respondents want their children to get good and higher education.

Tibet was one of the countries that has strongly ignored the importance of education during its hey day. But they woke up after being forced to seek asylum.

Now education has been given top priority in the Tibetan national agenda. The government-in-exile is responsible to provide better facilities for all Tibetan students taking keen interest in education.

Today, the main purpose of the modern education seems to help in growth of the economic prosperity. It seems that Tibetans have lost their original aims of education.

Anyone can see the drastic changes coming in the Tibetan youth which show a very pronounced, western influence. These changes are all due to modern education they are getting in exile. It was thus important to find out the places from where maximum Tibetan children got education :

Primary Education

Out of 200 respondents 179 respondents have completed their primary education. 63 respondents studied from Dehradun, 43 respondents from Mussoorie, 19 and 16 respondents from Dharamsala and Simla respectively. The rest 38 respondents studied from other places like Darjeeling, Mysore, Tibet, Mundgod, Orissa, Patna etc.

Junior High School

Out of 166 respondents 49 students studied from Dehradun, 30 from Mussoorie, 17 from Simla and 16 from Dharamsala. The rest 54 studied from other parts of the country.

High School

Out of 150 respondents, 38 respondents sutdied their high school from Dehradun, 31 from Mussoorie, 21 and 20 from Simla and Dharamsala respectively and the rest 40 studied from other places like Mundgod, Bylakuppe, Mysore, Pondichery, Dalhousie, Darjeeling etc.

Intermediate

Out of 110 respondents, 34 respondents studied from Dehradun, 32 from Dharamsala and Mussoorie collectively, 20 from Simla and the rest 24 from other parts like Bylakuppe, Dalhousie, Darjeeling etc.

Graduation

Out of 81 graduates 23 respondents studied from Dehradun, 16 from Chandigarh, 11 from Delhi and 11 from Bangalore. The rest 20 studied from other universities like Andhra Pradesh, Mundgod, Rajasthan etc.

Post Graduation

Out of 23 post graduate respondents, 7 studied from Dehradun, 4 from Chandigarh, 2 from Delhi and 3 from Banglore. The other 5 studied from universities of Kurukshetra, Dharamsala, Mysore, Simla and one from USA and 1 from Bosten.

Specialization

Out of 9 respondents 5 respondents specialized in various subjects from the university of Delhi, 3 from Dehradun and from Assam.

From the findings it is clear that some places like Dehradun, Mussoorie, Dharamsala, Simla, Delhi, Mundgod, Bylakuppe played an important role in the education of Tibetans.

These educational institutions, are located in good places of India. People in these places cannot ignore western life-style, therefore Tibetans too cannot remain uneffected; one can observe their inherent liking for western music, language and life-style. Tibetan youth can rarely be seen wearing "Chuba". Even their love for English language is more than their own language.

During interviews it is found that Tibetan males and females feel proud speaking English. Though they knew Hindi but pretend to be uneasy in speaking Hindi.

It is not only restricted to Tibetan youth, even the Tibetan children prefer to read and write in english. Tibetan school children read Enid Blyton, Nancy Drew, Biggles etc, and refuse to read Tibetan literature because it bores them to tears.

The absence of any Tibetan college is also the reason for the marked change in the attitude and ideologies of the new generation. After finishing the school, Tibetan children are forced to join the Indian colleges or other training institutes. Here the child spends next 3 to 4 years of his age when he is most vulnerable and his attitudes begins to take a definite shape.

Many of the Tibetan youth are not in a position to draft letter in Tibetan. This being very unfortunate. The objective to preserve Tibetan culture and tradition comes to an abrupt end after child finishes his high school. Therefore it is most important to set up Tibetan college or university.

Even the Tibetan leaders are very much concerned about this problem. The changing attitude of Tibetan youth has raised the question whether Tibetan youth will be able to preserve their religious entities and culture?

The Dalai Lama has also pointed out that enriching of Tibetan language is very important, using Tibetan language in daily conversation is not enough because when it comes to an important matter, they are compelled to use other languages.

It is then a matter of great shame. Therefore, the vernacularisation programme is an extreamely commendable thing. Whatever subjects are taught in the schools, they should be taught in the Tibetan language.

In order to deal with the problem of using Tibetan language TCV has set up an educational and development research centre in 1995. It is responsible to bring out books to facilitate teaching Tibetans in their own language. Tibetan schools in India are now using the same books and produce good results.

There are also some Tibetan institutions like the Astro-Medical Institute, the Institute of Performing Arts, the Norbulingka Institute and the Central Institute for Higher Tibetan Studies; which help to promote the cultural heritage of Tibet. Another thing which is observed is that social aspect for learning is now being fast replaced by the power of money.

Modern education has dragged the youth into the world where wealth and fame counts more than religious and spiritual devotion. Gone are the days when the youngesters would consider it his "duty" and "honour" to work, for his community regardless of salary and perks.

The respondents were asked if they feel education is a medium of earning good money, out of 200 respondents 110 respondents (55%) were in favour of the statement. According to them if they are highly educated they get good jobs and good jobs pay handsome amount, 76 respondents (38%) disagree with the statement. According to them it is not always necessary that if the person is highly educated he will earn more.

The remaining 14 respondents (7%) were uncertain, as shown in Table No. 7.8.

Table 7.8. : representing the opinion of the respondents on education as a medium of earning

Opinion of the respondents	No. of respondents	% of responses
Yes	110	55
No	76	38
Uncertain	14	7
Total	**200**	**100**

Source : Field-work.

From the Table No. 7.8. it is clear that still majority of Tibetans consider education as a means to earn good amount of money. It shows that education not only provides the link, between individual and society or functions in the transmission of norms and values of the society, it also teaches the individual specific skills necessary for his future occupation.

When the respondents were asked about what they think about the importance of education in the society :

(a) Very important (b) less important or (c) not important at all. The responses given are followed by

Table No. 7.9. Out of 200 respondents, 188 respondents (94%) say that education is very important. Another 12 respondents (6%) say that education is less important. The only important thing is that individual should be able to read and write. One should be technically perfect in some or the other field inspite of getting higher education.

Table 7.9. : Represents the opinion of respondents on importance of education

To what extent education is important	No. of respondents	% of responses
Very much important	188	94
Less important	12	6
Not at all important	—	—
Total	**200**	**100**

Source : Field-work.

It is clear from the Table No. 7.9. that Tibetans consider education very important to lead a better life. None of the respondent is against the importance of education.

Those responents who are educated when they were asked whether they are respected in the society? All the 179 respondents replied positively. According to them if they were not educated their life-style and status would be different from the present.

It is true that education of a person changes his/her status in the society. When the respondents were asked what sort of changes can be observed in their life-style if they were not educated.

Out of the four options as shown in Table No. 7.10. provided to them. 70.27% respondents gave their first preference to the third option which states that they would have done some different job 68.46% responses were given to the fourth option which states that they would have felt bad.

The next prefrence was given to the second option. 48.64% respondents states that they would have different friends and companions. The last preference was given to the first option 23.42% say that their status would be lower in society than it is at present.

Table 7.10. : Showing the prefrence of options given by the respondents

Type of change	% of responses
Status would be low	23.42
Different companions	48.64
Different job	70.27
Felt bad	68.46

Source : Field-work.

It seems that whatever position they are holding in society is because of the education. In a Tibetan society educational opportunities are open for all. The scholarships are also given to brilliant students regardless of their status in society. Sponsors from various countries like USA, Canada, Switzerland, France, Australia etc. have taken responsibility of the orphans. Tibetan refugee considers education as the only means to create equal and just society.

Attitude Towards Women's Education

It is true that men and women work in large numbers in the Tibetan society. But women tend to be less successful. Their number decreaes with every step upward in any profession. It is generally due to marital reasons that women drop their studies. The society's expectation that women have a primary obligation towards thier husbands and children rather than towards their own education and career.

Table No. 7.11. illustrates the educational level of women as compared to men in a Tibetan society. Those who are totally illiterate are 21, out of which 52.38% are males and 47.61% are females. Those who have completed their primary education are 13, out of these 30.76% are males and 69.23% are females.

Respondents who have studied J.H.S. and High School collectively are 56. Out of which 50% are males and 50% females.

It is clear from Table No. 7.11. that percentage of men at the level of intermediate, graduation, post graduation and specialization is 55.17%, 63.79%, 57.14 and 66.37% respectively. It is far more than that of women which is 44.82%, 36.20%, 42.85% and 33.33% at the level of Intermediate, graduation, post-graduation and specialization respectively.

Table 7.11.: Educational levels of males and females

Education	totoal No. of respondents	% of male responses	% of female responses
Illiterate	21	52.38	47.61
Primary	13	30.76	69.23
J.H.S.	16	50	50
H.S.	40	50	50
XII	29	55.17	44.82
Graduation	58	63.79	36.20
Post graduation	14	57.14	42.85
Specialization	9	66.37	33.33
Total	**200**		

Source : Field-work.

One can conclude from the data that at lower levels of education the women's attainment is greater than men's. At the higher levels it is found, women tend to drop out.

To know what people in Tibetan society, feel about the importance of education for women, respondents were asked to express their views.

Out of 200 respondents 119 respondents i.e. 59.5% agree that education is the best means for the progress and upliftment of women's status in the society. The reasons given for the importance of education for women are as follows:

(a) Men generally go out to earn the money and women stay at home and look after the family. If she is educated she will be able to guide her children for the future and manage the house properly.

(b) Secondly, people think that if the women are educated they can earn their livelihood they are not on the mercy of other people, they are always confident to face any circumstances in life.

On the other hand 40.5% Tibetans think that education for boys is more important than girls. The reasons for their negative perspective towards women's education were as follows :

(a) According to them, girls generally get married and look after their children and family. It is the duty of male members to earn money, to buy bread and butter for his family. If he is not educated he will be unable to run his family.

(b) These people are also not against the education of women. They think only those women should go for higher education who are interested in doing jobs of higher levels. Women after completing graduation or post-graduation just stay at home. This is really foolish according to them.

The Tibetan society believes that men are dominant by nature. Women are emotional rather than rational and calculative, they are passive rather than active and they are submissive rather than dominant.

EDUCATION AND MARRIAGE

Whenever the matter of marriage comes the boys want their wife to be educated, similarly the girls want their husbands to be highly educated than themselves. During the study it was asked from married respondents about the education of their spouses, whether husbands are more educated than their wives or wives are more educated than their husbands.

The total number of married female respondents is 51 out of 111, and total number of married male respondents is 60 out of 111.

In case of females

As shown in Table No. 7.12. out of 51 married female respondents, 19 respondents i.e. 37.25% say that their husbands are equally educated, 23.52% females say that their husband are less educated, 5.89% say that their husband are very less-educated, 11.77% respondents say that their husband are more educated and 9.80% females have highly educated husband as comparision to their education whereas there are 11.77% females who say that their husbands are illiterate.

Table 7.12. : Representing the education of husband in comparision to their wife

Educational level of husband	No. of female respondents	% of responses
More educated	6	11.77
Highly educated	5	9.80
Less educated	12	23.52
Very less educated	3	5.89
Equally educated	19	37.25
Illiterate	6	11.77
Total	**51**	**100**

Source : Field-work.

In case of males

Similarly when married male respondents were asked about the educational level of their wives, maximum respondents i.e. 41.66% say that their wives are equally educated. As represented in Table No. 7.13. The total 21.67% respondents say their wives are less educated but not very less educated in comparison 16.67% say that thier wives are illiterate only 15% respondents say that their wives are more educated whereas only 5% say that they are less educated and wives are highly educated.

Table 7.13. : Representing the educational level of wife as compared to husband

Educational level of wife	No. of male respondents	% of responses
More educated	9	15
Highly educated	3	5
Less educated	13	21.67
Very less educated	—	—
Equally educated	25	41.66
Illiterate	10	16.67
Total	**60**	**100**

Source : Field-work.

From the findings it can be said that the spouses are generally equally educated. It does not matter much even if the partners is less-educated or more educated, girls and boys are not worried even if their partners are illiterate.

Views on Indian Citizenship

It is true that policy of domicile does not allow Tibetan students higher educational opportunities in various professional colleges of India.

The educational standards in Tibetan schools are largely deteorating, lack of motivation towards study is the reason for this deteroration. The lack of motivation is because there is nothing for youth to look forward after schooling.

In such circumstances they feel nothing incorrect in getting Indian citizenship for the sake of their future. When the respondents during informal talks were asked whether they will accept Indian citizenship? All of them replied in negative. Getting citizenship of any other country means to loose their identity. India is a country where people of different sects and religion practice their own religious faiths and are also citizens of India eg: Muslims, Christians and Sikhs have different culture not identical to each other and are still citizens of one nation. Though I have comes across few Tibetan people (who were not my respondents) who are citizens of various countries like USA, Canada, Switzerland, Nepal and India. Yet, they practice their own religion and traditions. They live with their families own the community and are even fighting unitedly for independence of Tibet.

Problem of Unemployment

Though the Tibetan administration is giving best placement to their qualified and educated youth but it cannot be said for how long this process of absorption will continue. There are large numbers of students getting higher education in India and abroad. In future it will not be possible to absorb all of them. Time is not far when the Tibetan community will come across the problem of unemployment. Today the problem is under control, to avoid the problem in future, the demand for voccational and job oriented education has increased, findings also demonstrate that the schools lack adequate voccational education. The rapid expansion of the tertiory sector has provided on increasing demand for clerical, technical, professional and mangerial skills.

For Tibetan youngsters the CTA, must adopt the policy of "let go" and allow the Tibetans to seek employment outside the Tibetan community.

The students are more interested in voccational trainings and technical fields. They are not interested in getting higher education and degrees. Even the parents are keen to point out the stupidity of preserving studies too far.

8

Economy

The economy, is above all, a social institution. How a society produces and distributes goods and services, and the nature of goods and services so produced, helps to determine many of its important features.

Long back in 1956 Harrer Heinrich in his book "Seven years in Tibet" has written, despite the fact that the land is poor and unproductive, there was enough food for all and even though life on the high plateau is hard and austere, there is serenity and contentment, pervading the life of the individual and the community.

This may be because the population of Tibet was thin and stable therefore there was always excess land in proportion with the population and generally what was grown was kept stored for the bad weather.

In 1959, when Tibetans flew from Tibet, they could not bring anything with them except for those few people who were able to carry some goods during their flight.

It was the main priority for the Indian government at that time to rehabilitate them and set them to work to earn their livelihood. These refugees were initially sent to work in the road construction on the border are as of the Himalayas, but it took less time for them to get settled properly with the Indian community and raise their employments in various fields and maintain their standard of living.There is no doubt they have got various type of donations and relief aids from India as well as from other international organizations. It can be seen that now the average Tibetan had much better standard of living than the average Indian.

On getting an opportunity to visit their houses it was found that the houses contained full of modern commodities like Television set, cooler, refrigerator, washing machine, eatables of good quality and many other such things. Very few Tibetans say 2% to 3% were such who could not purchase the items mentioned. In the markets even one can observe them buying those things which an average Indian could not purchase.

When they were asked about their economic status in their native society, the responses received were classified into the category of -rich, very rich, middle class, poor, as also shown in Table No. 8.1. out of the total respondents, 36.5% belonged to the poor families in Tibet, while 30% were from rich families, 21% belonged to very rich families in Tibet, though 12.5% belonged to the middle classes.

Table 8.1. : Tibetans refugees in according to self-rating economic class Structure prior to migration

Category of respondents	No. of respondents	% of responses
Rich	60	30
Very rich	42	21
Middle class	25	12.5
Poor	73	36.5
Total	**200**	**100**

Source : Field-work.

It is also important to know that in the present economic conditions to what extent their economic status has changed either improved or declined.

In aggregate out of 200 respondents majority of 100 respondents i.e. (50%) say that their economic status has not improved at all. Another 52 respondents i.e. (26%) say that it has not very much improved, 37 respondents i.e. (18.5%) say that there is much improvement in their economic status and only 11 respondents i.e. (5.5%) say that their economic Status has not much improved.

Table 8.2. : Respondents views regarding improved economic status

Category of eco. Status in past	Total No.of respo-ndents	Present eco. status							
		Not Much	%	Very Much	%	Much	%	Not at all all	%
Very rich	42	3	7.14	—	—	1	2.38	38	90.47
Rich	60	8	13.33	—	—	2	3.33	50	83.33
Middle class	25	—	—	12	48	10	40	3	12.00
Poor	73	—	—	40	54.8	24	32.88	9	12.32
Total	**200**	**11**		**52**		**37**		**100**	

Source : Field-work.

Table No. 8.3. represents that out of 42 respondents who belonged to very rich families in Tibet 90.47% respondents feel that their present economic status has declined as compared to the past. 7.14% feel that their economic status has not declined at all and 2.38%, agree that their economic status has not much declined as compared to the past.

In the next category of respondents who belonged to rich families in Tibet are 60, out of these 83.33% respondents feel that there is a big decline in the economic status whereas 16.66% feel that there is not much decline in their economic status.

Another 25 respondents belonging to the middle class families have different opinions. 88% of such respondents observe no decline in their economic status, and on the contrary 48% feel their economic status has improved very much. 40% say that they have found very little improvement in their economic status and 12% respondents feel that their economic status has not improved at all.

The last category of respondents belonging to the poor families in Tibet are 73, out of which 87.67% respondents feel that at present they have observed no decline in the economic status but they found that their economic status in exile has improved only 12.32%respondents under this category say that their economic status has not improved at all and observes more decline in their living standard.

Table 8.3. : Respondents on the basis of their changed eco. status (declined)

Category of eco. Status in past	Total No.of respo-ndents	Decline in present economic status							
		Not Much	%	Very Much	%	Much	%	Not at all all	%
Very rich	42	1	2.38	38	90.47	—	—	3	7.14
Rich	60	10	16.66	50	83.33	—	—	—	—
Middle class	25	3	—	—	—	—	—	22	88
Poor	73	—	—	6	8.21	3	4.10	64	87.67
Total	**200**	**14**		**94**		**3**		**89**	

Source : Field-work.

While interviewing the respondents it was found that Tibetans who belonged to the aristocratic and noble families in Tibet considered poor people very low and did not like to sit and talk with them, but in refugedom all are equal. They all have more or less same economic status based on income and not on land- holdings.

There is no need to say that at present time , money making is one of the most common and omnipotent ways of social promotion. A successful money-maker is the greatest aristrocrat of the modern democratic society.

As it is already mentioned earlier that Tibetans are hard working and ready to do all type of work to earn their livelihood. Out of 200 respondents 163 are working i.e. 81.5% and only 37 respondents i.e. 18.5% are under the category of non-working respondents. On asking the respondents about the reason as why they are not working like other people, the various reasons given by the respondents are shown in Table No. 8.4. out of 37 non-working respondents, 27 respondents i.e. 72.97% are still studying and after the completion of their study they will definitely do some work. Another 5.40% respondents are illiterate and unable to do any work,13.51% say that they found no need to work because other family members are earning and there is no need for them to do any work. Another 5.40% respondents are housewives and are not interested to do any work.Their husband's are earing and they want to remain at home and take care of children.

The rest 2.70% respondents are of the same opinion that they are not going to do anything unless and until they got the job of their own choice. This category of respondents are interested in government jobs only and they are sure that one day they will definitely get the jobs of their choice.

Table 8.4. : Respondents on the basis of various reasons given by them on being remained unemployed

Various reasons for not working	No. of respondents	% of responses
Student	27	72.97
Illiterate	2	5.40
There was no need to work	5	13.51
Not interested	2	5.40
Did not get any job of choice	1	2.70
Total	**37**	**100**

Source : Field-work.

Out of 37 respondents, who are not working 27 are students, 2 illetrate, and 1 respondent who did not get job of the choice, when they were asked, if the opportunity is provided to them what would they like to do. As shown in Table No. 8.5. majority of respondents i.e. 36.66% wanted to become doctor, engineer, lawyer etc., another 33.33% wanted to serve the Tibetan government in exile, 6.66% students is dreaming of to become politicians and 23.33% say that they have not decided yet, but whatever comes to them in future and whatever be the circumstances, they will readily accept it.

Table 8.5. : Respondents on the various opinions given by them on the jobs they would like to do in future

What would you like to do	No. of respondents	% of responses
1. Politician	2	6.67
2. Govt. job	10	33.33
3. Whatever comes	7	23.34
4. Professional	11	36.66
Total	**30**	**100**

Source : Field-work.

The technical competence and personal ability of a person will place him in a position which he deserves and consequently the social mobility depends only on the merits of the individual there are it is necessary to provide better educational facility and technical training to them by the Tibetan government to achieve their aspirations and dreams.

When was asked to non working respondents as who runs the family or what is the sources of their income? The various responses were given by them is also represented in Table No. 8.6. Out of 37 respondents 21.63% respondents say that father is the only member who earns in the family, 13.52% say that only mother's income runs the family as they have no father and 27.02% are such families who's responsibilities are on the shoulders of both father and mother, 8.10% respondents say that husband is only the earning member on whose income they live and 13.52% respondents say that their children are running the house with their salaries they get from the work they do and 16.22% respondents say that neither parents, nor children and not even the spouses run the family. Their source of income are relatives which include chacha, maama, aunty, uncles etc.

Table 8.6. : Respondents on the basis of their source of income

Who runs the family	No. of respondents	% of responses
Father	8	21.63
Mother	5	13.52
Both	10	17.02
Husband	3	8.10
Wife	—	—
Children	5	13.52
Any other relative	6	16.22
Total	**37**	**100**

Source : Field-work.

When they were asked do you feel bad sitting at home? 32 respondents i.e. 86.48% say that do not feel bad about it. Out of them 27 are students who feel that it is not the right time for them to earn and after completing their studies they will definitely work. Another 8.10% respondents are females who want to give good moral teaching to their children therefore they also do not feel bad sitting at home and not work outside. The remaining 2 respondents i.e. 6.25% are old and now they feel , it is the duty of their children to take care of them. They had already worked for several years and now they wanted to lead life peacefully and happily.

Those respondents who feel bad sitting idle at home are 13.52%. They think that they are unable to serve their nation right at present, but if the opportunity knocks the door, they will definitely open it.

It can not be denied that the class - situation of any individual in the modern- urban- industrial society has certain financial aspects that impair social mobility. It is necessary to see the class- position of Tibetan refugees in different occupations.

Assessment of the status group has been carried out accounting to the income level of the respondents.

It is worth observing that there are 34 respondents who do not have their fixed income, but however asking their approximate income they are kept under different group levels. The Table No. 8.7. represents the relation between the occupation and their income, which will further helps to categorise them as to which category of class they belong.

In the income level of Rs. 1000 and below there are 22 respondents i.e. 13.75%, out of which 68.18% are doing business and 31.82% are employed in various offices.

In the second category of income level i.e. Rs. 1001-2000, there are 21.87% respondents out of which 45.71% are engaged in business, 48.57% are employees and 5.71% are from professional areas.

In the third category of Rs. 2001-3000, there are 22.5% respondents , in which 38.88% are engaged in business and 61.11% are professionals and there is no employee in this category.

The next income level is from Rs. 3001- 4000, which includes 34 respondents i.e. 21.25% out of them 85.29% are employees in different offices and 14.70% are professionals and there is no businessman in this category.

Then comes the income level between Rs. 4001- 5000 which includes 8.12% respondents. Out of these 7.69% are in business category, 38.46% are employees and 53.84% are professionals.

The next income level includes 3.13% respondents which lies between Rs. 5001- 6000. Out of these 40% are businessmen and 60% are professionals. There are no employees in this category.

The second last category 6.88% lies between the income level Rs. 6001- 7000, and in this income level group, 18.18% are business personals, 72.72% are employees and 9.09% are professionals.

The last income group is between Rs. 7001- 8000, in which there are 2.5% respondents, out of which there is an equal distribution between business persons and professionals, none in this category are employees.

Table 8.7. : Respondents in relation with income and occupation

Income in Rs.	Occupation			Total No. of respondents
	Business	Employee	Professional	
1000 and below	15	7	—	22
%	(68.18)	(31.82)	—	(13.75)
1001 - 2000	16	17	2	35
%	(45.71)	(48.57)	(5.71)	(21.87)
2001 - 3000	14	—	22	36
%	(38.88)	—	(61.11)	(22.5)
3001 - 4000	—	29	5	34
%	—	(85.29)	(14.70)	(21.25)
4001 - 5000	1	5	7	13
%	(7.69)	(38.46)	(53.84)	(8.12)
5001 - 6000	2	—	3	5
%	(40)	—	(60)	(3.13)
6001 - 7000	2	8	1	11
%	(18.18)	(72.72)	(9.09)	(6.88)
7001- 8000	2	—	2	4
%	(50)	—	(50)	(2.5)
Not fix	—	—	—	—
Total	**52**	**66**	**42**	**160**

Source : Field-work.

There are total 163 respondents working at present, out of which only 3 respondents i.e.1.84% are doing voluntary services. There is none in the category of 8000 and above.

Today in exile, the main determinant of one's social status is based on income a person has to run his/ her family. Thus according to the income level the respondents are categorized into following classes:—

i. 1000 - below - very very low class

ii. 1001 - 3000 - very low class

iii. 3001 - 5000 - low class

iv. 5001 - 7000 - lower middle class

v. 7001- 8000 - middle class

When class category of the respondents were determined in relation with their occupation and income the result found is illustrated in Table no : - 8 out of 52 business workers 30.76% belongs to very very low class, 59.61% in very low class, 1.92% in lower class, 5.76% in lower middle class and 1.92% are middle class.

In the second category of occupation i.e. employees, the total number of respondents are 66, out of which 10.60% are in very very low class, 27.27% in very low class, 48.48% in lower class, 13.63% in lower middle class but there is no respondent in middle class category.

The last category of occupation includes 42 respondents i.e. professional category. In this category there are no very very low class people whereas 59.52% are in very low class, 28.57% in lower class, 7.14% belongs to lower middle class and 2.38% respondents are in middle class category.

Thus the total 160 respondents out of 200, 14.37% are in very very low class, 46.26% belongs to very low class, 28.12% are under the category of lower class, 9.37% belongs to lower middle class and only 1.88% are under the category of middle class.

Table 8.8. : Class category of respondents with relation to occupation

Occupation	Class category					
	Total	Very	Very very low	Low low	Lower	Middle middle
Business	52	16	31	1	3	1
% of responses	(32.5)	(30.76)	(59.61)	(1.92)	(5.76)	(1.92)
Employee	66	7	18	32	9	—
% of responses	(41.25)	(10.60)	(27.27)	(48.48)	(13.63)	—
Professional	42	—	25	12	3	2
% of responses	(26.25)	--	(59.52)	(28.57)	(7.14)	(2.38)
Total	**160**	**23**	**74**	**45**	**15**	**3**
Total		**(14.37)**	**(46.26)**	**(28.12)**	**(9.37)**	**(1.88)**

Source : Field-work.

It has been found during the study that for few Tibetans whose status has been improved, exile conditions have proved favourable for them and for the others, whose status has been declined compared to the past, exile conditions have proved unfavourable for them.

It is found true, here, in the case of Tibetans that environmental conditions also influence the social class. It also suggests that change has both the functions and dysfunctions. A change which can be functional for one individual may be dysfunctional for the others.

Accquistion of land and live- stock are not the measuring scale for economic status. Today it is based on income as well as on the material artifacts a person possesses.

In the present changed, situation there is a great degree of occupational mobility which is entirely of new type Tibetans adopt different type of occupational roles which are also entirely different from those which existed in Tibet. In this context it is necessary to find out the difference between traditional occupation of the parents and those adopted by their children in exile.

In the case of Tibetan migrants, the occupation of the parents and that of their children is different. Many children whose parents were traders, nomads, agriculturists, teacher, craftsmen, have changed their occupation. Some are government employees, some others are businessmen and many are in professional occupation as represented in Table No. 8.9.

Only 3.06% of the Tibetans now are doing the work which is traditional as done by their parents in Tibet. Out of which 2 respondents are teachers like their parents and 3 respondents are in the craft business similar to that of the parents occupation.

Table 8.9. : Differences of occupation of that respondents and the occupation of their parents

Traditional occupation of the parents	Present occupation of Children Business	Employee	Professional	Responses	% of Responses
Traders	—	18	9	27	
		—	(66.67)	(33.33)	(16.57)
Nomads	33	27	10	70	
		(47.14)	(38.57)	(14.28)	(42.95)
Agriculturists	15	4	14	33	
		(45.46)	(12.12)	(42.42)	(20.24)
Nobles	2	2	5	9	
		(22.22)	(22.22)	(55.56)	(5.52)
Teachers	—	—	4	4	
		—	—	(100)	(2.45)
Craftsmen	3	15	2	20	
		(15)	(75)	(10)	(12.27)
Total	**53**	**66**	**44**	**100**	

Source : Field-work.

But one can not deny the fact that majority of Tibetans have switched over to different occupation which resulted in maximum occupational mobility among the uprooted Tibetans. In a refugedom, new generation has given up traditional class and occupations to achieve higher and newer ones. Hence result is upward mobility to large extent and uncountable change in society.

Tibetan refugees are businessmen and they are in strong competition with the local Indians. The main reasons for their success :–

i. Tibetans are hard working and they never wanted to sit idle unless they don't have any skill in work. In the present study, out of 200 respondents 81.5% are working and only 5% are not working. The rest 13.5% are students.

ii. The strength of women-folk - In Tibet trade and business was not only confined to men but women too actively involved in various business activities. Today in the refugedom one can see women working in various spheres of employment.

iii. The third and the last reason for the success of Tibetans in business is that they have been traders since ages and they have natural instinct for trading.

There are also various other methods adopted by the new generation to earn handsome amount of money. One such method of earning money is through smuggling. On visiting some local police station it was investigated that there has been few cases of brewing and selling of wine (chang) by Tibetans. Even the Indian administrative officials agree to it. There were also few cases recorded in the police files against Tibetans for the theft of scooter and motorbikes.

The deviant behaviour of boys of the Tibetans community cannot be ignored. When they were asked about the deviant behaviour of boys, majority of Tibetans respondents said that 'it is not true. It is found in every society then why specially Tibetans boys are noticed. It is totally unjust to say that Tibetan boys smuggle things'. On the other hand there were few respondents who agree that there are boys in the community who are engaged in all these things and because of them whole community has to suffer. People when talk of them don't simply say 'a boy has done this' they say 'a Tibetan boy' has done such wrong act.

But it is true that Tibetans specially boys are very mischievous and engaged in misdeeds too. It is not a misconception against them. Girija Saklani has provided the most suitable causes for their mischievous behaviour when she says, "Moreover in an uprooted community when the primary group control become loose, some of the deviant behaviour in the community is usually manifested.

Being a comparative study, it is also important to notice the difference of occupation among Tibetan refugees of Dharamsala and Dehradun. Table No. 8.10. indicates the type of occupation in which the Tibetan refugees are engaged in both these regions. The total number of respondents working in various fields in Dharamsala. Out of 92 working respondents 23.91% are in business sector, 48.91% are employees and 27.17% are professionals.

Table 8.10. : Respondents on the basis of their occupation in Dharamsala

Type of occupation	No. of respondents male and female	% of responses male & female
Business	22	23.91
Employees	45	48.91
Professionals	25	27.17
Total	**92**	**100**

Source : Field-work.

Similarly the working respondents in Dehradun and their distribution in various occupations is shown in Table No. 8.11. It was found that out of 71 working respondents in Dehradun 43.66% are engaged in business, 29.58% are employees and 26.76% are professionals.

Table 8.11. : Respondents on the basis of their occupation in Dehradun

Type of occupation	No. of respondents male and female	% of responses male & female
Business	31	43.66
Employees	21	29.58
Professionals	19	26.76
Total	**71**	**100**

Source : Field-work.

From the Table No: 8.10. and 8.11. it is clear that in Dehradun Tibetans engaged in business are 19.75% more as compared to Dharamsala. That means Tibetans are mostly dependents on business to earn their livelihood.

But it is also a fact that in Dharamsala Tibetans are mostly employees in government jobs and private jobs. The difference is 19.33% , as compared to Tibetans working in government as well as private jobs in Dehradun.

The reason behind the majority of Tibetans working as employees in Dharamsala is that the government-in-exile is located in Dharamsala and generally all the head offices are being channelized or controlled from Dharamsala and not from Dehradun.

Therefore, the place is of great importance. As the employees working in different offices in Dharamsala, their jobs are also transferable in nature and this is the reason why one cannot easily know about the exact population of the place.

In the professional category, the percentage of Tibetans from Dehradun and Dharamsala does not have much difference.

When the respondents were asked about the tax, they pay to the Tibetan government in exile or the Indian

Government All respondents replied in negative. They say they don't have to pay any tax neither to the Tibetan government in exile nor to the Indian government. But 90.79% respondents say that they are willing to offer 2% to 3% share of their income to the Tibetan government in exile. Nobody forces them to pay but it is a voluntary contribution. Few people are very poor and unable to pay the share.

Those Tibetans who are doing business in Tibetan market when they were asked if they pay some rent for their shops. They replied that initially when they started working they don't have to pay any rent but today pradhan (the head) of the shops collect money from the owner (which is also not fixed) and deposit it to the Indian officials about which they don't know.

They were further asked about the facilities provided to the individual to start new work either by the Tibetan government or by the Indian government.

According to the respondents Indian government has always shown interest to give them whatever they need. Indian Govt. provides them housing loans, funds for school, medical facilities and the most important is land.

The land is provided to Tibetans, so that they construct Tibetan colonies, shops, market etc. from time to time they also get aids and funds from the Indian government as well as from Tibetan government whenever need arises.

In response to they say that they don't have to face any difficulty in getting the loans or other facilities given to them by the Indian Government officials.

EDUCATION AND ECONOMY

Education has helped the younger generation of Tibetans to secure better jobs for themselves and to creat jobs for other too.

It is important to know about the occupation of the respondents who are illeterate or less- educated and those respondents who are more educated or highly educated. Out of 10.5% respondents who are not at all educated 4.76% are in Govt. jobs, 28.57% are in private jobs and 66.66% are doing their own business, either sweater selling business or running small restaurants.

Those who studied till primary are 6.5% out of which 38.46% are in government jobs, 38.46% are in private jobs and 23.07% are engaged in business.

Respondents who completed their education till junior High School are 8% out of these 12.5% are in government jobs, 18.75% are in private jobs and the 68.75% are doing their own business.

Those respondents who studied till High School are 20% out of which 22.5% are still studying and the rest 77.5% are engaged in different works. Out of these 77.5%, 70.96% are in Government jobs, and 29.03% are engaged in business. Nobody is doing private Job in this category.

The next category of respondents who have completed their intermediate are 14.5% out of these 23.07% are employees in government jobs, 30.46% are employees in pvt. Jobs and 46.15% are engaged in business.

Out of 29% graduates, 79.31% are employed in various fields. 89.13% are in government jobs 4.34% in private jobs and 6.52% are engaged in business activities.

Those young Tibetan respondents who have completed their post- graduation are 7% and all are engaged in some or the other work. Out of these 92.85% are working as goverment employees and 7.14% are in business field. None of the respondents is doing any private job.

The rest 4.5% respondents are specialized in different fields in different subjects and all of them are working as government employees.

It is therefore clear that Tibetans who are very well educated are employed and serving in Tibetan Government-in-Exile. The majority of respondents i.e. 58.90% are holding good position in Tibetan Goverment.-in-Exile.

The next important means of livelihood of most of the respondents i.e. 28.83% is business. This category includes both the educated, less- educated and illiterate respondents as represented in Table No. 8.12.

The last category of occupation with minimum number of respondents i.e. only 12.27% are in pvt. jobs, for eg. working in computer centre, at shops, coaching institute, STD booths, etc.

Table 8.12. : Respondents on basis of their occupation and their educational qualification

Educational qualification		Occupational status					
No. of respondents		Govt.	% job	Pvt.	% job	Business	%
Nil	21	1	4.76	6	28.57	14	66.66
Primary	13	5	38.46	5	38.46	3	23.07
J.H.S	16	2	12.5	3	18.75	11	68.75
H.S	40	22	70.96	—	—	9	29.03
XII	29	3	23.07	4	30.76	6	46.15
Graduate	58	46	89.13	2	4.34	3	6.52
Post-Graduation	14	13	92.85	—	—	1	7.14
Specilization	9	9	100	—	—	—	—
Total	**200**	**96**		**20**		**47**	

Source : Field-work.

When the respondents were asked as to what leads them to do this work, the reasons categorized were as such, it is their traditional work, it is more paying, they were interested in this particular work, no other job for them, they were not eligible to do any other job or somebody forced them to do the particular work. The responses given by the respondents are also expressed in Table No. 8.13.

The most satisfactory reason given by the respondents working in different fields is that they were interested in a particular job, they are doing at present which constituted 44.17% of the total respondents. The respondents under this category of reason are mostly professional and Govt. employees.

The next satisfactory reason given by 32.51% respondents say that they were not eligible to do any other job than that which they are doing at present.

This category of respondents are generally petty shop owners, sweater- sellers and are illiterate. They are happy that they are not dependent on others and they are not a liability on their Govt. who teaches everyone to be self-dependent.

Another reason given by 12.26% respondents was that, that their work is more paying and they are earning well. This work helps them to improve their living standard.

Another 80% respondents were not satisfied with their present occupation . If they got opportunity, they will switch over to another job of their choice and interest. This category includes those young respondents who are engaged in some petty business or doing some private job.

The negligible 3.06% respondents are engaged in their traditional business. They are also happy doing it. According to them to keep their traditional items alive somebody has to do it.

Long back their forefathers were also engaged in carpet- weaving, handicraft works, making of wine (chang) etc.

Table 8.13. : Respondents on the basis of the reasons given by them for the work they are doing

Reasons	No. of respondents	% of responses
Traditional	5	3.06
More paying	20	12.26
Interested	72	44.17
No other job	13	8.0
Not eligible to do any other job	53	32.51
Forced by someone	—	—
Total	**163**	**100**

Source : Field-work.

From the Table No. 8.13 it is clear that nobody forces their children to do particular work. All engaged in various type of occupation are their on own wish and choice.

When the respondents were asked whether they would like to continue their present work in future?

Out of 163 working respondents 83.43% said that they will not change their occupation but 14.11% said that they are not willing to do this work and they will definetly switch over to some other work. Whereas, 2.46% were not sure about it as shown in Table No. 8.14.

Table 8.14. : Respondents on the basis of their opinion about thier future work

Would you like to continue this work in future	No. of respondents	% of responses
Yes	136	83.43
No	23	14.11
Cann't say	4	2.46
Total	**163**	**100**

Source : Field-work.

Out of 163 respondents 83.43% are in favour of their occupation and this category of respondents basically includes professionals, few government employees and very few businessmen. According to them they are interested in their work because it is more paying and they can serve their nation by doing their work.

Those respondents who do not want to continue with their present work are 14.11%. This is because they are not satisfied with the amount they are earning and they wanted to earn more and raise their living standard.

Those who were not sure about their future prospects were 2.45% . According to them if the opportunity is provided they will change their occupation on they might continue with the same occupation. They were not sure about it.

Those respondents who replied in negative when they were asked that what else would you like to do. Out of 27 respondents 22.22% wanted to join politics. They are not oriented toward high salaries on good amount of money. They feel happy if they were given chance to be in the government. These respondents are generally engaged in business and government jobs. They think political platform is necessary to change certain ideologies and to introduce various policies and reformative programmes for the betterment of their countrymen.

Few Tibetans i.e. 3.70% are among those who are highly influenced by western countries and wanted to go to "States". Such Tibetans are young girls and boys. 44.44% Tibetans wanted to serve in Tibetan government jobs. The respondents under this category of opinion are educated. They are presently doing some business or some private job.

The respondents who wanted to do business are 18.51%. They wish to earn more and raise their living standard. The rest 11.11% respondents were not sure about their future work. What come's first, better they will opt it.

Table 8.15. : Respondents on the basis of their opinion about occupation

What else would you like to do	No. of respondents	% of responses
To serve in Tibetan politics	6	22.22
Wanted to go States	1	3.70
Govt. job	12	44.44
Business	5	18.51
Cann't say	3	11.11
Total	**27**	**100**

Source : Field-work.

From the opinion stated by the respondents in Table No. 8.15, one thing is crystal clear that they have a strong national feeling for Tibet. They wanted to serve their nation. They are neither greedy, nor lazy but always think of free Tibet and its future prospects.

9

Polity :
The Democratic Ideal

Within the past 40 years there has occurred a radical change in Political ideology of Tibetans. Whatever the form of government in exile, it seems the government is one of the effective agency of social change. The powers of the Tibetan government in exile functions towards shaping and modifying the character of Tibetan Society.

Dowse and Hughes states that Politics is about "power", Politics occur when there are differentials in power. In terms of this definition, any social relationship which involves power differentials is political. This is from a long way of traditional study of Politics which was concentrated on the state and the various institutions of government such as parliament and the judiciary[1].

The Assembly of Tibetan People's Deputies (the Parliament-in-exile) is located above the hill-town of Dharamsala.

In 1960, after one year stay at Mussoorie, Dalai Lama left for Dharamsala, where the first thought was to reconstitute the Tibetan government.

The first elections were announced in the early 1960's. Tibetans were totally ignorant about voting. They had never participated in the electoral process and it was a new experience for them.

In 1963, Dalai Lama announced the first written democratic constitution of Tibet based on socialistic guidelines along representative principles. All the old government titles and ranks were dropped.

The new constitution ensure equal distribution of wealth and democratic procedures for the working of representative government. It declared seventy - Seven articles and fundamental rights for all Tibetans which included those of universal suffrage, equality before the law, life, liberty and prosperity as well as freedom of religion, speech and assembly.

It was in the second Assembly i.e. in 1963, people were introduced to election committes, ballot boxes and female representatives. The older Tibetans found the new pattern of voting very difficult and complex. As lodi Gyari, Chairman of the Seventh assembly of deputies noted, "A lot of people got into the election tents and just pray to his Holiness". "I don't know any of these candidates, but please let me choose the right one to help the Dalai Lama and the people" Then they close their eyes, put their finger down and ask the election officer, "would you see who's name is here?" When they hear it, they reply, "Oh, its so and so. I'll vote for him[2]".

In Tibet, government gave no opportunity for democratic political practicipation to the commoners. It was autocratic and highly centralized in nature. In exile, the system has undergone a rapid process of democratisation and politicization.

The assembly was given independent authority in 1990, and was empowered to elect the Kashang (Cabinet) consisting of Kalons (Ministers) who were made responsible to the assembly.

After this the eleventh assembly became a full - fledged parliamentary body with effective power over the Executive.

In the 13th Asembly, the representative chosen are 46 in number. Out of these 46 deputies, 30 deputies are elected from three regions of Tibet (ten each from Amdo, Kham and U-Tsang). Another 10 seasts, to the five religious sects (two each are given to Gelugpa, Nyingmpa, Sakyapa, Kaygu-pa and Bōn) fo Tibetan Buddhism. It is mentioned in the book "The uproated Tibetans in India : a sociological study of continuity and change" by Girija Saklani (pg 309) that "Bonpos do not have their representation either on the council of religious affairs or on the commission of Tibetan People's deputies, which other sects and group have".

But today it is not correct to say so, as two representatives from this sect (Bōn) are representing the Tibetan People's deputies assembly.

To give representation to the exiled Tibetans of America and Europe two seats are reserved for exiled Tibetans one in America and one seat reserved for Tibetans in Europe. Another three deputies are nominated by H.H. The Dalai Lama.

The tenure of the 13the Assembly is for five years, The first session was on 1st June 2001. (see appendik iv)

CHARTER

The Charter of the Tibetans in exile is the supreme law governing the functions of Central Tibetan Administration which was drafted in 1990 containing 115 Articles. The Charter provides for a clear seperation of power among the three organs of the government :

Judiciary, Legislature and Executive. In the charter nine ammendements have been made.

Prior to refugedom all governmental positions were reserved for nobles. But today there is great mobility in political circulation. The change from feudal society to democratic one, facilitates a greater upward mobility among Tibetans. Intensive vertical mobility is one of the most remarkable characterstic of democratic societies.

Now anyone can hold the position of monk official, or become on officer at lay courts, irrespective of the position one, holds in a society. The criteria for being chosen to high position is education and ability of a person posseses rather than one's social and ritual position.

In a Tibetan society of today all positions are open to every one. There are no restrictions nor obstacles for a person whether religious or judicial in "climbing up or going down" from one social stratum to another. That is why present Tibetan society has become more stratified as compared to the past. In this ideal mobile society individuals position is allotted regardless of his/her parent's position.

Political participation means taking part in political matters to bring about desired change. It implies voting, attending political meetings, campaigning, supporting pressure groups, holding party offices, contesting elections and raising party funds etc.

To find out about the participation of the respondents in political matters they were asked as to what extent they participate in political matters. Out of 200 responses received, majority of 112 respondents (56%) say that they take interest in discussions about politics and vote during elections Another (44) respondents i.e. (22%) say that they attend political meetings and give financial contribution to social welfare. 30 respondents (15%) say that they are totally unaware about the political world around them only 14 respondnets (7%) say that they are working as political leaders themselves. It has also been represented in Table No. 9.1.

Table 9.1. : Level of Political Participation among Tibetan respondents

Level of political participation	No. of Respondents	% of Responses
Unaware literally to the political world around you	30	15
Spectators activity including voting and taking part in discussions	112	56
Attending political meetings and making financial contribution	44	22
Working yourself as a leader	14	7
Total	**200**	**100**

Source : Field-work.

As it has already mentioned that the basic principle of traditional Tibetan Political organisation was the obligation for a noble to serve the government. It meant that family background plays the important role in determining the level of political participation among Tibetans.

It is thus found necessary to know about the family background of those Tibetan respondents who are at present working as political leaders in Tibetan government in exile. Table No. 9.2. represents the family background of present Tibetan leaders : out of 200 respondents, 14 respondents i.e. 7% are serving in Tibetan goverment. in exile as political leaders. Out of these 14.29% respondents are from the family of traders who were not very rich nor they were poor 28.57% respondents are from the family of nomads 35.71% are among those whose parents were agriculturists in Tibet and 7.14% respondents are those who belong to the family of craftsmen with very poor financial background. There are only 14.29% respondents who belong to noble families and their parents were also holding high positions in the goverment offices of Tibet. None of the respondent belong to the family of proffessionals.

Table 9.2. : Political Leaders and their family background

Traditional occupation of the parents	No. of respondents belonging to a particular family background	% of responses
Traders	2	14.29
Nomads	4	28.57
Agriculturists	5	35.71
Nobles	2	14.29
Professionals	—	—
Craftsmen	1	7.14
Total	**14**	**100**

Source : Field-work.

It is clear from the Table No. 9.2. that family background is not the criteria to become, leaders and achieve high positions in the government.

It is found that every town and settlement has its own political leaders. They are elected by the families of that area. The person who are elected are those who are generally liked by the people. Therefore "elections" serve as the "Channel" of climbing up and going down of Individuals in a democratic society.

The electoral process is the logical outcome of the idea of equality. Elections conducted without force or coercion permit the majority to express itself, and in the end to rule.

Political theorists now agree that free and representative elections are a necessary condition for democracy[3]. Elections are therefore the indicators of Mobility.

EDUCATION AND POLITICS

It is important to know about the relationship between education of the respondents and their level of political participation. It will further help to study the role of education in making Tibetans aware about the changing political system.

It will also help to understand whether educational qualifications of a person is one of the criterion to participate in political matters or to become a leaders.

Therefore, the educational level of 200 respondents is studied in relation to their political participation which is followed by table no. 9.3.

(a) Respondents who were illiterate

Out of 21 respondents who are illiterate 6 respondents i.e. 28.57% were totally ignorant about the political world around them. 12 respondents i.e. 57.14% are included with in spectator category. They are interested in voting and political discussions 4.7% respondents barely attend political meetings but makes financial contribution. The rest 9.52% respondetns are themselves leader at local level politics.

(b) Respondents who studied till primary school

The total number of respondents in this category are 13 i.e. 6.5% out of which 3 respondents i.e. 23.07% are under the category "a" are unaware literally to the political would around them, 8 respondents i.e. 61.53% are under the category "b" spectators activity including voting and taking part in discussions the rest 2 respondents i.e. 15.28% lie under the category "c" attending political meetings and making financial contribution. None of the respondents is under the category "d" working themselves as a leader as it is clearly indicated in Table No. 9.3.

(c) Respondents who studied till Junior High School

Out of 16 respondents i.e. 8%, 31.25% are under the category "a" unaware literally to the political world around them 56.25% are under the category "b" spectators activity including voting and taking part in discussions and 12.5% respondents lies under the category "c" attending political meetings and making financial contribution.

(d) Respondents who have studied till High School

Under this category are 40 respondents i.e. 20% out of these 40% respondents are under the category "a" unaware literally to the political world around them another 40% are under the category "b" spectators activity including voting and taking part in discussions, 17.5% respondents and 2.5%, respondents are under the category "c" attending political meetings and making financial contribution and "d" working themselves as a leader respectively.

(e) Respondents who have completed their intermediate level education

They are 29 in number i.e. 14.5% out of these 17 respondents i.e. 58.62% are under the category "b" spectators activity including voting and taking part in discussions, 9 respondents i.e. 31.03% are under the category "c" attending political meetings and making financial contribution and 3 respondents i.e. 10.34% are under the category "d" working themselves as a leader.

(f) Respondents who have completed thier graduation

Their total strength is 58 i.e. 29% out of which 36 respondents i.e. 62.06% are under the category "b" spectators activity including noting and taking part in discussions, 19 respondnets i.e. 32.75% are under the category "c" attending political meetings and making financial contribution and 3 respondents i.e. 5.17% are under the category "d" working themselves as a leader.

(g) Respondnets who have completed their post graduation

They are 14 in number i.e. 7% out of which 11

respondents i.e. 78.57% are under the category "b" spectators activity including voting and taking part in discussions, 2 respondents i.e. 14.28% are under the category "c" attending political meeting and making financial contribution and only 1 respondents i.e. 7.14% are under the category "d" working themselves as a leader.

(h) The last category of respondents who are specialized in various fields of their choice

Total number of such respondents is 9 i.e. 4.5% out of these, 3 respondents i.e. 33.33% are under the category "b" spectators activity including voting and taking part in discussions, 2 respondents i.e. 22.22% lies under the category "c" attending political meeting and making financial contribution and the remaining 4 respondents i.e. 44.44% are under the category "d" working themselves as a leader.

Table no. 9.3 Showing the relation between education of the respondents and their political participation

Education	Total no. of respondents	Level of political participation			
		(a)	(b)	(c)	(d)
Nil	21	6	12	1	2
%		(28.57)	(57.14)	(4.76)	(9.52)
Primary	13	3	8	2	—
%		(23.07)	(61.53)	(15.38)	—
J.H.S.	16	5	9	2	—
%		(31.25)	(56.25)	(12.5)	—
H.S.	40	16	16	7	1
%		(40)	(40)	(17.25)	(2.5)
XII	29	—	17	9	3
%		—	(58.62)	(31.03)	(10.34)

		(a)	(b)	(c)	(d)
Graduation	58	—	36	19	3
%		—	(62.06)	(32.75)	(5.17)
Post-graduation 14	—	11	2	1	
%		—	(78.57)	(14.28)	(7.14)
Speciali-zation	9	—	3	2	4
%		—	(33.33)	(22.22)	(44.44)
Total	**200**	**30**	**112**	**44**	**14**

Source : Field-work.

From the Table No. 9.3. it is clear that those who are illiterate or less educated do not participate much in politics. Those who are educated know about the changing political scene around them. they are interested in political meetings, political discussions and making financial contribution for the welfare of the people. They are also leaders in Tibetan goverment-in-exile. Therefore, it seems that education is an important trait accquired to be possessed by a person if one has to "climb up" in politics in a democratic Tibetan society.

Though the old traditional leadership has undergone drastic changes, yet, the ultimate faith in Dalai Lama as the temporal and spiritual Head of a State cannot be wiped out. Still the Tibetans consider Dalai Lama as their Political head and the ultimate authority. His charismatic authority cannot be ignored at any stage. "Charismatic authority emanates from those leaders who inspire allegiance because of purely personal qualities they are thought to posses, independent of any office. It is irrational and elusive but still then it is powerful"[4].

Today the important traits of leadership are quite different from those in the past. While interviewing the respondents when they were asked about their opinion as to what qualities should a political leader must possess.

Out of 200 responses, the first preference is given to honsety. According to 117 respondents i.e. 58.5% leader should perform their duties assigned to them very sincerely.

The second prefrence is given to education of the leaders 49.5% respondents say that educated leader will be able to guide the commoners. It is a duty of leader to contact people outside the community and for this purpose leader should be educated.

The third preference is given to hardwork 39% respondents feel that leader should be hard working besides being educated and honest. Political leader should always be ready to look after the welfare of People and to solve their problems.

The fourth prefrence is given to the nature of the leader 16.5% respondents say that leader should be peace-loving, sympathetic and kind. Their ideal leader is H.H. Dalai Lama. The violent leader is not liked by one and all.

The fifth preference is given to the patriotic feeling in the leader. A leader should sacrifice his personal interests for the community welfare 10.5% respondents feel that leader should be patriotic.

The sixth preference is given to the knowledge a leader should possess. According to 3.5% respondents, it is a political leader who formulates plans and policies for the betterment of the poeple. New changes can be introduced if the leader has enough knowledge to plan everything. Only then one could set an example for others.

The last or the seventh preference is given to un-married status of the leader 1.5% respondents say that if the leader is un-married accquisition of welath, money, artifacts and such other things will become useless for him. This will help him to remain honest and unbiased.

All these qualities of a leader also mentioned in table no. 9.4. are considered perfect for a person to become a political leader.

Table 9.4. : Qualities a person should possess to become a political leader

Qualities of a Leader	No. of respondents	% of responses
Honesty	117	58.5
Education	99	49.5
Hard-working	78	39.0
Peace-loving	33	16.5
Patriotic	21	10.5
Knowledge	7	3.5
Unmarried status	3	1.5

Source : Field-work.

Next they were asked if the qualities mentioned by them are present in their leaders?

The responses were categorized into three level : (i) not at all (ii) very few; and (iii) almost all, as shown in table No. 9.5. out of 200 respondents the majority of respondents i.e. 99 persons (49.5%) replied possitively. These respondents are satisfied with the functioning of their leaders what even qualities they consider a leader should have, almost all of them are present in the present leaders of Tibetan goverment in exile. Though 90 respondents i.e. (45%) say that their leaders possess very few qualities mentioned by them. They are good and hard-working such leaders need to change their rough attitude towards local people of the community only, 11 respondents (5.5%) say that ther political leader do not possess the qualities they want to have in a leader.

It means that Tibetans are happy with the proper functioning of their leader. Some changes seems to be important. But otherwise in reply to to this which was asked by 200 respondents whether they are satisfied with the working of their leaders, 189 respondents 94.5% replied possitively and only 11 respondents i.e. 5.5% responded negatively.

Table 9.5. : Opinion of the respondents about thier present political leaders and qualities possessed by them.

Qualities possessed by the leader	No. of respondents	% of responses
(a) Not at all	11	5.5
(b) Very few	90	45
(c) Almost all	99	49.5
Total	**200**	**100**

Source : Field-work.

On asking the respondents about the availability of leaders to the local people 64.5% respondents agree that political leaders are easily availaible whenever they are needed by the people. Another 18.5% respondents say that political leaders are not easily available to listen their problems, 4.5% respondents say that officials at the lower level treat local people with differences and discourage them to meet senior officials.

Only 12.5% respondents feel that their problems are put forward to their leaders but they are not attended properly. They had to visit the office number of times to get their matter solved.

Table 9.6. : Represents the opinion of respondents on the availability of leaders

Availability of leaders	no. of respondents	% of responses
Easily available	129	64.5
Not easily available	37	18.5
With great difficulty	9	4.5
Not attentive	25	12.5
Total	**200**	**100**

Source : Field-work.

During the interview it is found that few political leaders do not pay any attention to the problems of the local people. But the majority of political leader listen to the problems of the people and they try to remove them.

On asking the respondents what sort of measures they will take if the leaders do not pay any attention to their problems. They were provided with the options :

1. Simply keep quite.
2. demonstrate on roads.
3. Appeal to higher authorities. There responses are shown in Table No. 9.7.

Out of 200 respondents 9 respondents i.e. 4.5% opt for first option. They will simply keep quite with out complaining against them or demonstrating on roads. They will not take any action against them. On the other hand 145 respondents i.e. 72.5% say that if they are not attended properly by their political leaders they will not keep quite. They will demonstrate on roads and raise flags and banners against them. The rest 46 respondents i.e. 23% say that they will either keep quite nor demonstrate on roads but they will appeal to higher authorities against those leaders to help solve their problems immediately.

It is clear from table no. 9.7. about the measures which respondents will take against the unattentive political leaders. Here, it is also important to know that respondents of which age-group has given what measures to remove their problems.

Table 9.7. : Representing the measures taken by the respondents if they are not attended by their leaders

Measures to be taken	No. of respondents	%of responses
(a) Simply keep quite	9	4.5
(b) Demonstrate on road	145	72.5
(c) Appeal to higher authorities	46	23
Total	**200**	**100**

Source : Field-work.

The categorization of age group is as follows (i) Respondents below the age of 20 years (ii) 21-30 yerars (iii) 31-40 years, (iv) 41-50 years (v) 51-60 years (vi) 61-70 yerars, and (vii) Above 70.

In the age-group 20-30 years there are 113 respondents. All these 113 respondents (56.5%) are in favour of the second measure i.e. if they were not attended properly by their leaders they will definitely demonstrate against them.

In the age-group of 31-60 there are 78 respondents (39%) out of which 16% respondents are in favour of demonstrating against the leaders if injustice is done to them whereas 23% say that they will appeal to higher authorities.

The age group of 61-70 includes 8 respondnets and in the age-group of above 70 there is one respondents. Out of these a respondents i.e. 4.5% nobody is in favour of using violence or demonstrating on roads. Neither they will appeal against the ill-atitude of the leaders. According to such respondents they will keep quite because leaders do what they like and they have no power to change their altitude. There is no use of complaining or demonstrating against them.

Table 9.8. : Relationship between age of the respondents and the measures taken by them against the unattentive leaders.

Age-group	no of respondents	Measures taken by them (a)	(b)	(c)
Below 20	10	—	10	—
%			(100)	
21-30	103	—	103	—
%			(100)	
31.40	35	—	20	15
%			(57.14)	(42.85)
41-50	31	—	10	21
%			(32.25)	(67.74)

		(a)	(b)	(c)
51-60	12	—	2	10
%			(16.66)	(83.33)
61-70	1	8	—	—
%		(100)		
Above 70	1	1	—	—
%		(100)		

Source : Field-work.

It is evident from Table No. 9.8. that youngsters have turned more violent and aggressive. They will easily exercise modern agitational methods like street demonstrations, shouting of slogans and closing down the shops and markets for political agitation or if their problems are not taken into consideration, for them moving from one table to another in offices with their applications is humiliating.

Middle-aged respondents feel that violence is not the correct method for them, appeal to higher authorities is the best solution to get their problems solved.

The elderly Tibetans are totally against violent activities of the youth. These senior Tibetans are unaware of the changing conditions so they don't want to interrupt in any of the activities related to politics. They simply keep quite if any problem arises. They feel that God will help them.

Youth, Non-Violence and Dalai Lama

The root meaning of violence comes from the latin "violentia" meaning 'vehemence', a 'passionate' and uncontrolled force, the opposite of a calculated exercise of power. Violence is so much a part of modern society that one is easily led to think of it as the dominant characterstic of times today.

Tibetan youth are living in the fast changing society and adopt new ideas and values of democracy, equality and liberty instead of traditional values prevailed longback in Tibet.

During the informal conversations it was found that youngsters wanted to remove the out-dated policies. Their political socialization took place in India and they realise their role in political development.

Tibetan Youth Congress (TYC)

Tibetan Youth Congress (TYC) established in 1970, has its branches all over India which are established under the name "Regional Tibetan Youth Congress".

The main objectives of this youth organisation are :

(a) To save their culture in diaspora,

(b) To maintain their religion, and

(c) To keep alive the issue of Tibetan freedom.

This youth organisation is more concerned about the third issue. In the year 1981 it has also launched a publicity campaign which "explains the Tibetan point of view and to warn that they should not accept any agreement between India and China which raised the Tibetan cause"[5].

According to the Tibetan youth the top priority is given to the matter of Tibetan liberation. They think "violence" is the right way to achieve their goal. This is sometning what Dalai Lama had never liked.

In one of the interviews Dalai Lama was asked about the radical attitude of the young Tibetans. He says that *"this is my main worry. The young Tibetans in and outside Tibet are less patient and some of the younger Tibetans outside of Tibet criticise me for being too mild. Tibetans of the new generation want things immediately. They are patriotic but less-patient."*[6]

This change in the attitude of young - generation is because they are born and brought up in entirely new and different environment. Another reason for the change in attitude of the youngsters may be due to the modern and liberal education provided to them in exile.

They even raise questions on the institution of Dalai Lama but they are few. Majority of them are still the blind believers of H.H. Dalai Lama. They are trying to take initiative to link Tibet with the modern world on the egalitarian basis.

Tibetans hope that one day Tibet will be a free nation and all of them will return back to their homeland. They will set-up their own political system which will be purely democratic in nature. On asking the respondents that in case they go back to their country, will the political system remain same, minor changes will occur, major changes will occur, or it will be totally different.

All of them say that changes will definitely come in the present political system, 26% respondents say that there will be minor changes, 55% say that major changes will come in the political institution and 19% did not say anyting. Table No. 9.9. also represents to what extent the changes will occur.

Table 9.9. : Opinion of respondents about changes in political system in future

To what extent the changes occur	No. of respondents	% of responses
(a) Minor changes	52	26
(b) Major changes	110	55
(c) Cann't say	38	19
Total	**200**	**100**

Source : Field-work.

It is clear from the perspective of Tibetans that changes will definately occur in the Tibetan political system. Since Indian government has not given them any formal recognition therefore it is known as Tibetan administration and the ministers came to be called as directors instead of minsters.

When the respondents were asked that if they were given the opportunity to become a political leader, what will they do for the society. The responses given by all 186 respondents out of 200 i.e. 93% were in the same manner. According to 156 respondents i.e. 78% the Tibetan constitution mirrors the Indian constitution. Here the democracy provides equal right to life, liberty and happiness to each individual. They say that they are not interested to accept the out-dated political and social institution. The most important thing which they want to give to all Tibetan citizens is freedom and political awareness.

On the other hand the rest 30 respondents i.e. 15% are among those who are not aware about the political happenings around them. If the opportunity to become a political leader is given them, the first thing they will do is to free Tibet from Chinese occupation, and they would bring about an equal distribution of wealth among Tibetans.

When respondents were further asked, whether political participation is directly proportional to income level, occupational status, educational qualification or any other factor they think to be appropriate. Table no. 9.10 represents that out of 200 respondents, 8 respondents i.e. 4% say that political participation is directly proportional to income level, 19 respondents i.e. 9.5% feel that political participation is directly proportional to occupational level, 76 respondents i.e. 38% view political participation is directly proportional to educational level. 70 respondents i.e. 35% say that there are various other factors which can be associated with political participation, and 27 respondents i.e. 13.5% did not say anything.

Table 9.10. : Respondents choice of factor which is considered directly proportional to political participaiton.

Factors	No. of respondents	% of responses
(a) Income	8	4
(b) Occupation	19	9.5
(c) Education	76	37
(d) Any other factor	70	35
(e) No Comments	27	13.5
Total	**200**	**100**

Source : Field-work.

It is seen from table no. 9.10. that political participation is directly proportional to income level, occupational status and educational qualifications. It has also been associated with various other factors.

These other factors include :

(a) Men are likely to have higher level of political participation than women.

(b) Middle aged or senior citizens of the community to have higher level of political participation than the youngsters.

(c) In case of local politics, long term residents to have higher level of political participation than short term residents in a particular locality.

These educated people have a high degree of political involvement. They are the people who are in a high occupational states and therefore they have the opportunity to come in contact with officials at upper levels.

It is easy for them to solve the problems effeciently than people with poor financial background who have a low level of participation. Poor people have less power and feel that their efforts will have little effect.

It has been found and often said by the respondents that political participation of men is higher than that of women. When they were as to what they think about political participation of women. Out of 200 respondents 195 respondents i.e. 97.5% say that if women has a capability to become a political leader she should definitely come forward. But 5 respondents i.e. 2.5% say that women should not participate in politics.

Respondents who feel that women's place is her home and not politics, are all male respondents above the age of sixty-five. One the other hand people readily accept the presence of females on political scene.

Females are also given representation in the Tibetan government in-exile at present.

The present political structure in exile have provided Tibetans a new ideology of "Political Equality". It implies political participation of each individual irrespective of his/ her native place, sect, sex, income level or occupational status.

References

1. Haralambos, M. and R.M. Herald - Sociology - Themes and Perspective. Published by - Neil O' Brien Oxford University Press - 1980 (Pg. 98).
2. Avedon, John. F. - In exile from the land of shows - (1959-60) (pg. 139).
3. Pennock, Ronald J. - Democratic Political theory, princeton, N.J., Princeton University Press. 1979 (pp. 6-11) as, quoted by Erich Goode-Sociology - second edition by prentice Hall - Inc - 1988. (Pg. 430).
4. Goode, Erich - Sociology, Prentice. Hall. Inc. 1988., New Jersey. (pg. 423).
5. Kumar Prem - "Foreign agents among Tibetans". The Statesman, N. Delhi. June 27. 1981 as quoted by Tanka. B. Subba - 1990 (pg. 160).
6. Tibet, China and the World - A compilation of interviews -The Dalai Lama. Narthang Publications 1989. (pg. 61-62).

Conclusion

In the forgone chapters attempt has been made to study analytically the process of social mibility and social change among the Tibetan refugee community. Though it is not an easy task to study all the aspects of the changing community in a single work, but efforts have been made to approach the problem in a comprehensive manner.

Traditional Tibetan society was by no means perfect and in need of changes. When the Tibetan refugees came to India they were in a extreme distress. They just followed Dalai Lama in state of confusion about what had happened in their peace-loving life. India being a land of Buddha, Tibetans always find themselves closer to India in terms of religion. They were very confident that India is a country where they could maintain their cultural identity for which they had fled their country.

Tibetans initally thought that they will be able to go back to their homeland and it will be just a short stay in India. But after sometime they realised the hard fact that it is not an easy task to go back to Tibet. Their stay in the host country would be of much longer duration. Tibetan had developed their own customs, institutions, behavioural, patterns which were suitable to their type of society which has different geographical conditions. But after taking asylum they had to face new sociocultural enviornment. They adopted new methods of life to adjust themselves. During the course of adjustments, in place of traditional customs they followed new ways of living.

Tibetans learnt the local language of the place of their settlements as well as English and Hindi. They adopted new methods of cultivation, acquired knowledge of modern techniques and accepted new type of clothing, education, food habits etc.

Today almost forty-five years have passed and this time is long enough in which no society can remain static or unchanged.

Social Adjustment Vs. Economic Adaptation

As Subba has quoted the study of Girija Saklani that "there is not much social interaction between Tibetans and local people and regards language as one of the barriers to this". Here I would like to say that things changes with time. The study of Girija Saklani was in early 80's. Now we cannot say that Tibetans are not in close contact with Indians. I have found many Indians in Tibetan settlements enjoying with their friends. Even the Tibetans can easily understand and speak Hindi but as I have already stated they feel proud in speaking English.

If Tibetans speak Hindi or English or any local dialect it does not mean that Tibetans have been influenced by it but it is the need of hour. Tibetans are not found speaking any other language than Tibetan in their homes or when they come across each other. This social intercourse between the guest and the host should not be mistaken with cultural assimilation. Still there is growing jealousy and conflict between the two communities.

I agree with Subba when he says that feeling of jealousy among Indians for Tibetans has grown because of the financial aid received by Tibetans from Indian and foreign agencies. It is true that many Indians are leading worst life than any middle class Tibetans On interacting with few Indians whom I found begging outside Tibetan colonies shows a feeling of hatered not only for Tibetans but more specifically towards the Indian government. The feeling of jealousy among Tibetans is also noticed in the study of Mundgod Tibetans by A.V. Arakheri. In his study he explains economic adaptations of Tibetans in the host society.

Tibetans have not only adapted socially and culturally with the host country but also economically. Economic adaptations were very stressful during the early years of their set-up. The sweated labourers had to face many problems in cultivating land. Agriculture is the main occupation adopted by Mundgod settlers (Karnataka region). The Tibetans were initially unaware of the techniques of cultivation and were also new to the crops they had to grow in their land. The main food in Tibet was barley which they could not grow in this land, so, growing wheat, maize and rice were quite difficult. For the purpose they asked Indian farmers to cooperate. Even the hot weather of south was not suitable for them, hence they hired Indian labourers to work for them. Indians found them innocent started cheating and stealing food grains from the grounds. All this was due to jealousy which Indian labourers had for Tibetans.

Dr. Subba in his study further indicated that Tibetans of Darjeeling, Sikkim do not compete with host in occupation nor do they have conflict between them. They maintain cordial relationship as such that they never thought themselves as outsiders or refugees.

Similarly the study of Claes corlin based on Nepal has highlighted the healthy relationship between the guest and the host. Here Tibetans are in sweeten relationship with the host that it would be incorrect to say them "Guest".

Marriages among Tibetans and local people have shown great adjustment capabilities between the two groups.

One of the basic reason behind such adjustments is the close resemblance of the two communities in respect of race, culture, traditions and practice of Buddhism in these areas. But If this is the reason then why Bhutanese are not in close proximity with Tibetans? Why every Tibetan wants to leave Bhutan despite such resemblence? It shows that individual's tendency of adaptation, the behavioural patterns, ethics and code of conduct is much important than physical, cultural and religious resemblence.

Tibetan studies in southern regions of India have indicated least social adaptability of Tibetans with local people.

A.V. Arakheri in his study has pointed out that Tibetans living in the Mundgod areas are not happy with its physical environment. Tibetans in this region suffer due to skin diseases, diarrhoea/dysentery, respiratory tract diseases, abdominal diseases and Tuberculosis. Even the Integrated development plan has shown a chart on disease incidence in 5 settlements in Karnataka.

Disease	**No. of cases**	**% of distribution**
Skin disease	2853	21.9
Diarrhoea/Dysentery	1413	10.8
Respiratory tract	3849	29.5
Abdominal disease	9499	7.2
Tuberculosis	744	3.7
Joint pain	1441	11.0
Fever and cold	1679	12.9
Ear and Eye	129	1.00
	13,052	**100**

Arakheri has also pointed out that Tibetans wanted to move from this region towards north as Dharamsala attracts them too much. In this region they have only shown adjustment towards material culture (artifacts). They follow certain rules made by Indian government from the security point of view but this has created psychological tensions among them. They start feeling themselves as outsiders and "aliens" and once this feeling arouses adjustment becomes difficult and more problematic.

Spatial mobility among Tibetans is also found in parts of Karnataka. They move from one place to another for business. This has brought Tibetans of various regions closer to each other. It has been stated earlier that in Tibet, Tibetans of different provinces like Lhasa, Amdo, U-Tsang, and Kham were not close and cordial with each other but now after coming to India this refugee circumstances have brought them closer and has given them opportunity to understand each other and stand unite for the cause of freedom of Tibet. Tibetans in far flung regions of south always seek the opportunity to shift towards north as they never liked the environment of the region.

Even the study of Mundakuppe by Melvyn Goldstein shows that relations between Tibetans and Indians were very formal and restricted to particular selfish motives. He studied, Tibetans in 1978 which was just after few years of their arrival. They were then in the condition of pot-luck. It is not a matter of surprise that people purely from different cultural and social background could easily understand each other. Nepal, Bhutan, Northern regions of India and border areas of Himalayas somewhat resembles Tibet and Tibetans either in respect of physical or religious environment or socio-cultural environment, hence, they had to face least difficulties in settling themselves in these areas. But they have faced tremendous problems in making them comfortable in southern parts of India, which has purely different culture of its own. This region does not show any resemblence with Tibetan culture.

Tibetans have adapted to new occupations throughout the country. They mainly are engaged in agriculture in southern areas of India whereas in Northern India agriculture is hardly practiced. Even the methods of cultivating lands in both these regions also differs. In North India business and service are practiced by majority of Tibetans. Here it would be important to explain the type of various business activities; most important of which is sweater-selling. They earn their living through selling woollen sweaters, jackets and other woollen garments. They directly bought them from Ludhiana and sell them in different parts of the region.

Other business activities include handicrafts. In Dehra Dun carpet-weaving is the most important work in which Tibetan ladies are engaged. They work in factories established in the Tibetan settlements and few women make carpets in their home. Wood work and metal work are also a means of good earning in this region though not much not in practice. They make various things out of the wood and metal and sell them at high prices in the Tibetan handicrafts showroom established by government in exile in various parts of India.

It is very interesting to notice that no one has never come across Tibetan handicraft work displayed openly in handicrafts festivals or various trade fairs organised by number of agencies in Dehradun. They are mostly found in Tibetan markets whether in Dehradun or Dharamsala or at Majnu-ka-Tilla Delhi. Even the "Chuba's" are not available in the Indian markets. They can be bought directly from Tibetan settlements only. Everywhere they are provided a separate place for their markets, Tibetan shops surrounded with Indian shops are never seen.

It can be said that even after such a long stay they are treated not as family but as "Tibetans" who have taken asylum in India and will one day go back to their country.

In the Northern areas, the high percentage of Tibetans are office workers. This is probably because of the closeness of Dharamsala. While studying about various settlements few conclusions can be drawn.

1. Firstly the conflict between Tibetan refugees and host country is universal. Though the intensity of conflict many vary at different places. As it is least in Northern India and highest in Bhutan. The reason behind this jealous nature of Indians is the economic prosperity of Tibetans.

2. Social interaction between two communities is more appreciable in Northern regions than in other parts of country.

3. Refugees living in far flung areas of the country, far from Dharamsala are less aware of their culture. In Dharamsala Tibetans are more patriotic, culturally and linguistically more educated and learned.

There is no second thought to the fact that economic adaptation by Tibetans is more than the socio-cultural adaptation.

Tibetan community has also faced new geographical, political and socio-cultural conditions. Due to this reason tremendous changes in their socio-cultural institutions, attitudes and values, can be observed.

In Tibetan family structure significant chages have taken place. Individual being closely knitted with the family had no identity of his own. The ultimate authority of the family was in the hands of the eldest male. In a refugee situation the structure and functions of traditional Tibetan family have lost their importance. The joint family structure existed in the past changed to nuclear type of families. Prior to refugehood there were (98.5%) joint families which have now declined to (7.5%), whereas prior to refugehood the conjugal type of families were only (1.5%) which have now increased to (92.5%). There are certain reasons behind this change :

(1) When they initially settled in India they did not have enough money and land-holdings to support the whole family under one roof.

(2) The houses provided to them in the settlement areas were too small to adjust large number of people.

(3) Those who where engaged in non-agricutural activities were highly mobile. They had to look for employment from place to place. They could not afford to take all the members with them. Thus, making money by following different occupations at different palces swayed away the growing generations from their parents.

Under these conditions, nuclear families were more suitable to their life-pattern.

These conditions had also loosend the kinship ties which were tightly knitted in the past (80.5%) respondents were of the opinion that now they are less affectionate and less attached to their sibilings and other relations. On the other hand, there are few (13.5%) who feel that present conditions have made them more closer to each other.

Even the polyandrous system which was considered a necessity in the past, has changed to monogamous system. Now a person can marry outside his/her group, for e.g. Amdo can marry a Khampa, Lhasanian can marry an Amdo. Few exceptions were also found wher Tibetans married Indians and Germans. But, despite such relaxity even today the majority of Tibetans marry within their own groups as found during the study.

In past, being a closed society members of the family had many restrictions imposed on them. Today, it is a free society and they are only few restrictions imposed on the children by the elders and the society. This is because of the :

1. Uprootedness of society,
2. They are very much influenced by the life-patterns of the host country.

One can see the youngsters wearing modern dresses, making different hair-styles etc. They have all modern type of furniture in their houses. As, now the financial position of Tibetans have very much improved, the material changes can be easily observed in the refugee community.

Tibetan society enjoys considerable freedom in relation with the opposite sex.

Drastic changes can be seen in the status of woman in the Tibetan society. Women are now given equal opportunities to work in different field of occupations. It is found that out of 163 working respondents 46.01% are females and rest 53.99% are males. They are goverment. employees, professionals, business women etc. They have accquired a high social staus and prestige and treat themselves equal to men. Women are more consious about their education. Equal opportunities are pvovided to them. There are 22.22% female respondents who are educated till High School level, another 23.33% have completed their graduation, 6.66% are post-graduate and 3.33% are specialised in different fields of education like teachers, doctors, senior TAS officials etc. In short, out of 90 women respondents only 10% are illiterate, which shows a Higher rate of literacy among women.

In traditional society women were not given opportunity to study and was considered down-trodden. Today, this view has faded away completely. They are now pretty consious about their position and rights. Even the democratic constitution of Tibet proclaims equality between sex. They now look at the problem of their status from a liberal perspective. Even men expect that women, should not sit idle at home if she is capable of doing job or business. The study has indicated that girls are considered necessary but it is more desirable to have a son in the family. Sons are expected to continue to live with family, unlike the daughters, are also looked as a carrier of families prestige and prosperity. Girls are considered superior to males. It is not only the story of Tibetans but also of that Hindu society.

It is often said that : "Bringing up a son is like watering a small plant in your home for when it grows it will give fruits and shade; but bringing up a daughter is like watering a plant in someone else home, for her services and love is meant for others". Often seen that the birth of a son is a joyous event; the birth of a daughter is something shameful and sorrowful. In stereotyped groups it is believed that women needs a life long protection and security and she is dependent for her whole life on her father in childhood, by husband in youth and by son in old-age. Though in modern times these type of stereotyped homes are not universal. There is small group of population who rejects this belief both in theory and practice. Coming up of modern thought and increasing education have brought about radical changes in the status of women. Women are economically independent as they have made their entry in various professions and services. Few working women themselves considers that sometimes they feel that they are neglecting their household responsibilities. But in the present conditions to make fairly economically and socially prestigious they have to work outside. Even men considers the working of women as unavoidable. Here the individual relationship matters much than traditional norms. If husband or father is considerate about his wife or daughter allows freedom to her and plays a significant role in helping her to raise her status in the society. Changes in the strereotyped images cannot be speedy and rapid. Tibetan society being highly traditional for centuries is growing towards democratic lines will definitely allow women to participate socially as well as economically in the community and national life. The change in this contemporary society has been mainly due to various factors.

(i) Firstly increasing modern and secular education rather than traditional and monastic education;

(ii) Secondly, occupational mobility and economic prosperity.

(iii) Thirdly and most important their positive attitude towards change and adopting new which is beneficial for them and is the present need.

Rapes and suicides were not reported during investigations. There was only one incidence of theft reported by the police personnel in Rajpur police station at Dehra Dun. In Dharamsala, while talking to an Indian administrative officer it was found that sometimes Tibetans indulge in illegal smuggling of goods at the border areas. The Tibetan youths have become use to spending money lavishly. They do not have enough money, hence sometimes they pursue illegal activities.

The cases related to fights and quarrels are generally solved within the settlements. They are not reported in police stations unless any localite is involved in the case. So, one cannot easily measure the criminality rate among Tibetans.

Religion being the core of Tibetan society, whole nation revolves around religion. Therefore, the role of religion cannot be ignored in the Tibetan community. As being stated earlier that being exposed to the modern society, ther has been remarkable changes in the ideology of the Tibetans. The changed values and beliefs helped in diminishing the influence of religion from the society. The concept of traditional sacred society has been replaced by the concept of modern secular society. 'Secularism' is now influencing the ideology of the youth.

In Tibet the number of Lamas and monks were invited to perform various rites and rituals in the families. They were provided with variety of food and were also given costly items in the name of gifts. In exile, due to lack of financial resources all such expenditures are avoided. Now only one or two lamas or monks are invited during various occasions and are paid little amount of money. Today, it is also not considered necessary to send at least one son from every family in the monastic life. Due to modern and scientific education old beliefs in superstitions have declined in practice.

Even the Lamas very often come in contact with the commoners. They are widely influenced by wordly comforts. Now, they are noticed wearing dresses (chubba) of different material suitable to them, stylish watches, watching movies, listening is in practice movie songs etc.

Owing to this the highly religious minded persons are afraid that whether the future generation would be able to retain their culture and religion in the changed circumstances.

Traditional methods of celebrating fairs and festivals have also changed. Now, they cannot afford to celebrate them for many days as they were usually practised in Tibet. During celebrations besides traditional meals, one can see Indian dishes like 'puri' etc. being served. Cold-drinks, cakes, pastries, chocolates, wafers, juices etc. are also provided to the guest. They play English and Hindi music songs on CD players and dance on the tunes.

Tibetans have a strong conceptions for purity and pollution. Traditionally they had separate altar room which was generally closed for the outsiders. It was not allowed for married couples also to sleep in the altar room. In the settlements, they are not provided with big houses to have seperate altar room. Today altar room is also used by them as store room and for various other purposes. But Tibetans who have private houses have still maintained this tradition.

In Tibet education was only for the nobles who studied by the private tutors. The monks were given religious education in monasteries and education was unknown to the commoners. In exile, the first and foremost necessity declared by Dalai Lama was the proper education of the children. Hence, Tibetan children are given free and compulsory education through Tibetan schools established by government of India with the help of various sponsors from different parts of the world. Initially traditional minded Tibetans thought that the modern education will lead their upcoming generation towards western culture and take them away from their traditional values and customs. This is where they were slightly correct. The majority of Tibetan youth studying in good schools and colleges of India and abroad have a strong bend towards the western life-style. They now started feeling their culture to be inferior and sometimes their attitude seems to be more arrogant. On the other hand this modern and secular education is playing a vital role as a means of increasing social mobility among Tibetans. This is only due to education that they have been able bring to reforms in their social structure.

It has also been observed that among the Tibetan refugees income acquired by professional skills has become the main criterion for defining one's social position in the society. Even the majority of respondents (94.5%) consider that education is necessary for all, to lead a better life in the society and to upgrade their social status. The traditional aristocracy based on rental incomes of land and property have suffered a sharp downfall in their social and economic status. Instead education proved to be an important channel of vertical social mobility. The traditional society which was based or ascribed values has shifted to accquired values and achievement oriented society.

There were three broad aspects of traditional Tibetan economy i.e. Agriculture, pastoral and animal husbandry and Barter and trade. After coming to India some of them were provided with small pieces of land to cultivate and the rest others were engaged in road construction work on the border areas. The present economic conditions have widely changed. They have followed many new occupations. 'New occupations' here refers of the occupations adopted by the Tibetan refugees of Dharamsala and Dehra Dun :

(1) Business : 32.55% respondents are engaged in business. Their business activities are not confined to settlement premises but also to the local Indian markets. They are in competition with localites. Sweater-selling being their main business in these areas helped them a lot to improve their economic

status. Besides selling sweaters they also sell clothes, shoes, cosmetic items etc. The handicrafts again is entirely monopolished by the Tibetan refugees. They now prefer to use machines and technical tools for the purpose. Though in few settlements this work is also done manually. Few Tibetans had open restaurants specially where 'momos' and 'chang' is served. The other eatable items are snacks, sweets, cakes, salted tea, cokes etc.

(2) Government services : other refugees are engaged in jobs provided to them mainly by the goverment in. exile. They do not earn enough money being a goverment. employee but the main charm behind it is that they feel proud in serving their government and nation.

(3) Professionals : Some are doctors, teachers, law officials, civil servants etc.

(4) Traditional occupations : Only (3.06%) respondents are such who are still doing their 'fathers' occupation.

Thus, they have not only exhibited a high occupational adaptability but also a strong instinct of survival by making a very rational choice of occupations. These vast changes in the occupational structure have uprooted the strong foundations of old traditional pattern of social stratification.

(The role of religion has been neutralised in terms of economic growth. Though it is one of the factors affecting economy of a society but not an individual variable which influences the promotion or retardation of economic growth. As weber in his book "Protestant Ethics and the spirit of capatalism" have considered religion as the major variable for economic growth of the people. There are various example where traditional occupations have been discontinued by the upcoming generations among Hindus, Brahamins are traditionally given to priesthood and engaged in learning but they took advantage of job opportunities. They are now engineers, doctors, lawyers etc. Similarly Marwaries have shown remarkable tendency to switch over to business activities and today being the most orthodox Hindus are brilliant businessmen.

The major cultural problems which affects the economic growth of Tibetan society are its ascriptive order, sacredism, ritualism present in the social structure. Tibetans in exile have adopted the strategy to remove these cultural problems and to link their traditional values to the new era, like Marwaris and Brahamins. They have respondent positively to the new system of economic opportunities. They have been able to overcome quickly from difficult conditions and grabbed every opportunity which was favorable for them. They have taken up modern values in several areas and shown remarkable brilliance to pickup economic gains of modernization. Occupational mobility results in change in attitude and values. The change in economic order is likely to bring alternations at the level of awareness and emotion also.)

Another significant change can be observed in the political structure of the Tibetan society. In Tibet nobles could become the village heads and they were respected and obeyed because of their high birth and financial status. It was more like a feudal system. Monastic institutions also played a vital role in the matters of politics and every decision was taken by the name of Dalai Lama. It was found during the study that after refugehood Tibetans have undergone a quick process of 'politicization'. To be more specific one can call this changing process as 'democratisation'.

The traditional values and beliefs are now being critisised as outdated and irrelevant. Those Tibetans brought up in India blames the traditional political structure for their present conditions. The democratic framework has brought radical changes in the present Tibetan polity. Now, the leaders at any level (village, sect, state or regional level) are elected through proper voting system. Educational qualifications and leadership qualities are the only bases for anyone to become a leader.

In the closed Tibetan society, politics was not to be discussed by the commoners. But, today it has become the most hot topic of discussion. Every young and old person is interestingly involved in voting and keeping an eye on the activities of the political leaders elected by them. The commoners are free to express their views in matters of political decisions taken by the government in exile. Even the institution of Dalai Lama has put to question. Many respondents expressed in favour of democratic polity without even mentioning the name of Dalai Lama as their political head. Majority of respondents feel that politics should not interfere in religious activities and vice-versa. They should be completely seperated from each other. This could only start with the office of Dalai Lama. Even Dalai Lama decleared that he might be the last Dalai Lama.

Despite all these changes in the political structure, Dalai Lama continues to remain as a symbol of Tibet's religious and political unity. It is remarkable that the concept of freedom, equality, nationalism, democracy which were almost unknown to them have now become a part of their life. There is no doubt that Tibetans showed tremendous ability to adopt to new situations.

Prior to refugehood the class system was a closed one based on ascribed status. Their was hardly any social mobility present in the system. The class system has now become open and achievement oriented where any person irrespective of his/her sex, birth, wealth can move up and down from one social stratum to another.

The main determinants of social mobility are educational achievements, professional and occupational skills and income.

The speedy change in the occupational structure not only weekend the bases of old social stratification pattern but also served as a means of social mobility among the individuals.

Whenever the traditional social structure is replaced by the new social set-up, the role of youth cannot be left unignored. They are the one who questions the old traditional customs and values. Therefore, while analysing the changes and the pattern of social mobility in a Tibetan refugee community it is necessary, to keep in view the role of new generation emerging in a different social set-up.

The new generation has almost different opinions in regard to institutions of marriage, education, religion and politics. The Tibetan youth now studying in schools and colleges exchange views with the local Indian youth. They enjoy cinema, hotels and parties. The older people think that intermingling of these two traditions are spoiling their youth.

The inter-generational differences among the Tibetans are almost narrowing. The parents and the children brought up in the same social environment have hardly any conflicts between them. But the grand-parents brought are up in Tibet still attached to older values, customs and traditions and are in continues conflict with them. It is found that at several times the children call their parents and grand-parents ignorant, old-fashioned, orthodox etc. and considers them responsible for their present conditions.

It is also true that the young generation have embeded in them a strong feeling of nationalism. They feel themselves proud it they could do anything for their country. But their are few youngsters who are neither emotionally attached to their motherland nor they want to go back to Tibet. They have only superficial emotions while they talk of Tibet and its culture.

The new generations of Tibetans are more educated and has a wide vision towards every aspects of society. Every young Tibetan is of the view that religion should be kept away from politics. They feel that 'free Tibet' should be capable enough to defend itself from any foreign aggression. They want their political authorities to play a decisive role in the international scenario. They try to develop an egalitarian society. Traditions are often cursed by the Tibetans youth for their present conditions. But there are several evidences which has shown remarkable capacity of traditions to respond positively towards change and innovations. Traditions along, cannot be a cause for poor development of the nation. Long-term planning which is purposeful is far more rational than a blind attack on traditions. Though, some aspect of culture may be functional in one social system and may be dysfunctional in other. Hence, if culture of society come in contact with other culture, the dysfunctional aspects of tradition need changes. It is not necessary then for the entire social system to change. For the purpose to be fulfilled it is important to excavate those elements of traditions more cautiously.

One can see the examples of third world countries (South-East Asia) where sticking to traditional values have caused failure of the strategies of development. Traditions with concept of modernity can go together; it can be witnessed in the progress of various Asian countries. Person working in one sector of life with values and attitude of modernization can also follow strictly his traditional ethics and codes. This is what H.H. Dalai Lama has been continuously conveying in his messages. He wants his people to learn about modern techniques and innovations without forgetting their traditions and culture. The latter is more important for the survival of their identity. This was the ground reason for which they fled from Tibet. Thus they have to make the choice as to which traditional values to be kept and which all to be left out. It is the time to check that modernity does not sallow traditions. If the functional parts of old traditions and modernity are combined together, the pain and strain Tibetans are facing in exile will definately be minimized.

Everything in tradition is not harmful and immoral. There are several characteristics of traditions like welfare of all, selfless motives, sympathy, concern for the suffering of others, etc. which were not useful for the past only but they hold strong identities for the future also. hence they should be given proper respect and place in the changing scenario too. A society without spirit of culture and tradition will become a source of mirth and degradation. A sudden loss of traditions can lead to anomie, rootlessness and alienation. It is essential to reconsider, therefore, many of the important traditional values and institutional patterns of the society. It is also important because the uncertainity of the future of Tibet cannot be visualised at present and even difficult to predict.

The Tibetan youth feel that some reformations in the Tibetan educational system should be made. As introducing computer education in schools, opening vocational training institutes in large numbers, providing technical training to the children are few important suggestions given by the respondent. These will lead to better employment opportunities and further it will help to improve their living standards. There is no doubt that youth is the future of 'Free Tibet'.

On the basis of a comparative study of Dharamsala and Dehra Dun, some significant generalizations can be drawn:

(1) The sense of nationalistic feeling, cultural consciousness, linguistic awareness are more stronger in Dharamsala than in Dehra Dun. This is because Dharamsala is considered as 'little Lhasa' which is a residence of Dalai Lama.

(2) Dharamsala has a large number of lamas and monks who are more religious, oriented, than those residing in Dehra Dun. In Dehra Dun Lamas are more inclined to materialistic things.

(3) Different community groups reside in Dehra Dun and Tibetan refugees community is one of them. Therefore, they have adopted the life-style of the localities which was hardly noticed in Dharamsala.

(4) The Tibetans in Doon Valley are in better economic position and many of them have their own private houses either in the settlement area itself or outside the settlement. The refugees in Dehra Dun are in some way able to ignore the directives from Dharamsala but those living in Dharamsala can not afford to do so.

(5) The Tibetan refugees in Dharamsala are engaged in goverment jobs and those in Dehra Dun are mostly engaged in business. This is becomes the goverment-in-exile is situated in Dharamsala as well as all the officers have their headquarters at Dharamsala. Related to this very reason the educated people are more found in Dharamsala than in Dehra Dun.

(6) The Tibetans in Dharamsala are more inclined to religious activities and feel that religion is still a core of their society. In Dehra Dun Tibetans find religion as one of the uniting force in the exile condition. But they are more modernised as Dehra Dun is itself a cosmopolitan city where people from various communities reside.

(7) It was observed that Tibetans living in Dharamsala do not have close relations with others local people. As the Tibetans in Dharamsala are more mobile due to their transfers from one place to another. Contrary, to this Tibetans in Dehra Dun have close relations with local people as they are less mobile in nature.

Thus one can conclude that Tibetans in Dehra Dun represent the characteristics of an open society and on the other hand those living in Dharamsala represents those of a closed society.

Tibetan refugees in Dehra Dun are having great expectations from the newly formed government of Uttaranchal state. During study it was found that after the formation of Uttaranchal state, the state goverment has not provided any new of official aid to the refugee community.

Tibatars too have not put forward their demands to the state, as they know that, presently state itself does not have enough finances in her pocket. It shows that they are concesred about the India goverment also This feeling expresses their love for the indian people.

But they suggested that goverment. should look after the health and education problems at priority.The goverment. should provide land to those scattered refugees who the still need proper settlement areas. The Tibetan refugees feel that no taxes should be levied on them and they should be given maximum rebates.

WIZARDS

The Tibetan refugees passing through a critical phase of transition have been working unitedly for the liberation of Tibet from the clutches of communism.

Infact prior the arrival of Dalai Lama the Buddhist groups already existing in India adopted the way of Hindus. This is because Hindus considered Buddhism as a part of their own religion hence Buddhist too, never fell they have to protect their identity in India and among Indians.

On coming of Dalai Lama to India, the Tibetans recognised their individual identity which further encouraged them to revive their traditions in their original form.

They have come across many difficulties during the various phase of change. India is their second home and it has helped them at every stage to re-adjust themselves. Here it would be important to appreciate the Role of Mass Media (print and electronic media) which performs the dual function - Firstly in uniting the Tibetans scattered throughout world and secondly by maintaining and preserving their traditions and customs and bringing them forth to the outside world.

Mass Media : While planning the future of free Tibet the role of Mass of Mass media cannot be ignored. Communication is now recognised as an important factor in the process of development, the strategies of economic growth and technological change evolved by the developing countries invariably have a strong communication component.

In the developing societies the inter-personal network of countries has to be strong. Face to face communication carries a considerable volume of Changes. Studies in media have suggested that messages originally received in a mass media get substantial diffusion through the interpersonal networks. The function of media is to promote socio-economic development of the country. It feels the responsibility to exercise there functions in environmental surveillance, consensus building and socialization in order to strive for the protection of sustainable environment. Media is an instrument of social change and national cohesion by upholding progressive values and involving a community in a free dialogue.

The media programmes carried at ethnic, religious, linguistic and cultural groups may concern within the country and also those outsides, producing different results in different settings. Media like radio and television have to be careful about what they offer in their broadcasts. Music, dance and drama; fiction, poetry and other forms of religious and general literature, and plastic and graphic arts form and important part of TV offerings.

In reference to the Indian society media educates about gender issues and equality, common empowerment issues; health and hygiene issues; exploitation, corruption, favouritism and nepotism issues etc. India being a country of different religious sects and communities, it is obvious in such environment, that onflicts are bound to arise, media plays an important role in promoting the communal harmony.

Tibetans the developing community have also stressed on the role of media to communicate their views and ideas. In the context of Tibetan community media is playing an important role in process of development by conveying information and persuasive messages of H.H. Dalai Lama to their people, scattered throughout the world.

The words of Dalai Lama have a strong impact on the heart and minds of millions of refugees. Speech is no doubt the most effective vehicle of human communication. The spoken word has a sanctity of its own. Before the advent of printing technology, traditional beliefs were communicated orally. The preachers in ancient days used the oral technique for propogating their point of view. Language used in this method of communication is of great importance. This importance of language can be understood by an example - When the Brahamin priests used highly sanskritised language which carried an aura of scholarship and erudition. Their teachings were confined to the elite group far beyond the understanding of the general masses. Thus it laid lesser impact. On the other hand the religious preachers known as parivrajakas (Wandering monks) travelled from one place to another, delievered lessons and teachings on religious matters, epics and scriptures. They communicate them through local language. People were thus more receptive to the Buddhist mode of communication.

Traditional Media

Since ages traditional medium has been communicating wide variety of messages, the traditional folk drama and theatre has its deep roots in the society, only because it strictly adheres to the traditional themes have always been changing but never was there any departure from tradition. Tibetan Institute of Performing Arts (TIPA) established in 1959 is one of the oldest institutions which promotes Tibetan folk culture. The display of regional costumes, musical instruments, mask and arts is the speciality of this institution. In desire to maintain cultural identity and to retain links with the past have kept the folk cultures alive even in exile.

The traditional media occupy an important place, through modern education and the inroads made by the mass media have diminished their power. They consist many folk forms of dance, drama, narrations and entertainment which have hitherto performed two functions; they have been principal instruments for the transmission of cultural heritage and also major providers for entertainment. They can be used as powerful instruments of mass education and of diffussion of developmental ideas.

Tradition represents both continuity and change. Each generation re-evaluates it in terms of the new reality that it has to encounter. Insensitive handling of tradition can promote orthodoxy and obscurantism.

To preserve a democratic way of life it is essential that people should have a freedom to express their feelings and to make their views known to the people at large. Hence press should be free to play its role in building a strong viable society

Books is one of the most important means of print media to understand any society. Various Books on Tibet and Tibetan Culture gives a wide understanding about the Tibetan society. "Tibet Past and Present", "People of Tibet", "My land and my People", "Daughter of Tibet", "Religion of Tibet", etc. (endless names to quote) are few Tibetan classic books which provides the indepth knowledge about the Tibetan Society "The Tibetan Book of the Day : A way of life - Part I" is a film in which Dalai lama himself gives His views on the meaning and importance of Books.

The Department of Information and International Relations (DIIR) publishes periodical journals in four language : Tibetans Hindi, English and Chinese. In addition to this, this department brings out audio and video programmes on Tibet, DIIR serves as a protocol office of the CTA and liaises with the international media and Tibet support groups throughout the world.

The Indian press is characterised by pluralism and range of diversity in terms of socio-economic, linguistic and cultural interests. The press in India is freest in the world which has emerged as a strong pillar of democracy and rights of citizens. The Tibetan youth have widely accepted the mode of media to transmit their views and ideology about the freedom of Tibet. The TYC has brought about number of articles in "Tibetan Review", "Tibetan Bulletin" and "Lugta" to highlight their opinions on various statements of national and international importance. H.H. Dalai Lama has also given number of interviews to the print media. It can be said that even Dalai Lama accepts the vitality and importance of various means of media in the struggle of freedom. One cannot deny that number of India's great, social reformers, leaders and crusaders in the struggle of freedom movement used press for furthening their philosophy and causes they espoused.

Framing slogans is another important method to convey our ideas and motives to the masses. A slogan is most effective, if, it conveys some basic idea or theme which continuous for a long time, for example - Tibetans suffering from China's domination speaks - "FREE TIBET". This is one of the most popular slogan which provides a sense of unity among various sects and classes of Tibetans residing all over the world. Hence press should be free and denial of freedom of the press would necessarily undermine the power to influence public opinion and be counter to democracy. In the modern society films have great impact on the audiences. Films like (1) KUNDAN by Martin Scotsese is a story of Tenzing Gyatso the 14th Dalai Lama. The viewers here come across sadness and pain and realise what has been lost by Tibetans.

(2) "Why are we silent" a documentary film by Garthwait Griffin supports for the freedom the Tibet from communist Chinese.

(3) "Tintin in Tibet" story by Herge imparts knowledge about Tibet and Tibetans.

(4) "The Cup" a film in Tibetan language by Khyentse Norbu is a story of Tibetans life in exile and how other are greatly influenced by the modern world in which they have took asylum.

All films and T.V. programmes in one way or the other, project certain life styles. Its true that no innovation is problem free Tibetan youth have also innovated number of techniques to promote not only their culture and tradition but also what Chinese have illegally done to their country and countrymen.

Tibetans have made number of adjustments in their culture in order to survive in the refugedom. On the other hand they have maintained their identity too, so that whenever they go back to free Tibet they may not be considered as 'outsiders' in their motherland. It is true that if they return back to free Tibet, the new generation of Tibetans will bring major changes in their social system. New social system will come in existence different from what it was prior to refugehood and also different what it is now in India.

Bibliography

Arakheri, A.V. : Tibetans in India - *The uprooted people and their cultural transplantation,* Reliance Publishing House, New Delhi, 1998.

Avedon, John. F. : *In Exile from the Land of Snows.* 1959-60.

Bailey F.M. : *China-Tibet, Assam - A Journey,* London, 1945.

Barber, Noel : *The Flight of Dalai Lama,* Hodder & Stoughton, London, 1960.

Bell, Charles : *Religion of Tibet,* Oxford, 1931.

Bendix and Lipset : *Class Status & Power.* Routledge & Kegan Paul Ltd., London, 1967.

Bergel, Egon Ernest : *Social Stratification,* McGraw-Hill Book Company. Inc. 1962.

Bhattarcharjee, Ajit : *Tibetans in Exile - The Democratic Vision.* Tibetan Parliamentary and Policy Research Centre, New Delhi, 1994.

Blau & Buncan : *The American Occupational Structure,* New. York, 1967.

Chhetri, Ram Bahadur : *Adaptation of Tibetan Refugees in Pokhara, Nepal. A study of Presistance & Change.* 1990.

Corlin, Class. : *A Nation in Your Mind - Continuity and Change among Tibetan Refugees in Nepal.* 1975.

Dahrendorf : *Class & Class Conflict in Industrial Society.* Routledge & Kegan Paul Ltd. London, 1959.

Damle, Y.B. : *Reference Group Theory and Mobility in the Caste System.* Movton & Co. The Hague, 1968.

Das Sarat Chandra : *Journey to Lhasa & Central Tibet.* Cosmo Publications, New Delhi, 1988.

David, Macdonald : *Tourning in Tibet & Sikkim.*

Davie, Maurice R. : *Refugees in America,* Harper & Brothers, New. York. 1947.

Desai, A.R. : *Rural Sociology in India.* 1959.

Dreyer, O. : *Cultural Changes in Developing Countries.* Progress Publishers, Moscow, 1976.

Elliot & Merrill : *Social Diorganisation* III Edition. Harper & Brothers. Publishers, New York, 1950.

Erich Goode: *Sociology,* Prentice Hall, Inc., New Jersey, 1988.

Etzioni & Etzioni : *Social Change Sources, Patterns and Consequences.* Basic Book, Inc. Publishers, New York, London, 1964.

Fairchild, H.P. (ed.) : *Dictionary of Sociology,* 1962.

Fichter, Joseph H. : *Sociology.* University of Chicago Press, 1957.

Fletcher, Ronald : *The Making of Sociology - A study of Sociological Theory,* Vol. 2. Michael Joseph Ltd. London, 1971.

Gold, Peter : *Tibetan Reflection Life in Tibetan Refugee Community.* London, 1984.

Haralambos, M. and R.M. Herald : *Sociology -Themes and perspectives.* Neil O'Brien, Oxford University Press, 1980.

Harrer, Heinrich : *Seven Years in Tibet.* Rupert Hart, Davis, London, 1953.

Haveman & West - The College Graduates in America Today, Harcourt Brace, New York, 1952.

Havser, R.M. & Thomas. N. Daymont : *Schooling Abilities & Learning Sociology of Education.* July, 5. 1977.

Hetzel, Ralph V. : *A Tibetan Refugee Problem.* Spring Semester Publications. 1968.

Huthcesing, Raja : *Tibet Fights for Freedom,* Orient Longman, New Delhi, 1960.

Inkeles, Alex : *What is Sociology - An introduction to the Discpline and Profession.* Prentice Hall of India Pvt. Ltd., New Delhi. 1987.

Keller, L. Stephen : *Uprooting and Social Change - The Role of Refugees in Development.* Manohar Book Service, New Delhi, 1975.

Kuppuswamy - *Social Change in India,* 1972.

Lamo, Rinchen : *We Tibetans,* New Delhi, 1997.

Lapiere, Richard T. : *Social Change.* McGraw-Hill Book Company, USA, 1965.

Lasswell, Harold D. : *Politics Who Gets What, When and How.* New York, Mcgraw Hills, 1936.

Lipset & Bendix : Social Mobility in Industrial Society. University of California Press, 1959.

Loomis & Loomis : *Modern Sociological Theories.* Affiliated East West Pvt. Ltd. New Delhi, 1961.

Macdonald, David. : *Cultural Heritage of Tibet.* Light and Life Publishers New Delhi.

Martindale, Don : *Social Life and Cultural Change.* D. Van Nostrand Company, Inc. 1962.

Miller, S.M. : *Comparative Social Mobility.* 1960.

Moore, Wilbert E. : *Social Change.* Prentice - Hall of India Pvt. Ltd. New Delhi, 1965.

Mukherjee, D.P. : *Diversities,* Peoples Publishing House, Delhi, 1958.

Mukherjee, R.K. : *The Rise & Fall of East India.* Berlin, 1958.

Norbu Chophel : *Folk Culture of Tibet,* LTWA, Dharamsala, 1983.

Norbu, Namyang : *Warriors of Tibet,* Wisdom Publications, London, 1986.

Norbu, Thumpten : *Tibet is My Country,* Dutton & Co. London, 1961.

Orans, M. A. : *Tribe in Search of A Great Tradition,* Man in India. 1959.

Palakashappa, T.C. : *Mundgod Tibetans - A study in the process of Adjustment,* New Zealand, 1976.

Pandey, Devki Nandan : *Glorious Glorious Dehradun.* Tuhina Publication House, Dehradun. Aug. 2000.

Panikkar, K.M. : *Hindu Society at the Cross Roads.* Asia Publishing House, Bombay,1955.

Parelius & Parelius - *Sociology of Education,* Prentice Hall, 1978.

Parkin, F. : *Class Inequality of Political Order.* London, 1972.

Parson, T. *The Social System.* Free Press. New York, 1964.

Patel, Srisha : *The Tibetan Refugees in Orissa - An Anthropological Study.* Punthi Pustak Publication. 1980.

Pennock, Roland J. : *Democratic Political Theory.* Princeton University Press, 1979.

Prasad, Narmadeshwar : *Change Strategy in a Developing society - India.* Meenakshi Prakashan, Meerut.

Prem Hari Har Lal : *The Doon Valley Down the Ages.* Interprint, New Delhi, 1993.

Richardson C.J. : *Contempory Social Mobility.* Nicholas Publishing Company, New. York, 1977.

Richardson, H.E. : *A Short History of Tibet,* Dutton & Co, Inc. New York, 1962.

Richardson, H.E. : *Tibet and its History.* Oxford University Press, Toronto, 1962.

Richardson, H.E. *Tibet & Its History.* Shambhale, 1984.

Rider : *The Theory & Practise of Mandala,* 1961.

Rigzin Tsepak : *Festivals of Tibet,* LTWA, Dharamsala, 1993.

Robert, E. Park & Miller Herbert, A. : *Old World Traits Transplanted.* Harper & Brothers. New York, 1921.

Rogoff, N. : *Recents Trends in Occupational Mobility,* Free Press, 1953.

Rudolph & Rudolph : *The Modernity of Tradition.* Orient Longman Ltd., New Delhi, 1969.

Saklani, Girja : *The Uprooted Tibetans in India - a sociological study of continuity and change.* Cosmo Publications, New Delhi, 1984.

Saksena, R.N. and P.S. Jayasinghe : *Refugees - A study in changing pattern.* Asia Publishing House, Bombay, 1961.

Sandberg Graham : *The Exploration of Tibet,* Cosmo Publications, Delhi, 1986.

Selltir, Jahoda, Deutsch, Cook : *Research Methods in Social relations.* Holt, Rinehart & Winston, Inc., 1962.

Sen Chanakya : *Tibet Disappears,* Asia Publishing House, New Delhi, 1960.

Shiromany, A.A. : *The Spirit of Tibet - Universal Heritage.* Allied Publishers. 1995.

Silverberg : *Social Mobility in the Caste System in India.* Mouton, The Hague, 1968.

Singh, Surajit : *Tribal Cultures of Penninsular India : As a Discussion of Little Tradition in the study of Indian Civilization,* Man in India, 1957.

Singh, Yogendra : *Social Stratification and Change in India.* Manohar Publications, New Delhi, 1977.

Smith, William Carison : *Americans in the Making.* New York, 1921.

Snellgrove, David : *A Cultural History of Tibet.* Prajan Press, 1980.

Stein, Burton : *Social Mobility & Medieval South Indian Hindu Sect* - The Hague, 1968.

Stein, R.A. : *Tibetan Civilization,* Faber & Faber, London, 1972.

Subba, B. Tanka : *Flight and Adaptation 'Tibetan Refugees in The Darjeeling - Sikkim Himalayas.* LTWA, 1990.

The Information Office of H.H. The Dalai Lama : *Tibetans in Exile.* Information Office Central Tibetan Secretariat, Dharamsala, 1959-80.

Theodore Brameld : *Japan - Culture, Education & Change in Two Communities.* Holt, Rinkhart & Winston Inc. USA, 1968.

Tibet A Political History. Yale University Press, 1967.

Tibet Today - The Facts : TYBA, Dharamsala, 1990.

Tibet, China and the World : A compilation of interviews - The Dalai Lama. Narthang Publications, 1989.

Trungpa,.Chogyan : *Born in Tibet,* London, 1987.

Tsung, Lien Shen & Liue, Shen-Chi : *Tibetans* Stanford, 1951.

Tucci Guiseppi : *The Religions of Tibet.* University of California Press, Berkeley, 1980.

Van Walt, Van Praag : *The Status of Tibet,* Westview Press. 1987.

Vine, Margaret Wilson : *An Introduction to Sociological Theory.* Longmans Green & Co. Toronto, 1959.

Weber Max. (Hans. H. Gerth and Wright Mills, trans & ed.) From Max Weber : *Essays in Sociology.* New York, Oxford University Press, 1946.

Young. P.V. : *The Pilgrims of Russian Town.* Chicago. University of Chicago Press, 1932.

Appendix-1

A. The Flag of Tibet

During the reign of King Songtsen Gampo, in the later half of the seventh century the war-banner was introduced which later came to be recognised as the National flag of Tibet. In 1912 during 13th Dalai Lama modifications were introduced in the flag. Initially the Rising Sun and the twelve stripes in red and blue were the features of the flag.

After modifying it the main features of the present flag of Tibet are snow mountain at the base with a pillar of lions in white (with green mares and tails) in the foreground, a rising sun in the golden yellow with twelve rays radiating from the top of the mountain, each ray alternately in red and blue.

Every component in the flag has its special significance. The snow mountain symbolizes the Himalayan ranges surrounding the country.

Pair of lions in the foreground symbolizes the dualistic system where temporal and spiritual rule functions with co-operation. The wishing gem in the paws of lions express the rule of law based on the principles of cause and effect underlying the Ten golden percepts and Sixteen Human principles, which are the ultimate source of benefit and peace.

The three jewels flaming over the revishing gem symbolises the idea of devotion to the three gems symbolising Buddha, Dharma and Sangha endowed with twenty four transcendental attributes. The rising sun and its rays symbolizes democracy, freedom, happiness and prosperity. The twelve stripes in red and blue symbolize the twelve descendants of the six obriginals of Tibet. The colours red and blue signifies the great support of the two guardian deities - Mar - Nag. The golden border on the three sides of the flag specifies the spread of the golden ideals of Buddhism.

B. Sacred Objects of Tibet

(I) *Tharchock*

Where there are Tibetan settlements one can see the tharchock (Prayer flags) bearing different colours flying on houses on hill topes so that one can easily recognize the Tibetan colony or Tibetan house. The Prayer Flags are printed on unglazed paper brought from Banaras. The various coloured flags symbolizes long-life, material prosperity, defeat of the evil spirits, prayers for the well-health of Dalai lama and the undying continuity of the Tibetan tradition. Prayer flags at the roof top indicates the continuation of Bon practice; incorporated in Tibetan Bhuddhism.

(ii) Sacred Books

The sacred five books-of the Tibetans known as **shungchenKapyunga** are kept on the domestic altar and worshipped. They are not read by the common people as they are not easily understandable. The books generally read by commoners are:

(i) Tamering Chemo

(ii) Ngarming Chemo

(iii) Sagyen Peja

(iv) Khatang Tenga

(iii) Rosaries

In Tibetan rosaries is known as **ten-wa** or **mow**, since it contain beads in it. There are hundred and eight beeds in a rosary, the extra eight beads are called **mdo-dsin**. Then there are pair of strings of ten small pendant which help to count the cycle of the beeds.

(iv) Prayerwheels

Tibetans are seen turning prayer-wheels and prayer cylinders while meditating. These prayer-wheels are rotated in a clock-wise direction and in every Tibetan settlement one can see elderly people especially women rotating their prayer wheels with the right hand and counting the beads with the left hand. Inside the Prayer wheels are written the sacred Syllables-**"Om Mani Padme Hum"**.

C. Tibetan Kha-ta

A Tibetan Kha-ta (scarf) is a loosely woven white silk or cotton strip and varies in size, quality and colour. Higher the status of the person to be honoured the best type of Kha-ta is used.

Kha-ta is a common object used by Tibetans in expressing their gratitude, friendly and respectable feeling towards the honorary. Tibetans offer such Kha-ta even to friends who visit the family to express their warmth. When a letter is sent to a friend, relative or an officer a Kha-ta is also sent along with it, and without it the act is considered improper. On the other hand a letter accompanied by a Kha-ta is an indication of "submission with a God's robe" to support it. Now a days owing to the public postal facilities sending of the Kha-ta is discontinued.

There are mainly three modes of offering the scarves. When a scarf is offered to a superior it should be raised to the level of his forehead and offered. When offered to an equal it is raised to shoulder level. It is spread on the nape when given to a person who is lower in status.

Now owing to poverty the different varieties have gone and only white, silken and the cotton Kha-tas are found. Cotton Kha-tas are even presented to senior most lamas, which in the past was used only for the commoners.

Tam-den the person who disposes off the dead generally called under- taker. He occupies the lowest position in the social hierarchy. His presence is sign of ill luck. He is the one who earns his living by the dead peoples.

Tsampa - Flour of roasted wheat or maize offered to the fire God by Tibetans.

Appendix-II

Traditional Dances of Tibet

CHAM : Traditional mask dances toward off evil forces, by the Tibetan monks from Zonkar Choede Monastery The tradition of "Cham" dates back to the 13th century. It began from guru Chopel Sangpo (the first abbot of Zonga Choede monastery, the largest monastery in upper Tibet) who encountered attacks from the Toh-Hor anti-religious force. To ward off the force, the Guru initiated special retreat and prepared sacrificial oblation for protection. During this retreat a wonderful miraculous vision appeared to him, it was a joyful dance of the monastery's guardian deity Mahayaksha and the retinue, Dharmapala, guardian deities and the solitary.

NGONPA : The ritual dance of the hunters and masked dancers representing the Buddhist deity of Chakna Dorjee (Vajrapani) the destroyer of evil.

TASBI SHOELPA : The white beard mask dance is the realization of the dream of the great fifth Dalai Lama.

RALPA : The dance of the wanderers who travel from village to village singing and dancing, has poetry and wisdom collected, while in their journey.

CHANGSHAE : The song of drinking weaves poetry and wit in celebration of joy and happiness. (Chang is the Tibetan drink fermented from cereals).

DROKSHAE : The dance of the nomads is the celebration of nature. Men and women sing and dance while grazing yaks and sheep in the green pasture of Changthan the great Northern plain of Tibet.

Appendix-III

A. Tibetan Religious Festivals

Ganden Ngam-chho : According to the Tibetan Calendar, Ganden Nagam-che fall on the 25th day of the 10th month. Ganden Ngam-cho celebrates the birth and death anniversary of rJe Tsong-kha-pa, the founder of the Gelug-pa Sect of Mahayana Buddhism in Tibet, popularly known as the Yellow Hat Sect. *Ngam-cho* means "worship of the 25th" because rJe Tsong-kha-pa was born on the 25th and also died on the 25th. This is primarily a day of worship and prayer when Tibetans remember the teaching of the great saint scholar. They visit the monasteries and chant the prayers of rJe Tsong-kha-pa. In the evening it is customary for people, both monks and laymen, to light thousands of butter lamps on the terrace of monasteries, in towns and villages.

Nganpa Guzom : This is actually a festival lasting two days celebrated on the 6th and 7th day of the 11th Tibetan month, which are observed as holidays. The first of these is *Nganpa Guzom*, meaning "Nine Evils". This is a day of solemn observance when Tibetan reflect on the nine principal evils. The second day is known as *Sangpo Ghuzom*, meaning 'Ten Good Fortunes." This is the antidote day to the first, and it celebrates the ten good fortunes which may befall a man. As time passed the original name of the holiday, Nganpa Guzom, was popularly substituted with the more pleasant Sangpo Chuzom.

The Sangsol Ceremony: The Sangsol Ceremony falls on the second or the third day after the New year (the exact date depending on astrological calculations). The ceremony is an act of purification. Tibetan families invite learned lamas to their homes so that special prayers are said on the house tops to invoke good fortune. Incense is burnt and the old prayer flags are replaced by fresh ones.

Guthok Ceremony: Since the 29th day of the 12th month of the Tibetan Calendar is considered the end of the year by Tibetans, observances on that day include special prayers to drive away evil spirits. The day is an official holiday and specific religious ceremonies are performed. On this day the monks of Namgyal Dratsang monastery give a performance of Tantric dances. The dance is based on the prayers of the Togyag-a ritual for driving evil spirits away. In the evening all members of Tibetan families get together and eat a special broth called Guthung. Small balls of dough, each containing a piece of charcoal or a piece of broken china, wool, salt and pepper are added to the broth, as also small symbol of the sun, crescent moon and stars and two pieces of thread twined clockwise and one anti-clockwise. Each symbol has a significance, for example, the symbol of the sun stands for happy days to come; the crescent moon stands for prosperity. On this day all families in Tibet make it a special point to clean their homes. The dust and the dirt are gathered and thrown far away along with the left overs of the broth. Tibetan believe that if they do this all the unhappiness and misery of the old years will be removed and they will be ready to welcome the new year.

Choeng a choepa : is the celebration of the offsprings on the fifteenth day of the first month of the Tibetan calendar. This is to mark the triumph of lord Bhuddha over six non-Bhuddhist teachers who challenged him in performing miracles. The tradition got way from the fourteenth century with lama Tsongkhapa, who was a great Tibetan reformer.

On this day huge butter sculpture are created and mounts of "khapse" are heaped up for offering. After they are distributed to the lamas and the lay people. In the Indian context because of hot climate monks use ghee mixed with wax rather than butter. It is generally completed in not less than one month. It is traditional belief that by making such offering create a possitive collective Karma which overcomes natural disasters in the world and promotes peace and harmony.

In India this celerbration is most colourful at Dalhousie, the seat of the Tibetan Mahayana Tantric Colleges and the miniature Densum monastery, representative of the three great Monasteries of Tibet. The monks of these monasteries make intricate designs of flowers, cloud formations, the sun and the moon, images of Bodhisattvas and of holy personages, all fashioned in butter and painted in various colours. This is a unique art practised mainly by the monk section of the Tibetan people, and forms a part of the rich cultural heritage of the Tibetans.

In Lhasa these figures were erected all along the Bakor, the sacred Inner Path surrounding the Tsug Lag Khang, the holiest place in Tibet. They were entered from the various monasteries in the suburbs of Lhasa and made up a grand exhibition. Towards the evening His Holiness the Dalai Lama would arrive in state and inspect each of the butter towers. The best among them would be given a lavish prize by official proclamations.

Drugpa-Tse-shi : (Fourth day of the Sixth Month). This day commemorates the event when Lord Buddha first preached the Four Noble Truths after attaining the supreme enlightenment beneath the Bodhi Tree at Bodh Gaya. In Buddhist terminology, it is commonly known as the (first Turning of Wheel). Religious services, sermons, public meetings, and visits to high lamas form the main part of the celebrations.

Trel-Da tse-shi; (Birth Anniversary of the birth of Guru **Padma-sambhava**). The anniversary of the birth of Guru **Padmasam-bhava** falls on the 10th of the 5th Tibetan month. Guru Padmasambhava was a great Indian Tantric teacher who revitalized Buddhism in Tibet in the 8th century A.D. He was also the founder of the Nying-ma Sect of Mahayana Buddhism in Tibet. The present Dudjom Rimpoche is regarded as the successor of Guru Padmasambhava.

Zamling Chisang : This festival is celebrated on the Full Moon Day of the 5th Tibetan month. On this day the people gather on a high, vantage spot and join in the burning of stacks of juniper leaves-a traditional ritual which most probably had its origin in Bon, the Shamanist cult of Tibet and in the mass prayer conducted for peace and prosperity in the land.

Lhabab Duchen : This festival is held in commemoration of the descent of the Buddha to the human world from the Tushita Heaven. It is celebrated on the 22nd of the 9th Tibetan month.

Monlam Chenmo : (The Great Prayer): The Great Prayer, the most significant of Tibetan religious festivals is held annually in the first Tibetan month, a few days after the onset of the Tibetan New Year. These are dedicated to the peace and prosperity of the land, and also commemorate the miracles performed by Lord Buddha. The concluding period is devoted to prayers to the Maitreya Buddha, the next Buddha to come, pleading for his speedy advent into this world.

The highlight of the Great Prayer Festival is the holding of the annual examination in the Geshey degree (doctorate degree in Psycho-Ethical Philosophy). The examination is conducted before a board of the highest and most learned scholars of Tibet. Only the most brilliant of the candidates appear in the Great Prayer examination and naturally they are the most respected ones. The first Great Prayer in India was held at Bodh Gaya, Bihar, in 1961. More than 700 monks from Burma and other places participated in the festival.

B. Kalchakra Puja

The word "Kalachakra" means "Cycle of time". The Kalchakra is a preformed Bhuddhist system of teaching and practice. The tantra was taught by the Bhuddha in India two and a half thousand years ago. Within the Bhuddhist tantras, the practice of highest yoga tantra leads to perfect Bhuddhahood; the Kalchakra teachings found only in Tibet were the heightst tantra yoga preserved and practiced as a living tradition after the decline of Bhuddhism in its nature land of India.

The Mandala is the residence of Kalachakra deity and retinue of deities surrounding him, all of which represents the components of a single individual person in purified form a fully enlightened being. The Mandala is actually three dimensional, being a five storeyed divine Mansion at the centre of which stand the Kalachara deity, the manifest state of Enlightment.

On entering the Mandala through one of the outer doors at the first level, that of the body mandate, walking in through the outer walls, which are transparent and in five layers and coloured from outside to inside, yellow, white, red, black and green. On further entering in and climb up the steps to the second level, the *Speech Mandala*, also surrounded by five transparent coloured walls; up another set of steps to the third level, the *Mind Mandala* surrounded by three transparent coloured walls. Inside mind Mandala there is a square platform. The fourth level, the *Prinstine Conšciousness Mandala*. On this platform is another platform the fifth level, the great *Bliss Mandala*. On this is the green eight-petalled lotus on which Kalachakra stands. A repoesertation of this Mandala is used by a practitioner of the Kalachakra tantra for the purpose of visulalizing in meditation.

The material used in sand Mandala are coloured sand and minerals. They are filled inside a cone with a tiny hole at the tip. With a single line of sand grains to the exquisitely grand sand Mandala, its a completion of an abode of a deity.

Once started making Mandala should be finished at one stretch. For the purpose number of monks work by shifts as it take weeks to complete one Mandal.

Whoever just take one glimpse of this Mandala is thought to establish his/her relation with this tantra. The positive seeds sown upon the mind seen of the observer will ripen beneficially in future as the events of out world system manifest as predicted in Kalachakra teachings.

(C) Festivals of Tibetan Refugees celebrated in India throughout the year

1. Indian Republic day 26th January
2. Tibetan New year or losar - A lunar festival somewhere near February or March.
3. Tibetan uprising day - March 10
4. Day of offerings (cho-trul Duechen) - A lunar festival in month of March.
5. Opera festival (by TIPA, to celebrate the coming of spring) Shoton Festival - Its a week long celebration in April.
6. TIPA foundation day - May 27

   Established in 1959, one of the oldest institution in exile is a home of Lhamo, a colourful and unique opera of Tibet. It promotes the music, dance and theatrical traditions of Tibet. The institute has a modern theatre troupe which puts on contemperory plays. It maintains its own workshops for making constumes marks and musical instruments. It also runs a school which both modern and cultural tibetan education is provided to children.

TIPA holds an annual folk opera festival in March or April. A number of folk operas, dances and programes, plays and concernts are presented on this occasion. Recently TIPA has started a special programme to teach Tibetan performing Arts to non Tibetans also.

7. Saka-Dawa - Celebrating Bhuddha Shakyamuni's Birth, Enlightment and parinirvara in month of June.

8. Birthday of H.H. Dalai Lama - 6th July.

   His Holiness the Forteenth Dalai Lama of Tibet was born on july 6, 1935 to a Yeoman family in the small farming village of Taktser in the province of Amdo, northeast Tibet. At the age of two, following a nationwide search, the child named Lhamo Dhondup was recognized as the reincarnation of his predecessor, the Thirteenth Dalai Lama. He was brought to the capital, Lhasa, on October 1939, and formally installed as the head of state of Tibet on February 22,1940. The Dalai Lama lineages are manifestaions of the Bodhisattva of Compassion, Chenrezig.

9. Choe-Khor Duechen - In July/August when Bhuddha Shakyamuni gave first Teaching.

10. Independence day of India - August 15

11. Democracy day of Tibet - September 2nd

12. Gaddi Fair at Dal Lake in September

13. Gandhi Jayanti - October 2

14. Diwali - Festival of Hindus in October/November.

15. International Himalayan Festival - A festival of music and dance in December 10 to 12 since the awarding of the Noble Peace Prize to H.H. Dalai Lama in 1989, this day is celebrated as an important day. It is also observed as a Human Rights day.

Appendix-IV

(A) Central Tibetan Administration

The Central Tibetan Administration (CTA) is recognized by Tibetans. both in and outside Tibet, as their sole and legitimate government. It is more widely known as the Tibetan Government-in-Exile.

The CTA was first established in Mussoorie on April 29, 1959 soon after His Holiness the Dalai Lama reached India . Then in May 1960 it was moved to Dharamsala, and is now located halfway between Kotwali Bazar and McLeod Gunj, in an area named Gangchen Kyishong. It is a Tibetan Phrase meaning "happy valley of snow".

Right from its inception, the CTA has set itself the twin task of rehabilitating Tibetan refugees and restoring the freedom of Tibet. Education has been on the top of the rehabilitation agenda. Simultaneously, the CTA decided to experiment with modern democracy in preparation for future Tibet. On September 2, 1960 the Tibetan parliament-in-exile came into being. It was then known as the

Commission of Tibetan People's Deputies. Later its name was changed to the Assembly of Tibetan People's Deputies.

In 1990 His Holiness announced further democratization of this elected body.The Assembly was then empowered to elect the Tibetan Kashag or the Council of Ministers, which was made answerable to it. Similarly, the Tibetan judiciary, known as the Supreme Justice Commission, was instituted. The newly-empowered Assembly of Tibetan People's Deputies then issued the constitutional document for exile Tibetans under the title of *the Charter of the Tibetans in Exile.*

Today, the CTA functions as a veritable government and has all the departments and attributes of a free democratic administration. It must be noted that the CTA is not designed and groomed to take power when Tibet become free. In *Guidelines for Future Tibet's Polity and Basic Features of its Constitution,* His Holiness the Dalai Lama states that the present exile government will be dissolved as soon as Tibet regains her freedom. His Holiness also states that there will be a transitional government in future. Tibet which will be headed by an Interim-President, elected or appointed by him. To this Interim-President His Holiness will transfer all his temporal power. The Interim-President, in his or her turn,will be required to hold a general election within two years, and devolve power to a popularly-elected government.

(B) Constitution

The Charter of the Tibetans in exile is the supreme law governing the functions of the CTA . It was drafted by the "Constitution Redrafting Committee" and referred to the Assembly of Tibetan People's Deputies for approval. The Assembly adopted the Charter on June 14, 1991.

The Charter professes to adhere to the Universal declaration of Human Rights as specified by the United Nations and to provide all Tibetans with equality before the law and enjoyment of rights and freedom without discrimination on the basis of sex, religion, race, language or social origin. The Charter provides for a clear separation of power among the three organs of the government: judiciary, legislature and executive. Before the charter came into being, the CTA, functioned roughly on the lines of draft democratic constitution for future Tibet, promulgated by His H.H. Dalai Lama on March 10, 1963.

(C) Judiciary

The Tibetan Supreme justice Commission is the highest judicial organ of the CTA. According to the Charter, the Commission is responsible for adjudicating all civil disputes in Tibetan communities . The Commission, however, does not entertain any case if doing so is seen to be in contravention of the laws of the host countries. Similarly, the Commission does not handle criminal cases as this is the preserve of the host government.

The Supreme Justice Commission is headed by the Chief Justice Commissioner (CJC) and two other Justice Commissioners, all of whom are nominated by His Holiness the Dalai Lama and referred to the assembly for its approval. If the assembly does not reject the nomination by a two-thirds majority, His Holiness will confirm the appointment. The Commissioners hold office till the age of 65. However, the assembly is empowered to impeach them by a two-thirds majority if they lose its confidence before the expiry of their term. The CJC and the other two Commissioners have equal power in adjudicating cases. The difference is that the CJC is also the administrative head of the Supreme Justice Commission.

According to the draft judicial code and civil procedures, there will be three tiers to the justice Commission: the Supreme Justice Commission, Circuit Justice Commissions (equivalent to a state-level high court) and Local Justice Commissions (lowest-level or magistrates' courts). It is proposed that there will be 62 Local justice

Commissions one in each of the major Tibetan settlements and scattered communities. In addition, there will be five Circuit justice Commissions to cover the six different zones into which the Tibetan exile communities are divided.

The most important cases heard by the Supreme justice Commission are those between the administration and people. When His Holiness first suggested setting up a judiciary, He specifically pointed out that it should become a forum where the people can voice its grievances against the administration.

(D) Legislature

The Assembly of Tibetan People's Deputies is the highest legislative organ of the Tibetan refugees community. It was instituted in 1960. The creation of this democratically-elected body was one of the major changes that His Holiness the Dalai Lama brought about in his efforts to introduce a democratic system of administration. The assembly consists of 46 elected members. U-Tsang, Kham and Amdo, the three traditional provinces of Tibet elect 10 members each while the four schools of Tibetan Buddhism and the traditional Bon faith elect two members each. Three deputies are elected by Tibetan in the west: two from Europe and one from North America. In addition, three members with distinction in the fields of art, science, literature and community service are nominated directly by His Holiness the Dalai Lama. The Assembly of Tibetan People's Deputies is headed by a Chair and a Vice-Chair, who are elected by the deputies.

Any Tibetan who has reached the age of 25 years has the right to contest elections to the assembly. The elections are held every five years and any Tibetan who has reached the age of 18 years is entitled to vote.

Sessions of the assembly are held bi-annually, with an interval of six month between the sessions. However, His Holiness can summon extraordinary sessions of the assembly in case of emergencies. There is a standing committee of 12 members: two members from each province. One member from each religious denomination, and one member who is directly nominated by His Holiness the Dalai Lama.

As representatives of the people, the deputies of the assembly undertake periodic tours to Tibetan communities to make an assessment of their return, they bring to the notice of the administration any specific grievances and matters. The assembly of Tibetan People's Deputies keep in touch with people also through Local assemblies established in 38 major Tibetan communities. The Charter provides for the establishment of a Local assembly in community having a population of not less than 160. The local Assemblies are scaled-down replicas of the assembly of Tibetan People's deputies. They keep an eye on the activities of their respective settlement/welfare officers. They also make laws for their respective communities according to the latter's perceived needs. The laws passed by the Local assembly must be implemented by the respective settlement/welfare officer.

(E) Executive: the Kashag (Cabinet)

It is the apex executive body of the Central Tibetan Administration. It exercises its executive powers subordinate to His Holiness the Dalai Lama. Members are elected by the assembly of Tibetan People's Deputies for a term of five years.

The Charter of the Tibetan in Exile stipulates that the kashag should have eight members. One chairs the kashag while the remaining seven head one department each. The Chair is elected by the kashag from amongst its own members. The members of the kashag have equal powers and responsibilities. One of the main responsibilities of the kashag entails spearheading the Tibetan freedom movement.

The Kashag is serviced by a Secretariat which, amongst other things, runs the Tibetan Computer Resource Centre to provide computer services to all departments, organizations and individuals in Dharamsala. The secretriate also runs the Planning Council, set up to optimize the use of Tibetan human, physical and financial resources.

DEPARTMENTS UNDER KASHAG

(i) **The Department of Finance** runs 25 business enterprises in India, Nepal and the United States to generate funds for the running of the CTA. An important source of its income is the annual voluntary contribution of Rs24, plus two percent of income, from all the exile Tibetans. The department also formulates the annual budget of the CTA.

(ii) **The Department of Education** administers 84 Schools in India, Nepal and Bhutan, serving 30,000 children, which form 70 percent of the children in exile. A further 15 or 20 percent goes to private schools.

Out the 84 schools administered by the Department of Education 30 schools come under the Central Tibetan Schools Administration (CTSA) of the Government of India. The Tibrysn Children's Village in Dharmsala and Tibetan Homes Foundation in Mussoorie are autonomous bodies under the Department of Education. While the Tibetan Children's Village administers 15 schools with over 10,000 students, the Tibetan Homes Foundation runs 2 schools with 1,500 students.

The Department of Education also has a major child sponsorship scheme, which receives funds from individuals and organizations. Under this scheme, the Department provides scholarships for higher studies to deserving school graduates.

(iii) The Primary responsibility of the **Department of Security** is to ensure the security of His Holiness the

Dalai Lama. The Department has a Branch Security Office which deals mainly with the arranging of public audiences with His Holiness the Dalai Lama and help Tibetan refugees in seeking renewal of their refugee residential certificates from the Government of India. The Department also runs a research unit which monitors the developments in occupied-Tibet and China.

In addition, the Department of Security runs a Reception Centre to look after the growing number of new refugees arriving from Tibet. The refugees usually arrive first in Nepal, from where they make their way to Dharamsala and other Tibetan communities via Delhi. There are branch reception centres in kathmandu and Delhi where new refugees are given food and lodging, and guided to their onward destinations. The Reception Centre also helps the new refugees to find employment, join schools and monasteries, or start small business enterprises in exile.

(iv) **The Department of information and International Relations (DIIR)** educates the Tibetans and international public opinion on the political, human nights and environmental conditions in Tibet. Under the DIIR are representative offices in 12 countries. These offices function as the embassies of the CTA and are based in New Delhi, Geneva, New York, Tokyo, London, Kathmandu, Budapest, Moscow, Paris, Canberra, Pretoria and Taipei.

(v) **The Department of Health** runs 61 Primary Health Care centres and six referral hospitals in almost all the Tibetan communities in India and Nepal. The Department meets the cost of emergency health care needs and treatment of poor Tibetans. The Tibetan Medical and Astro institute in Dharamsala is an autonomous body under the auspices of the

Department of Health. The Tibetan Medical Institute has 36 branch clinics in various parts of India and Nepal to provide traditional Tibetan medical care to Tibetans and the local populations.

(vii) **Department of Home** is responsible for rehabilitation schemes for Tibetan refugees. It looks after 21 agricultural settlements, 11 cluster units, 8 agro-industries and 4 carpet-weaving cooperatives in India. In adition there are 20 Tibetan settlements and handicrafts societies in nepal and Bhutan which are looked after by this department. It works in close cooperation with Government of India and other international organisations. Employment generation and promoting self-reliance among the refugees is the main task of this department.

(F) **Constitutional bodies :** The power and functions of the Election Commission are to conduct and oversee elections of the Tibetan Assembly, Local People's Assemblies, the Chair of the Kashag. If the CTA decides to call a referendum to get people's verdict on a matter of extreme importance, it will fall upon the Election Commission to conduct the referendum. Although the settlement and welfare officers of most Tibetan communities are appointed by the CTA, people have the right to elect them if they so wish, in such a case, the Election Commission will conduct the election of settlement/welfare officers as well. To ensure the independence of the Election Commission, the Charter provides for the appointment of the Chief Election Commissioner by His Holiness the Dalai Lama. Two additional Commissioners are appointed by His Holiness during the general election of the Assembly of Tibetan People's Deputies. The Chief Election Commissioner holds office for a term of five years unless impeached by the assembly by a two-thirds majority.

(G) **The Public Service Commission :** is responsible for recruitment, training, appointment and promotion of the civil servants of the CTA. The Chair of the Commission is appointed by His Holiness Dalai Lama for a term of three years.

(H) **The Audit Commission :** is responsible for auditing the accounts of all the CTA departments and its subsidiaries. It also audits the accounts of most of the public institutions such as cooperatives, trading concerns, educational institutes, hospitals, health centres. The Commission also evaluates efficiency, propriety and management performance. In short, the Audit Commission functions as a watchdog of the CTA. It is headed by an Auditor General, who is appointed by His Holiness the Dalai Lama for a term of ten years.

Appendix-V

TIBETAN ORGANIZATIONS

(a) **The Tibetan Youth Congress** (TYC) is a worldwide non-governmental organization with over 10.000 members, It is the largest and one of the most politically active Tibetan organizations in exile. To provide a forum for non-Tibetan to assist its activities. TYC has started, the international Friends of TYC.

(b) **Tibetan Women's Association** (TWA) is a non-profit organization of Tibetan women working to raise public awareness of the ongoing abuses faced by Tibetan people, particularly women. In Tibet in 1995 TWA successfully participated in the controversial UN World Conference on Women in Beijing. In exile TWA serves the Tibetan community as a whole assisting groups and individual women on a day-to-day basis, and launching projects to address specific needs such as education and welfare, care of the elderly and children. They are involved in the rehabilitation and education of nuns escaping from Tibet, and hold workshops and seminars to raise the political awareness of Tibetan women in order to encourage them to participate fully in the political process in the exile community.

Their "Stitches of Tibet" project provides a one-year training course for underprivileged Tibetan women in tailoring, health and hygiene. It also runs an English-language course for Tibetan women. This retail outlet sells, Tibetan chubas for women, men's and women's shirts trousers and bags. TWA receives its funding from membership fees, sponsorship, and friends of TWA.

(c) **The Tibetan Centre for Human Rights and Democracy** (TCHRO) is a non-governmental organization founded in 1996. TCHRO was established in response to a need for effective monitoring of the human right situation in Tibet and the promotion of democracy in the Tibetan community. TCHRO submits its reports to the UN Human Rights Commission, participates in UN human right conferences and other national and international fora, organizes seminars and workshops on human rights and democracy in the exiled community and conducts campaigns for victims of human rights violations in Tibet.

Appendix-VI

Tibetan Medical Tradition

Over a period of 2500 years, lineages of Tibetan doctors (amchis) have perfected a sophisticated medical tradition based on the holistic mind and body concept. Tibetan medicine is today has been recognised as one of the richest areas of the nation's cultural heritage. Tibetan medicine maintains that disease or disorders in the human body are caused when there is a disequilibrium of physcological and physical energies. Tibetan doctors normally follow three methods of diagnosis : visual observation, interrogation and pulse - reading. Tibetan medicines normally come in hard pills or powder, and mostly bitter in taste. The ingredients are herbal, but precious stones and metals are also used; the stones and metals are burned and de-toxified through an intricate and secret process of alchemy. Tibetan medicines cures various chronic diseases. Its effectiveness in curing hepatitis is miraculous. Tibetan medicine is also known in curing chronic sinus-related diseases, although one has to be on medication for a long time.

Index

Index

❑❑❑